Gilberto Freyre

The Past in the Present

Editor in Chief

Francis Robinson, Royal Holloway, University of London

Peter Burke
Maria Lúcia G. Pallares-Burke

Gilberto Freyre

Social Theory in the Tropics

Peter Lang Oxford

Cover illustration: Government employee leaving home with his family and servants, from *Voyage pittoresque et historique au Bresil,* engraved by Thierry Freres, 1839/ The Bridgeman Art Library
Cover design: Dan Mogford

First published in 2008 by Peter Lang Ltd
International Academic Publishers, Evenlode Court, Main Road,
Long Hanborough, Witney, Oxfordshire OX29 8SZ, England
© Peter Lang Ltd 2008
www.thepastinthepresent.com, www.peterlang.com

The right of Peter Burke and Maria Lúcia Pallares-Burke to be identified as the Authors of this work has been asserted in accordance with the Copyrights, Designs and Patents Act 1988.

British Library and Library of Congress Cataloguing-in Publication Data: A catalogue record for this book is available from the British Library, UK, and the Library of Congress, USA.

ISBN 978-1-906165-04-8 (Paperback)
ISBN 978-1-906165-09-3 (Hardback)

Printed in Hong Kong

For Gláucio Veiga,
intellectual brother and sparring partner
of Gilberto Freyre

Contents

The past is never over; the past continues.
(O passado nunca foi; o passado continua.)

    GILBERTO FREYRE

The further backward you look, the further forward you can see.

    WINSTON CHURCHILL

List of Abbreviations

A&R G. Freyre, *Aventura e Rotina*, 1953; new edn, RJ: Topbooks, 2001

AAM G. Freyre, *Além do Apenas Moderno*, 1973; new edn, RJ: Topbooks, 2001

BI G. Freyre, *Brazil: an Interpretation*, New York: Knopf, 1945

BVGF Biblioteca Virtual Gilberto Freyre, BVGF.fgf.org.br

C&P G. Freyre, *Como e Porque Eu Sou e Não Sou Sociólogo*, Brasília: Editora Universidade da Brasília, 1968

CFA *Gilberto Freyre; sua ciência, sua filosofía, su arte*, RJ: Olympio, 1962

CGS G. Freyre, *Casa Grande e Senzala*, 1933; 40th edn, RJ: Record, 2000

CUP Cambridge University Press

DP *Diário de Pernambuco*

EC G. Freyre, *Casa Grande e Senzala*, Edição Crítica, ed. Guillermo Giucci, Enrique Rodríguez Larreta and Edson Nery da Fonseca, Paris: Allca XX, 2002

Imperador Joaquim Falcão and Rosa Maria Barboza de Araújo (eds) *O Imperador das Idéias: Gilberto Freyre em questão*, RJ: Topbooks, for Colégio do Brasil, UniverCidade and Fundação Roberto Marino, 2001

Escravo G. Freyre, *O escravo nos anúncios de jornais brasileiros do século xix. Tentativa de interpretação antropológica*, Recife: Imprensa Universitária, 1963

FGF Fundação Gilberto Freyre, Apipucos, Recife (the home of Gilberto Freyre's library and archive)

HAHR *Hispanic American Historical Review*

I&R G. Freyre, *Insurgências e Resurgências Atuais. Argumentos de Sims e Nãos num mundo em transição*, Porto Alegre and RJ: Globo, 1983

IB G. Freyre, *Ingleses no Brasil*, 1948: 3rd edn, RJ: Topbooks, 2000

M&S G. Freyre, *The Masters and the Slaves*, trans. S. Putnam, New York: Knopf, 1946

Mansions G. Freyre, *The Mansions and the Shanties*, trans. H. de Onís, New York: Knopf, 1963

Meneses Diogo de Melo Meneses, *Gilberto Freyre*, Recife: Casa de Estudante do Brasil, 1944

Meucci	Simone Meucci, 'Gilberto Freyre e a sociología no Brasil: da sistematização à constituição do campo científico', doctoral thesis, University of Campinas, 2006: contasabertas.uol.com.br/noticias/imagens/quarta2.pdf
NE	G. Freyre, *Nordeste: aspectos da influência da canna sobre a vida e a paisagem do Nordeste do Brasil*, 1937; 2nd edn, RJ: Olympio, 1951
O&P	G. Freyre, *Ordem e Progresso: processo de desintegração das sociedades patriarcal e semipatriarcal no Brasil sob o regime de trabalho livre, aspectos de um quase meio século de transição do trabalho escravo para o trabalho livre e da monarquia para a república*, 1959; 5th edn, RJ: Record, 2000
Order	G. Freyre, *Order and Progress: Brazil from Monarchy to Republic*, ed. and trans. R. W. Horton, New York: Knopf, 1970 (an extremely abbreviated translation)
OUP	Oxford University Press
PBA	G. Freyre, *Problemas brasileiros de antropologia*, 1943; 3rd edn, RJ: Olympio, 1962
PT	G. Freyre, *The Portuguese in the Tropics*, Lisbon: Commission to Commemorate Prince Henry, 1961
QP	G. Freyre, *Quase Política*, 1950; 2nd edn, RJ: Olýmpio, 1966
R&T	G. Freyre, *Região e Tradição*, 1941; 2nd edn, RJ: Record, 1968
RJ	Rio de Janeiro
S&M	G. Freyre, *Sobrados e Mocambos: decadencia do patriarchado rural no Brasil*, RJ: Olympio, 1936; new edn, RJ: Record, 2000
Skidmore	T. E. Skidmore, 'Gilberto Freyre and the Early Brazilian Republic: Some Notes on Methodology', *Comparative Studies in Society and History* 6 (1963–4), 490–505
SL	G. Freyre, 'Social Life in Nineteenth-Century Brazil', *HAHR* 5 (1922), 597–630
Sociología	G. Freyre, *Sociología: introdução ao estudo de seus princípios*, 1945; 2nd edn, RJ: Olympio, 2 vols, 1957
SP	São Paulo
TA	G. Freyre, *Tempo de Aprendiz*, 2 vols, SP: IBRASA, 1979
TM	G. Freyre, *Tempo Morto e Outros Tempos*, 1975: 2nd edn, SP: Global, 2006
UP	University Press
USP	University of São Paulo
VF&C	G. Freyre, *Vida Forma e Cor*, 1962; 2nd edn, RJ: Olympio, 1987
VSN	G. Freyre, 'Vida Social no Nordeste', in *Livro do Nordeste*, 1928; 2nd edn, Recife: Secretaria da Justiça, 1979
VT	M. L. Pallares-Burke, *Gilberto Freyre: Um vitoriano dos trópicos*, SP: UNESP, 2005

Preface and Acknowledgements

One of the strengths of Gilberto Freyre, as will be argued later in this book, was that he saw Brazil from the viewpoint of an outsider as well as an insider. The authors also happen to combine these viewpoints, since one is Brazilian and the other English. One of us encountered Freyre in the footnotes to Fernand Braudel's famous book on the Mediterranean, and read *Casa Grande & Senzala* – in English – before hearing the author lecture at the University of Sussex in 1965. Ironically enough, the other, although Brazilian, encountered Freyre's work later, in the 1980s. In her generation, which went to university at the end of the 1960s, he did not attract much interest, since his support for the military dictatorship (1964–85) alienated many students. We would like to think that, as an Anglophile who was also passionately Brazilian, Freyre would have welcomed our joint approach, even if he would not have agreed with all our conclusions.

In our many discussions of Freyre over the years, even when we began from different points of view, we have usually come to agree – but not always. To use Freyre's own terms, we have aimed at an equilibrium of conflicting opinions rather than a completely smooth or bland interpretation. Our compromise has affected the style of the book as well as its content. The reader may sometimes notice a contrast between a more prolix Latin style and a more concise British one. The result is a hybrid book, not inappropriate in the case of a study attempting to mediate between a Brazilian thinker and an English-speaking or, more exactly, English-reading public.

The idea of writing this book together was a result of the celebrations of Gilberto Freyre's centenary in 2000, when we each wrote several papers about him and felt that we had already written half the book – though as it turned out, most of the research as well as the writing was still to come. Maria Lúcia's book about the young Freyre both postponed and assisted this second project.

In the course of our research we have been fortunate enough to receive assistance from many quarters. Our thanks go in the first place to

Freyre's family and to the staff of the Fundação Gilberto Freyre in Recife, where we worked in Gilberto's house, and to the British Academy for the Small Research Grant that allowed us to spend two months there. We are also grateful to the archivists and librarians at Baylor University, Columbia University and the Catholic University of America for their help. Our work was supported by fellowships at two research institutes, the Getty Research Institute in Los Angeles and the Netherlands Institute for Advanced Study in Wassenaar, giving us the opportunity for intense writing against a background of Californian sunshine and Dutch snow.

Our special thanks go to Edson Nery de Fonseca and Gláucio Veiga in Recife. The first has long been an admirer of Freyre's, who said that for him reading *Casa Grande & Senzala* was like a psychoanalysis. The second was once an adversary, 'the most terrible anti-Gilberto in the world', as Freyre himself once remarked, but became a 'fellow scholar', whose Marxism was no longer an obstacle to 'our *rapprochement*'. Our conversations with both Edson and Gláucio helped us come closer to Gilberto the man as well as the scholar.

We should also like to thank our friend José de Souza Martins for his encouragement and help, and especially for his critical reading of a draft of the chapter on social theory; Simone Meucci, for sending us her doctoral thesis, 'Gilberto Freyre e a sociología no Brasil'; Julietta and John Harvey, Philip Howell, Christel and David Lane, David Lehmann, Marcos Chor Maio and Thiago Nicodemo for references and comments; the audiences of lectures and seminar papers in Cambridge, Colchester, Florence, Heidelberg, London, Madrid, Marília, Mexico City, Oxford and San Diego, where we tried out some of our ideas; and the anonymous publisher's reader, whose comments we received at the last moment. Our thanks also go to our family and friends for their patience whenever the conversation turned to Freyre, as it often did, as well as for answering our questionnaire about blocks of flats, maids and service lifts in São Paulo today.

1 The Importance Of Being Gilberto

What was or is the importance of Gilberto Freyre? He has some claim to be regarded not only as a leading social thinker and historian but also as the most famous intellectual of twentieth-century Brazil or even, as one enthusiast suggested, of Latin America. However, in his long life (1900–87), Freyre played many other parts. In the language of Lewis Mumford, a thinker whom he much admired, he was a 'generalist' rather than a specialist. When he was presented for an honorary degree at the University of Sussex in 1965, Asa Briggs called him someone who 'spans the disciplines'. In fact, he was a 'one-man-band' (*homem-orquestra*), as Freyre himself sometimes described people whom he admired, among them the American poet Walt Whitman.

In his reading, Freyre transgressed the frontier between the so-called 'two cultures' of science and the humanities, referring in his historical works to studies of physiology, climatology, nutrition and medicine. He was active as a sociologist, a historian, a journalist, a deputy in the Brazilian Assembly, a novelist, poet and artist (ranging from caricatures to watercolours). He was a cultural critic, with a good deal to say about architecture, past and present, and a public intellectual, whose pronouncements on race, region and empire – not to mention sex – made him famous in some quarters and notorious in others. It is difficult to imagine how he found the time for so much reading and writing, as well as other activities, despite the support team of family, friends and disciples who typed his manuscripts (originally written in pencil) or copied documents for him in the archives.

In Brazil he is best known as the author of one of the most influential interpretations of that country's culture and history, *Casa Grande & Senzala* (1933: literally 'The Big House and the Slave Quarters', translated into English under the title *The Masters and the Slaves*). Its central argument about the importance of miscegenation in Brazilian history and of the importance of the Indian and more especially of the African contribution to Brazilian culture – virtually denied before *Casa Grande & Senzala* (henceforth *CGS*) appeared in 1933 – helped his compatriots to define their identity. Later books continued the project of interpreting Brazil from the perspective of social history or historical sociology. From the 1930s onwards, the author was commonly described, like Henry James, as 'The Master', or alternatively 'The Master of Apipucos' (his little 'Big House' in a suburb of Recife). A documentary about his life was launched under that title.[1]

Freyre knew how to appeal both to academic readers and to a wider public. *CGS* was received with enthusiasm by the anthropologists Alfred Métraux and Georges Balandier, the critic Roland Barthes and the historians Fernand Braudel, Asa Briggs, Lucien Febvre and Frank Tannenbaum. In Brazil, the book's twenty-fifth and fiftieth anniversaries were marked by academic celebrations. *CGS* also enjoyed a popular success that few history books can match. Besides more than forty editions and translations into nine languages, this study has been 'translated' into a comic book and a television mini-series, while two directors (one of them Robert Rossellini) planned to turn it into a film.

As for Freyre's later publications, a newspaper survey made in 1948 showed that his new book about the British in Brazil, *Ingleses no Brasil* ('The English in Brazil'; henceforth *IB*) was the best-seller of the week, ahead of a new novel by the Scottish writer A. J. Cronin (then at the height of his reputation) and the autobiography of Rachel Mussolini, the wife of the late Duce, telling the story of her life with Benito. Another historical study, *Ordem e Progresso* (*Order and Progress*; henceforth *O&P*) sold 10,000 copies in the six weeks following its publication in 1959.

Freyre has been described as a 'national monument' and – by the modernist writer Oswald de Andrade – as 'our literary totem' (*nosso escritor totêmico*). No wonder then that the Committee on Education and Culture of the Chamber of Deputies chose him as Brazilian candidate for the Nobel Prize for Literature in 1947, or that the Brazilian government declared the centenary of his birth, 2000, to be 'The National Year of Gilberto de Mello Freyre', in which a postage stamp was issued in his honour. Less attention was apparently given to the five-hundredth anniversary of the discovery of Brazil by the Portuguese than to the discovery of Brazil by Freyre for the Brazilians. Gilberto – as he is often called, even by people who never knew him – has also become a local hero. In 2004 the new international airport in his native city of Recife, in the state of Pernambuco, was christened 'Gilberto Freyre Airport'. School parties regularly visit his house, while taxi-drivers, proud of their local celebrity, offer to take tourists there.

The totemic writer was also a breaker of taboos. His colloquial style offended some of his first readers in the early 1930s. His blunt writing about sex was condemned as pornographic. His statements about the influence of African culture on Brazilians – all Brazilians, without exception – were quite shocking at the time that they were first put forward.

Freyre deserves the attention not only of readers concerned with Brazil or South America but also of readers with a general interest in history or social theory – even if he is better described as a 'quasi-theorist', as we shall explain later. Essential to his project was the focus on the everyday, on private life, or as Freyre himself said (following the Goncourt brothers) 'intimate history' (*historia íntima*). Intimate history, including the study of food, clothes, housing and the body, was a reaction against the traditional assumption of the 'dignity of history' and a plea for the study of 'the Cinderellas of history', ordinary people, as well as humble objects and apparently trivial yet significant details. This style of history has enlisted many recruits in the last few years under the banner of the 'new cultural history', but in the 1930s and 1940s it was still relatively unusual, if not downright eccentric.

One of the central arguments of this book is that the histories of historical writing, histories that emphasize contributions from the 'centre', in other words Europe and North America, need to be redrawn in order to take account of the pioneering work of this gifted sociologist-historian from the periphery. However, the fact that he was a pioneer of approaches that are now acceptable or even orthodox is not the only reason or even the best reason for reading the former heretic today. Some of his ideas are more shocking now than when he first put them forward. Others have not been taken up, or taken up only to be abandoned – yet we can still learn from them.

Freyre was a major social theorist or more exactly – given his aversion to system – a major social thinker, one of the few who have not come from Western Europe or the United States. It has often been noted that social, cultural and political theories that claim to describe the human condition are usually formulated on the basis of the experience of those parts of the world alone. How different would the history of sociology or anthropology have been if Max Weber (say) had come from India, Emile Durkheim from Cuba or Norbert Elias from Martinique? The problem is that even when social and cultural theories have been produced in the 'Third World' – by M. N. Srinivas, for instance, Fernando Ortiz or Frantz Fanon – they have taken a long time to travel to the Western centres of social studies. Even today, despite the rise of Postcolonial Studies, these ideas of the three scholars are not as well known in the West as they deserve to be.

A similar point might be made about Brazil and about Freyre. Brazil's Carnival and popular music (not to mention sex and violence) are in the limelight of publicity, but the country's scholars and thinkers remain in the shadows, Freyre among them. Best known in his own country for his positive evaluation of miscegenation and cultural hybridity, together with his controversial theories or quasi-theories of 'racial democracy' and 'Luso-Tropicalism', he also put forward original and provocative ideas on such topics as the sociology of architecture, language, medicine, leisure and time and the problems of post-industrialism, post-capitalism and – to use a term that he was employing long before it became fashionable – 'postmodernism'. His career shows that problems and controversies that we often think belong to our own time alone have been discussed for generations, while the analyses and the solutions that he put forward have not lost their relevance.

In a recent study of Islamic fundamentalism, Roxanne Euben has argued the case for what she calls 'comparative political theory', in other words the introduction of 'non-Western perspectives into familiar debates about the problems of living together, thus ensuring that "political theory" is about human and not merely Western dilemmas'.[2] To write about Freyre's work is to make a contribution to a comparative social theory in the same spirit.

Freyre's ideas are of particular relevance today for both political and academic reasons. His suggestion that Brazilians should accept themselves as a mixture of ethnic groups and cultures, rather than fragment into Italo-Brazilians, German-Brazilians, Afro-Brazilians and so on, remains a topical issue in Brazil, but globalization has made it relevant to many other parts of the world as well. In the academic world, his mixture of sociology and anthropology with history and literature (another form of hybridity!), was unorthodox in his own time – the moment of the rise of quantitative methods – but is taken more seriously today. His interest in gender, ethnicity, hybridity, identity, cultural patrimony and the problems of the periphery ensure that his ideas are still topical.

Freyre's achievement has been assessed in very different ways. It has often been simplified, thus ignoring its paradoxes and ambiguities and it has sometimes been utilized to support some cause, regional, national or ideological, as in the notorious case of the Salazar regime in Portugal, to be discussed in detail later in this book.

His admirers have presented Freyre as if he had always been a follower of the great German-American anthropologist Franz Boas, replacing race by culture as the key to the interpretation of Brazil, thus suppressing the many hesitations, qualifications and ambiguities in Freyre's thought.[3] In opposed yet similar fashion, critics, especially Marxist critics, have focused on – and in a sense invented – a reactionary Freyre, ignoring his many references to social antagonisms and treating his famous trilogy about Brazil as a simple description of a society marked by social harmony, consensus or 'racial democracy'. These opposite interpretations are equally reductive and simplistic.

Freyre himself might be described as an accomplice in this process of simplification. The invention of Freyre included his self-invention. For example, he too presented himself as if he had been a follower of Boas ever since his student days. He liked to spread rumours about himself, such as the story current in the early 1930s that he was about to marry the daughter of an American millionaire and was going to buy an island, a sugar factory and a major newspaper in Recife. In the 1940s, he was criticized in a newspaper for his 'exhibitionist' pleasure in appearing in public and posing for photographs.

Thanks to this tendency, Freyre left a great deal of material for future biographers – the first biography (written by his cousin Diogo Meneses) appearing as early as 1944, when the protagonist was in his early forties.[4] The prefaces to his many books include a good deal of autobiographical material. As he grew older, Freyre wrote and spoke about himself more and more. In his sixties, he published reflections on his career under the title *Como e porque sou e não sou sociólogo* ('How and why I am and am not a sociologist'). In his seventies, he published what he claimed was a slightly edited version of the diary that he kept as an adolescent and young adult, a text that is now known to be a later autobiography in diary form.[5] At eighty, he gave interviews to the press (including *Playboy*) in which he spoke openly about sexual experiments.

As in the case of all self-presentations, it would obviously be a mistake to interpret these texts literally or believe every claim that they make: claims to have been the first to put forward certain ideas, for instance, to have been close to famous writers such as W. B. Yeats or H. L. Mencken, or to have been the victim of a conspiracy of silence. On the other hand, since self-images play an important role in everyone's life, they have a place in any biography or portrait. In any case it is quite difficult to say something about Freyre, even something critical, that he had not already said himself somewhere or other: about his lack of system, his penchant for calling long books 'essays', his mania for prefaces and so on.

In spite of his egocentrism, it is fair to say that there are signs, dispersed among Freyre's many writings, of a person who did not take himself too seriously and even made fun of his notorious vanity. He was quite

aware that he could perform too much and mocked the way in which he
savoured praise 'like a child savouring sweets'. In fact, his friend Simkins
made a perspicacious remark about Freyre's sense of humour when referring to his self-presentation as a 'Federal Senator of Brazil' in the 1940s. 'As
he struts and poses I am sure there is at least one person laughing. That
person is the senator himself.'[6]

Another major source tells us about Gilberto the reader. To the
despair of librarians and the delight of his biographers, Freyre was an active reader who often dog-eared the pages of his books. He had the habit
of reading with a pencil or pen in his hand in order to mark passages of
particular interest. When a pencil or pen was not within reach, he not infrequently scored passages with his fingernail. He also wrote comments in
the margins of books, allowing us to catch his thought in flight, as it were.
Thanks to this evidence, together with his letters, it is possible to identify the thinkers most important for Freyre's development, his 'masters',
as he sometimes called them, and to see more clearly than before what
attracted him to these thinkers and how he used, qualified or developed
their ideas.

Among the conclusions that emerge from this source, two should
be singled out here at the start. The first concerns Isaiah Berlin's much-
employed distinction between two types of intellectual: the hedgehog,
concerned with one big idea, and the fox, who is many-sided. At first sight
Freyre is a classic instance of a fox, a voracious reader with many interests, a 'intellectual sponge' as the writer Bruce Chatwin once called him,
soaking up ideas as well as information, absorbing them and making them
part of himself. [7] However, some of his annotations reveal the hedgehog
inside the fox, showing that when he was reading about England or the
United States, for instance, he was thinking about Brazil. Reading G. M.
Trevelyan's *English Social History*, he marked the pages on country houses,
travel and child labour. Reading Wilbur J. Cash's well-known study of the
United States, *The Mind of the South* (1941), he sometimes wrote in the
margin 'Brazil'. His mind was less of a sponge than a filter, selecting what
would be useful for his work.

Freyre was not a marble statue but human, sometimes 'all too human', in his intellectual life as in his life more generally. In this study we
aim at being critical, at pointing to what we consider to be the weaknesses
of our protagonist. However, we also consider it our duty to present his
point of view and to concentrate on his strengths, the positive aspects of
his work from which readers from different cultures can still learn today.

What follows is not an intellectual biography in the strict sense – that
is, a chronological account of the development of an individual, like the

detailed account of the young Freyre that one of the authors has already published, *Gilberto Freyre: Um vitoriano dos trópicos* ('Gilberto Freyre: a Victorian from the Tropics'; henceforth *VT*). What we offer is what Gilberto himself might have called a 'semi-biography'. It presents an intellectual portrait of Freyre in the manner of the portrait of Max Weber by the American sociologist Reinhart Bendix.[8] In other words, this is a book concerned more with the thought than the thinker, and consequently organized by themes rather than by decades.

All the same, it would be a mistake to ignore the intellectual development of a man whose publications were spread over some seventy years and whose views changed more than he ever cared to admit, most obviously in the case of his conversion from a belief in the importance of race, and in the superiority of the white race in particular, to a belief in the importance of culture, including the contribution of the slaves to the culture of their masters. To reinforce this sense of development we have included a brief chronology of his life and writings. This intellectual portrait is also the portrait of an intellectual in the sense of an individual who, as we have said, was attracted not only by literature and scholarship but also by public affairs, moving between the two realms with apparent ease.[9]

Freyre often thought in a comparative mode. In order to understand Brazil better, he made comparisons and contrasts with Spanish America (especially with the plantations of Cuba), with the United States (especially the South), with Britain (noting a similar art of compromise, but also, he thought, a lack of adaptability to the tropics). Viewing Brazil as a kind of tropical Russia, a huge country with slaves instead of serfs, he acquired books about Russia, from Georgi Plekhanov to Richard Pipes. In order to help identify Freyre's distinctive approaches and achievements, we have adopted a similar approach, suggesting comparisons between his work and that of other Brazilians (Mário de Andrade, Jorge Amado and Sérgio Buarque de Holanda, for instance) and Latin Americans (Jorge Borges, Fernando Ortiz).

Freyre's work also has affinities with that of some European historians and theorists. As a portrait of an age, we might – and indeed will – compare *CGS* to the Dutchman Johan Huizinga's *Autumn of the Middle Ages*[10]. In other ways its approach resembles that of Philippe Ariès, the French historian of childhood and the family. As a social theorist, Freyre's style resembles that of Georg Simmel, a master of the impressionistic approach to sociology; while his interests in the history of material culture and everyday life ran parallel to those of Norbert Elias. Like Pierre Bourdieu, he viewed his own culture with foreign or anthropological eyes and focused on what Freyre called the 'insignia' of social distinction.

In fact, Freyre had a life-long interest in foreign writers and thinkers, especially the English and French, appropriating and transforming, or as he said, 'tropicalizing' their ideas. His gradual discovery of this intellectual world is the main topic of the chapter that follows.

2 Portrait of the Artist as a Young Man[1]

Precisely because of his wide curiosity and interests, the young Gilberto Freyre found the Recife of his time too narrow for his cultural ambitions. He saw not only his 'village in the provinces', as he called his city, but the whole country as too backward to offer the educational opportunities he longed for. 'Why was I not born an Englishman, a German or American?' he once lamented to a friend.[2]

Freyre's close relatives were willing to help him to overcome the obstacles to his development and, following a long tradition among the Brazilian elite of sending their sons to study abroad, paid for him to live five years away from home. Indeed, to travel and study abroad was, not only for Freyre but also for his family, a means for the unquiet, talented and promising youngster to develop his great potential fully and realize his ambitions. As his older brother made clear in a letter sent from the United States to the sixteen-year-old Freyre in Recife, to study abroad for a few years was a necessary step for his important, albeit still unknown, future role in the country's so much needed development.

Freyre was born in Recife in 1900 into a relatively impoverished upper-middle-class family that had been part of the rural aristocracy of the state of Pernambuco in the North-East of Brazil, which was once the most important region of the country. His mother Francisca was descended from one of the most distinguished plantation owners, the Wanderleys of Serinhaém, their Dutch name, Van der Ley, going back to the Dutch occupation of Pernambuco in the seventeenth century. His father, Alfredo, was a judge as well a professor of political economy in the Law Faculty of Recife. Despite this academic background, it did not seem at first that Freyre was destined to achieve any intellectual success. Like W. B. Yeats, Einstein and so many other great men, the young Gilberto did not excel right from the start. His grandmother, as his father recalls, had died almost certain that the young Freyre was 'mentally retarded'. Indeed, much more interested in drawing than in the three Rs, he learned to count, read and write only at the age of eight, thanks to an English teacher, Mr Williams, who recognized his 'unusual intelligence', stimulated the boy's enthusiasm for English literature and culture and would be always remembered with gratitude by Freyre and his father for the stimulus and understanding he had provided.[3]

The Education of Gilberto Freyre

Freyre's school, where his father also taught, was the American Baptist College in Recife, which attracted children of the best families of the region. Baptist schools, which had been founded in different parts of Brazil, were part of the Protestant missionary project of the late nineteenth century. Although they failed to convert large numbers of people, as they had hoped, the Baptists were successful in their educational enterprises, which were open to Catholics. The Freyres chose the Baptist school for their children on account of its high academic standards and innovative methods, not its religious affiliation. All the same, Freyre did become a Protestant for a short time in his late teens, to the dismay of his mother, for whom Protestantism was equivalent to heresy. At that time, as he later confessed, he had been seduced by the example of the missionary and explorer David Livingstone, who was, for a time, his great hero. His school years were years of voracious and precocious reading (including Tolstoy, Kant and Nietzsche) not to mention writing for his school magazine and even, at the age of fifteen, giving a public lecture on Herbert Spencer.

It was thanks to the connections of the American College with sister institutions in the United States that Freyre was sent to Baylor, a Baptist university in Waco, Texas, known as the 'Baptist Vatican', which had already accepted a number of Brazilian students, some of them from the leading families of Recife. Europe would have been his family's first choice for him, and his too, but the year in which he turned eighteen was 1918, not exactly the ideal moment for a prolonged stay in France or England.

Freyre found Baylor and Waco very disappointing and, ironically for someone who was trying to escape from the narrowness of Recife, 'terribly provincial', as he put it. The majority of his fellow students he considered mediocre and, although he admitted that the racial prejudices he shared with the Brazilian elite grew even stronger in Texas, the violence against black people that abounded in the region was certainly disconcerting. It was there that he lost his brief enthusiasm for Protestantism, having realized that there was little in common between his admired Livingstone and the students – whom he described as 'Bible-maniacs' – who were being prepared to become missionaries. He rejected the pretentiousness of their claim to be 'giving lessons' to the Catholics.

On the other hand, Freyre's interest in books in general and in English literature, in particular, was greatly encouraged by the one professor at Baylor whom he admired deeply and who became his most long-lasting American friend and interlocutor, the head of the English Department, Andrew Joseph Armstrong, a convinced anglophile, at least as far as literature was concerned. Armstrong shared with his students his belief in the power of books to enlarge one's mind, stressing in his lectures that by reading widely, without prejudice against this or that cultural tradition, an individual would not only live his own limited life, but would be able to 'live the lives of every race!'

Thanks to this professor's dynamism, Baylor, and even Waco, was spared from the total monotony and 'banality' of a province, as Freyre soon noticed. The many concerts, plays and visits by major cultural figures, national and international, that Armstrong organized on the campus – more than a hundred of them in the course of his academic life – were a way for him to widen the horizons of the students, one of the main roles of a university, as he saw it. During Baylor's Jubilee, in 1920, Freyre was delighted to hear lectures by W. B. Yeats and the American poets Vachel Lindsay and Amy Lowell, who would all play a part in his development as a writer.

In Armstrong's department, which was far from conventional, Freyre studied – along with Shakespeare – authors as different, for instance, as Dante, Tasso, Ariosto, Goethe, the medieval German poets known as the *Minnesinger*, the now obscure German novelist Sudermann and three genres of English literature that would be extremely important for his intellectual development: the novel, the essay and the travelogue. All of these were approached, in a typical Armstrong style, not only through their formal or literary aspects, but as a kind of cultural history.[4]

Freyre's passion for English literature certainly took root at Baylor, although he did not devote all his time to its study. He followed courses in history and sociology, he read widely on his own, and he wrote regular articles for a Recife newspaper, the *Diário de Pernambuco* (founded in 1825, making it the oldest newspaper in Latin America). He also observed the culture around him, that of a small town in the American South, with its wounds from the Civil War still unhealed, at a time when the First World War was ending, the Ku Klux Klan growing and the lynching of African-Americans was not uncommon.

When the time came for him to decide where to go and what to study after graduation, Freyre chose the Faculty of Political Science at Columbia University. His letters reveal his excitement at living in a metropolis and participating in its rich cultural life after two years in a small town. New

York itself, as he told his newspaper readers, was 'full of educational opportunities' and in the middle of it he felt as a 'greedy child in front of a huge bowl of ... pudding'. Another reason for his choice of university was his intention of writing a dissertation on the history of South America under the supervision of a leading Columbia historian, William R. Shepherd.

Disappointed with his performance in the English language, which was not as outstanding as he wished, and aware of the limitations that a foreign language entails for someone with high literary ambitions, the young Freyre soon decided to give up the successful career as a 'new Conrad', on which Professor Armstrong had wagered, turning his efforts to the study of a discipline in which he had received better grades at Baylor. 'I can walk in English, but not dance on tiptoe. I have to content myself with walking – nothing more – and even then, badly; falling down sometimes', he lamented. Little did he know that the great Conrad also fought a daily battle with English grammar and syntax.

In 1921 and 1922 the majority of the courses that Freyre took at Columbia were in history, including some given by Carleton Hayes, who, like Charles and Mary Beard and James H. Robinson ('one of the great innovators in the study of history', as Freyre wrote later), was associated with the early twentieth-century movement known as the 'New History', drawing on the social sciences in order to analyse economic, social and cultural as well as political aspects of the past. For example, in a study of the Germanic invasions of the Roman Empire, Hayes emphasized 'the contact between religions rather than between races'.[5]

At the same time, Freyre was following courses in sociology given by Franklin Giddings, and courses in anthropology by Franz Boas. Giddings is more or less forgotten now, but at this time he enjoyed a reputation as one of the leading American sociologists. A follower of Herbert Spencer who dedicated most of his writing and teaching to the spreading of his mentor's ideas, Giddings' most original contribution was to stress the importance of identity, which he called 'consciousness of kind'.[6] Boas, who continues to enjoy a high reputation, was the leading anthropologist in the United States. Nevertheless, he was not successful at that time in the almost solitary battle that he fought against the growth of racism and its institutionalization throughout the country. Trained in geography in Germany, and at home in museums as well as in universities, Boas was not only an outspoken critic of racism but also of simple evolutionary theories that had no place for regional variation.

It is worth emphasizing that at this point in time both sociology and anthropology were closer to history than they would become a generation later. In their lectures in the early 1920s, both Giddings and Boas devoted considerable attention to the development of civilization. The introductory course in anthropology attended by Freyre, for example, stated very clearly that one of its aims was to deal with the 'problem of the progress of civilization, and of the controlling causes that influence characteristic lines of cultural development'.

An important event in Freyre's Columbia days was the lecture he heard in November 1921 by the British classicist turned pacifist campaigner, Alfred Zimmern, on the relation of Greek political thought to modern problems. So relevant was this encounter for his development that in his later memoirs Freyre misremembered it as a course that he had followed at Columbia. Author of the once famous *The Greek Commonwealth* (1911), a work that Harold Laski considered essential reading for the new generation, Zimmern had the unusual gift of making the past come alive and of showing its relevance to the present. As his former student Arnold Toynbee confessed, this talent made Zimmern's lectures 'one of the most sensational experiences' of his Oxford years.

Zimmern's major work was extremely innovative in its attempt to understand ancient Greek politics as the result of geographic, economic and social factors. Like other pioneer classicists from Cambridge and Oxford, among them Gilbert Murray, Robert Marett and Jane Harrrison, Zimmern had an anthropological approach to historical understanding. For instance, he considered the Greek patriarchal family to be an extremely resilient social and religious system which remained in vigour from the age of Homer to that of Plato.

For Freyre, the experience of hearing Zimmern was, although brief, extremely significant. This was perhaps the first time that he had heard a historian who did not exclude from his interest everything that was not political or military and who would not hesitate to mix history with poetry and philosophy, citing writers such as Browning, Nietzsche, Unamuno and Tolstoy in order to 'extract truth from fiction'. Freyre was soon reading Zimmern's major work and drawing analogies between the histories of ancient Greece and Brazil, two societies composed of masters and slaves and of patriarchal families.[7]

It would take some time for other ideas of Zimmern's to bear fruit – such as the harmony and humanity that counteracted conflict in the relationship between master and slave – but Freyre's later development reveals the rich contribution they made to his new paradigm for the interpretation of Brazil. It is interesting to note that the expression 'Big House', which Freyre would make emblematic of the Brazilian patriarchal system and of the 'feudal' power of the plantation owners, was used by Zimmern as a synonym for the master of the Greek patriarchal family.

Also important for the intellectual development of the young Freyre were two friends he made in the Columbia years. Together with Armstrong and the Brazilian diplomat and historian Manoel de Oliveira Lima, then living in Washington, DC, who were Freyre's oldest and dearest mentors and confidants, two students of history whom he met in 1920 became important interlocutors for him for many years to come.

Francis Butler Simkins (born in 1897) came from South Carolina, went to Columbia to write a Ph.D thesis on the history of his own state and became a respected historian of the Old South. Rüdiger Bilden (born in 1893), was an immigrant from Germany, who impressed his teachers at Columbia by his humanist education, analytical capacity and rare linguistic knowledge, but for many reasons, mostly beyond his control, he did not succeed in the career in which he seemed so promising.

Bilden was writing a doctorate under Shepherd's supervision on the history of Latin America, but having a wide range of interests, from ancient history to American political theory, he became a kind of mentor to his friends, introducing Freyre, for instance, to a number of German writers and thinkers. It was perhaps thinking of Bilden that Freyre wrote to a friend that he was determined to study like 'a Friar or a German'. Aware that both of them owed a great deal to Bilden, and regretting the difficult life of the most promising of the three friends, Simkins reminded Freyre of their great debt years later: 'God knows, Rüdiger helped educate you and me, and we owe him something.'

In his New York period, although Freyre's studies were aimed at achieving a doctorate in history, he continued his love affair with English literature, voraciously reading works of fiction, literary criticism and biographies of artistic and literary figures. It is revealing of this love that when writing to friends, Freyre's enthusiastic comments about what he was reading refer almost exclusively to literary and biographical texts.

The long list includes works by or about Oscar Wilde, Matthew Arnold, Lafcadio Hearn, H. L. Mencken, John Ruskin, William Morris, George Moore and Walter Pater.[8] In the case of Pater and Wilde it was especially their aesthetic approach to the world that attracted Freyre, an interest that was also revealed in his bohemian appearance. As his friend Simkins put it, 'he had almond eyes, the black and heavy hair of a part South American Indian, and the shabby and unseasonable clothes of the bohemian. One expected him to write decadent verse which no one could understand.'

It was thanks in part to Pater that Freyre developed an interest in the history of childhood. Reading, in the early 1920s, the beautiful autobiographical and allegorical story 'The Child in the House', Freyre was made aware, perhaps for the first time, of the importance of childhood experiences for the mental and spiritual trajectory of all human beings.[9] No fewer than four of the articles he wrote for *DP* in the 1920s were concerned with children and their books and toys. Visiting New York Public Library, for instance, Freyre was impressed by the section devoted to children's books and contrasted the situation with that obtaining in Brazil. The history of the child seems to have interested him partly as an opportunity to discuss his own childhood, and partly as a microcosm of the history of Brazilian culture, while the house, discussed so sensitively by Pater, would become a major theme in his later work.

Freyre abandoned the idea of taking a doctorate for financial reasons. He had to content himself with a master's thesis, which seems not to have upset him, since he was never much interested in academic grades for their own sake. The most tangible result of Freyre's New York years was the historical essay he wrote on a theme that was probably stimulated by homesickness, the social history of his own region, Pernambuco. The dissertation, published in 1922, was entitled 'Social Life in Nineteenth-Century Brazil' and offered a brief discussion of a number of themes that would continue to preoccupy the author for most of his life.

One of these themes is childhood, more exactly the lack of a real childhood for the sons and daughters of the planters. Another is the Big House and its furnishings. A third theme that would recur in Freyre's later work is what some German thinkers have called 'the contemporaneity of the non contemporary', in other words the idea that different social groups in the same society live effectively in different periods. 'In their material environment and, to a certain extent, in their social life', he wrote, 'the majority of Brazilians of the [18]50s were in the Middle Ages: only the elite was living in the eighteenth century.' Elsewhere in the essay the author refers to 'medieval landlordism', 'baronial style' and 'feudal' plantations. Finally, this essay already argues for the existence of a relatively gentle slaveholding regime in Brazil. In his usual vivid style, Freyre writes that 'The Brazilian slave lived the life of a cherub if we contrast his lot with that of the English and other European factory-worker [*sic*] in the middle of the last century.' The confident judgements of the young man are also worth noting, from the 'almost total absence of critical thought' in Brazil from 1848 to 1864 to the description of the plan of the *sobrado* (mansion) as 'a masterpiece of architectural stupidity'.

Some of the points just mentioned had been made by earlier writers, among them the parallel between the Brazilian slaveholding regime and European feudalism, already noted by the statesman Joaquim Nabuco. Again, when the author suggested that nineteenth-century Brazilian slaves were treated better than European factory workers, he was probably, as he later suggested, 'unconsciously following the lead of José de Alencar [a famous novelist of the nineteenth century], whose books I had read with enthusiasm, even fervour, as a child'. The older Freyre also noted that the comparison had been made by English travellers of the time and also by Carleton Hayes, 'my old teacher in Columbia University'.[10]

Despite these precedents, 'Social Life' remains a master's thesis of remarkable precocity and originality, which was published almost immediately as an article in the *Hispanic American Historical Review*. This social history of Pernambuco was constructed from travelogues, memoirs and what is now known as oral history, Freyre's sources including his father's father, described as 'a sugar planter', and his mother's mother. In its concern with everyday life, unusual at this time, the essay reveals the inspiration of the New History, Giddings (on 'consciousness of kind') and Walter Pater, from whom he borrowed the phrase which sets the tone of the work in the very first paragraph, saying that in studying history his ambition was the same as the British essayist, who wanted to know 'how people lived, what they wore and what they looked like'.

The Scholar Gypsy

If being unable to take a doctorate did not bother Freyre, the possibility of not going to Europe worried him a good deal. For someone like him, so self-conscious about the importance of his formative years, a trip to the Old World was essential. From Nietzsche, as the marginalia he left in his copy of *Human, All Too Human* reveal, he had learned that talent or even genius was not enough by itself to produce a great man. A great deal of effort and experiences would have to be added. On the same lines, Freyre's mentor Oliveira Lima emphasized that his education would be incomplete without the experience of Europe. When the rise of the dollar against the Brazilian currency made his family consider cancelling the so much awaited visit to the Old World, the young Freyre was disconsolate and talked about going there anyway, even if it meant travelling like a 'tramp'. His plans for the trip were extremely ambitious and seem to follow Nietzsche's recommendations about the importance of seeing the world from different perspectives (*verschiedene Augen*). Inspired by Matthew Arnold's poem, *The Scholar Gypsy*, Freyre confesses in his notebook that he planned to travel as a 'scholar gypsy' [*cigano de beca*], looking for a variety of contacts with the objective, as he put it, of 'understanding the most diverse points of view'.[11]

Although his family was unable to finance a doctorate, they eventually found enough money for Freyre to visit Europe for a few months before returning to Brazil. He arrived in Paris in August 1922 and was immediately taken by all the beauty and tradition which surrounded him and which he absorbed with 'all the greed of a starving man', who had missed it all his life. Despite its monumental technological innovations, the New World, where everything was new and 'smelled of varnish or fresh paint', could not compete with these traditions and so lost much of its attraction. While in Paris, he wrote about the enriching experience of meeting people from very different backgrounds, such as 'a Catholic student attracted to the idea of *Action Française*, a Tolstoyan woman in love with Romain Rolland', a representative of the old aristocracy, a federalist poet from the provinces, French students, Oxford students and so on. In Germany, where he was impressed by the museums and the Expressionist movement, one of the things that most attracted him was a toy factory he visited in Nuremberg.

However, what seemed to have pleased him most in his early European days was how close he was to the source of great talents. While in Paris, for instance, he felt that the whole city – its walls, pavements and even air – was impregnated with literature. The cafés and bars named after Racine, Victor Cousin, Voltaire and Claude Bernard made him feel 'as if he had been dipped' in literature, he commented. And in England, he was thrilled with the experience of tracking down his English literary heroes, like Samuel Johnson when in London, and Pater when in Oxford.

Notwithstanding these attractions, the postwar climate proved to be somewhat depressing and the French academic world rather disappointing ('Paris appears banal nowadays', he says), when compared to England and especially Oxford, the places in Europe which turned out to surpass his already great expectations.

The prejudice in favour of British culture had been developing in Freyre since his childhood, thanks to the influence of his teacher Mr Williams and of his father as well as the traditional anglophilia of his native Pernambuco, so intense that some nineteenth-century critics were led to complain that the influx of English products and ideas was 'Londonizing our land'. Extremely revealing of his early enthusiasm is the fact that the first essay that Freyre wrote, on a theme of his own choice, for an advanced secondary history class, concerned British civilization. The admiration that he always felt for the country was a kind of 'premonition', he once admitted.

However, his experiences as a traveller must have made Freyre's anglophilia even stronger. To begin with, Armstrong strongly recommended Oxford to him as an appropriate destination for a talented young man, were he to follow the advice of giving up the idea of writing in Portuguese and trying instead to become a great writer in the universal English language.

In any case, English literature and especially the English tradition of the essay, the principal means through which he was learning to admire some features of the culture – the sense of humour, the history of bloodless revolutions, the tendency for stability, equilibrium and compromise instead of extremes, the gift for 'checking and balancing antagonisms', the taste for history and tradition, the peculiar combination of tradition with modernity, etc – created a horizon of expectations that encouraged Freyre to find in England what he was ready to discover.

Immediately on arrival his premonition was confirmed, as he confided to friends. The uniqueness of the English experience started at the customs, where he felt as if he had left 'this planet'. Instead of treating the travellers with suspicion, as if they were all 'smugglers, anarchists and carriers of microbes' – as the Americans, French and Germans did – the English immigration officers treated the new arrivals 'as if they were all gentlemen', he reported to his newspaper readers.

Freyre's later interest in studying the role of the English in Brazil can also be in part explained by his anglophilia. One of the aims of his *IB*, published in 1948, was to correct what he considered to be the stereotypes and distorted views of the British held by the Brazilians. In this work we can see Freyre defending the British with passion against those who accuse them of being irreparably hypocritical, ethnocentric, insular and greedy. Those who describe them as such, he argued, are only seeing 'half-truths'.[12]

Part of the reason for this rosy view of England can be found in references Freyre occasionally made to the painful experience of being a foreigner, and not of Nordic stock, in an America which was in the middle of a campaign to keep 'America for the Americans', that is for the WASPs (White Anglo-Saxon Protestants). Perceived as a 'Dago' or a 'damn foreigner' – 'I like you so much that I even forget you are a foreigner', an American girl once told him – the young Freyre could not avoid a certain degree of disillusion with a country that in other respects had many cultural benefits to offer him. All the same, for some years this occasional disappointment would not be strong enough to prevent his sharing the widespread view about the 'problem of race', a topic in which he was immersed, as we shall see.

To friends Freyre confessed that spiritually he felt he belonged to England. 'Doesn't the spirit have a genealogical tree?' he asked, only to answer that his 'dearest mental grandparents were the English writers' and that Shakespeare or Milton meant more to him than the famous Portuguese poet Camões.

The other Latin American author who immediately comes to mind when we think of anglophilia is the Argentinian Jorge Luis Borges, who was born the year before Freyre, in 1899, would die the year before him, in 1986, and who, like Freyre, was bookish from early boyhood.[13] The similarities between their education and tastes are striking, and apart from the importance of international figures such as Nietzsche and Whitman in their formation (as in that of many other young intellectuals at the turn of the century), the impact of British authors was overwhelming.

For Freyre, the admiration that he felt for the English language and English culture was such that, as he confessed very early, 'sometimes I think and even feel in English.' A similar admiration made Borges say that the English language and literature were 'among the greatest adventures of mankind.' In the same way that the young Freyre had felt as if 'dipped into literature' while in Paris, Borges said that when in England he could feel in the air that 'the greatest poetry of all time' was written by the English. Again, like the young Freyre who had eagerly followed in the footsteps of his English literary heroes, Borges, already in his sixties when he spent some time in England, followed the footsteps of his own heroes – in De Quincey's Manchester, Johnson's Lichfield, Arnold Bennett's Hanley, etc. – with the enthusiasm of a teenager.

The fathers of both Freyre and Borges were convinced anglophiles – like many members of the Latin American elite at this time – and great admirers of Herbert Spencer, a widespread enthusiasm in Latin America that they passed on to their sons. The anglophilia of the Borges family was, one must say, even greater than that of the Freyres, since their English pedigree (via the mother of Jorge's father) made them stand out in a predominantly Latin environment. The family's pride in their Englishness was so great that Borges' father made him wear an Eton collar and tie when he attended a state school in a poor district of Buenos Aires, an ill-considered decision which made the young boy the object of merciless bullying, but, surprisingly enough, did not affect his love of England.

Mr Williams' decisive role in Freyre's early education was replicated in the case of Borges by his English grandmother Fanny and his governess Miss Tink, from whom he heard stories and thanks to whom he became fluent in English. Voracious readers from an early age, both Borges and Freyre were amazingly eclectic and even apparently chaotic in their interests, encountering many books by chance and reading them on impulse.

In spite of this, as well as the impact that authors from different cultures had on their education, the references to British writers, mostly from the nineteenth century, in the articles that both men wrote for periodicals from the beginning of their careers, are rather impressive. Borges referred to English literature as 'the richest in the world' and used to describe himself as 'a Victorian person'. Oscar Wilde, Thomas Carlyle, Samuel Johnson, James Boswell, George Moore, George Bernard Shaw, Arnold Bennett, Robert Louis Stevenson, Samuel Coleridge, Thomas De Quincey, Charles Lamb, Algernon Swinburne, John Keats, Rudyard Kipling, William Morris and W. B. Yeats, among others, are present in the works of both Freyre and Borges.

The British essayists played a crucial role in the education of both writers, who would become brilliant essayists themselves. From early days Freyre showed his admiration for a literary genre which was, as he saw it, free from pedantry, empty erudition or blustering rhetoric, and combined common sense, poetry and philosophy in the discussion of the 'essential problems of humankind and society'. He would remember all his life the privilege he had had of hearing one of the greatest British essayists alive, G. K. Chesterton, lecture at a theatre in New York, when he was beginning his courses at Columbia University.

In fact, the author of *Father Brown* stands out as a common hero for both Freyre and Borges, while De Quincey seems to have been for Borges what Walter Pater was for Freyre: a 'spiritual grandfather'. 'To no one do I owe so many hours of personal happiness' and 'my debt to him is so huge' that it would be difficult to specify it, said Borges of De Quincey. Freyre's praises of Pater were equally warm. 'My most dear Walter Pater' was referred to by Freyre as a very close friend who had become part of his life and who relieved his solitude by cheering him up in his 'intellectual exile in the tropics'.

The 'physical and at the same time mystical love' that Freyre confessed to feeling for England was due, in great part, to his brief but intense visit. In fact, one could say that in England and Oxford the brevity of the visit preserved much of the enchantment of the experience. While young, Borges had been to the island only *en passant*, in 1914, on the way to Geneva with his family, and again on their return to Argentina in 1924. Only when visiting England in 1963, as an established writer, would he feel the intense emotion of being in 'the' country of literature he had learned to love so deeply. With Freyre, it was different, and one may say that his short but intense experience of England in 1922 was decisive for his whole intellectual trajectory.

Arriving in Oxford, a place in which he immediately felt 'at home' and where he lived the 'most paradisiacal period of his life', as he later confessed, Freyre participated, as a guest, in many features of university life, attending lectures, seminars and sporting events and even giving a talk to the Oxford Spanish Club.

What he observed there, the particular tendency of English youths for 'intense friendships' that involved passion, sensibility and eroticism, captivated him profoundly, just as it had captivated the philosopher-essayist George Santayana, and explains much of his intense anglophilia. Freyre, a person who described himself as being 'hungry for tenderness', found that friendship 'in the manner of the young men of Oxford' was deeper and more affectionate than any he had ever encountered before. Repeating Santayana, he described friendships of this kind as 'brief echoes of that love of comrades so much celebrated in antiquity' and 'a union of one whole man with another whole man'. As early as 1924, he commented in a newspaper article that 'we', the Brazilians, are 'a people of companions, that is, of easy companionship: but not of great affections. We shun great affections.'

Much later in life, Freyre would still recall his Oxford days with nostalgia and even attempt to admit in public a very meaningful, though ephemeral experience with a youth of the same sex that he had had there in those unforgettable days, a 'brief adventure of homosexual love, in the best sense of the term, without any vulgarity', as he put it. As we shall suggest later, the experience definitely left marks on his future work as a social historian. He was also impressed by the traditions and the beauty of Oxford and not least by the combination of tradition with modernity, symbolized for him by students wearing gowns and riding bicycles (in 1923 a bicycle was still a symbol of modernity, at least for a Brazilian).

Reading may be regarded as a form of travel, travel of the mind, especially in the case of Freyre since he was voraciously reading – and marking – so many foreign books at this time, Spanish, French, German and especially English and American.[14] The idea stressed by Armstrong in his lectures at Baylor, that books could transport one to other periods and places, seems to have left an indelible mark on his Brazilian student.

Before leaving Recife, Freyre was already aware of the importance for his education of travel to other countries. During his years abroad, he seems to have become even more aware that books were essential to the person he would become; in other words, as Primo Levi puts it, that what some people are depends to a great extent on what they read.[15] Freyre – who 'loved books voluptuously', as he confessed, often referring to them as 'my brothers' and 'my friends' – reminds one of people like Anatole France, whom Levi describes as an extreme case of a book-dependent individual.

In many of Freyre's own books, the marks he made bear witness to his increasing self-awareness and his determination to follow the example of famous people he admired. The 'great chance' of one's life, but unfortunately one often missed, lies between the ages of seventeen and twenty-seven, remarked George Gissing in *The Private Papers of Henry Ryecroft*, a book carefully read and annotated by the young Freyre. In similar fashion, Havelock Ellis, one of the first English thinkers to bring the ideas of Nietzsche and Freud to the English-speaking public, and another writer whom the young Freyre read with attention, insisted that 'when one is young, to read is as it were to pour a continuous stream of water on a parched and virginal plain. The soil seems to have an endless capacity to drink up the stream.'

As if unwilling to miss this 'great chance', Freyre consciously and avidly immersed himself in reading in his years abroad. From Oxford, he confessed to friends that he had been reading so much that he would need a holiday. 'But whoever was born to be a Benedictine will always be a Benedictine – especially when one is in such a congenial environment', he commented. At this stage Freyre was extremely conscious that imitation was a necessary prelude to originality. He had learned this from some of his favourite writers – Arnold Bennett, W. B. Yeats, Lafcadio Hearn, William Morris – who all confessed that during their formative years they had imitated other writers or artists, sometimes in a quite servile way.

Yeats, for instance (with whom Freyre was extremely proud to have exchanged a few words at Baylor in 1920) openly admitted that he began by writing poems in imitation of Shelley and Spenser, and that his paintings were for a long time greatly indebted to the example of his father and others around him. As for William Morris – whose life Yeats once admitted that he would like to have lived, poems included, had he been offered the choice by an angel – he too confessed with pride that for years he had longed to imitate the Pre-Raphaelite Rossetti as closely as he could.

The essays on Shakespeare that Freyre wrote in 1920 reveal that the imitative aspect of the learning process impressed him greatly, especially because this was visible even in one of the greatest dramatists of all time. Writing about *The Two Gentlemen of Verona*, he says that the play 'represents Sh's [sic] dramatic genius in its earliest stage of evolution. Genius – like everything else in this world – evolves. And in the development of genius what we see is this: gradual freedom from imitation to glorious independent personal creation.'[16]

It was in this frame of mind that the young Freyre read widely and seriously – as he said, like a Benedictine – during his period abroad. Following some of his mentors, he developed the habit of acknowledging the books and authors who had inspired him, acknowledgements that of course tend to be more genuine when they are made while young, at a time when they are not yet idealized by nostalgia or harnessed to the production of a specific self-image.

The Spanish books that Freyre found inspiring included the reflections on Spanish identity by Angel Ganivet, Miguel Unamuno and others, provoked by the crisis of 1898 in which Spain lost her colonial empire. Ganivet, for example, praised the regional culture of Granada, and the English author so much admired by the young Freyre, Havelock Ellis, may have first called his attention to Ganivet's advice to his compatriots. In his copy of *The Soul of Spain*, Freyre marked a passage in which Ellis referred to Ganivet's urging the Spaniards to search in themselves and in their best traditions for the means of the country's salvation.[17]

In the case of the French, the writers who attracted Freyre at this time were either aesthetes or regionalists. Among the aesthetes were the Goncourt brothers, to whom he had already referred in SL, and Marcel Proust, to whom he would refer again and again later on (an author, it should be pointed out, whom Freyre considered to be 'almost English', because of the importance of English authors in his formation). The leading regionalist was Maurice Barrès, whom Freyre described at one point as his 'hero', but whose 'narrow nationalism' he soon rejected. Barrès was the author of a novel about seven young men from Lorraine, *Les déracinés* (1897), whose lives are ruined when they leave the provinces and become rootless cosmopolitans in Paris.

Freyre did not know the language well enough, at least at this time, to read German texts in the original, but he had already read some Nietzsche in French translation and with Bilden's encouragement he discovered, probably later in his career, the work of the sociologist Georg Simmel as well as Oswald Spengler's *Decline of the West*. But it was definitely at this early stage that he read, in translation, a novel by a now virtually forgotten regionalist author, Hermann Sudermann, *Frau Sorge* ('Dame Care') recommended by Armstrong in a course on 'English' literature. On the flyleaf of this book, which he bought in New York in 1921, he wrote, 'I swear I had the idea of the psychology of the prematurely old boy before I read this book!'[18]

It is extremely significant that in this novel, which impressed Freyre so much that he recommended it to friends with enthusiasm, the symbolic importance of the house in the life of an individual was strongly emphasized. The nostalgia that the young Paul Meyerhofer felt for the 'white house' where he was born, but which his ruined family had had to leave, was so intense that it became a representation for him of 'what "paradise lost" is for humanity'.

Freyre's knowledge of Anglo-American culture included his 'masters' in social science, Boas and Giddings, as we have seen, and the iconoclastic journalist H. L. Mencken, perhaps the most outspoken critic of North-American Anglo Saxon culture in the early part of the twentieth century. All his life Freyre would refer with pride to the letter of incentive he received from this 'American Nietzsche', in return for a copy of the master's thesis that the young student boldly sent to the famous critic.

Freyre was also reading and admiring Anglo-American authors that he would later be embarrassed to admit to having attracted his attention, not to mention his praise. Understandably, he would not acknowledge in his later recollections the deep impression left on him in his youth by eugenicists such as Madison Grant and Lothrop Stoddard, authors of two highly acclaimed books of the early 1920s aimed at popularizing the so-called 'scientific racism' that was a powerful paradigm (in the Kuhnian sense) at that time. Grant's *Passing of the Great Race* (1916), a book that Hitler confessed to taking as his 'Bible', discussing what the author called 'the racial basis of European history', together with Stoddard's *Rising Tide of Color* (1920), expressing a fear that the age of white supremacy was over, appealed to the young Freyre for revealing what he saw then as the healthy reaction of the United States to the problem of race. According to the ideas that these authors were popularizing, the innate superiority of certain races and the inferiority of others, like the undesirability of racial mixture, were established by science. As a character in Scott Fitzgerald's *The Great Gatsby* (1925) put it, 'It's all scientific stuff, it's been proved.' Only people of the 'inferior races' were expected not to accept this as truth, Grant wrote.

One must remember that at the time Freyre was living in the United States, the old metaphor of the 'melting pot' was increasingly questioned, while the 'one drop rule', originally part of the Southern ethos, had contaminated the whole country. Racist ideas, legitimized by science, permeated the press, fiction, the film industry, popular culture, children's stories, and so on. Freyre arrived in the States a few months before the end of the First World War and saw the intensification of the campaign for the restriction of immigration led by the eugenics movement with the support of many respectable biologists, psychologists and anthropologists. The debates he witnessed led eventually to the Immigration Restriction Act of 1924, a law that was to regulate the admission of immigrants until 1965. The act favoured the older Nordic stocks over the newer immigrants, mainly from Southern and Eastern Europe, and excluded Japanese altogether. It was therefore understandable that Freyre would take these racist opinions as if they were proved scientific facts and that, following the majority of people around him, his prejudices would grow stronger.

Still a long way from being the champion of miscegenation he would later become, Freyre was positively impressed for a while by the immigration and anti-miscegenation policies that the 'science of race' was backing, so as to regenerate the American people. Contrary to the relative passivity with which Brazil was facing its reality of being a country with a growing mixed population, the United States was actively discussing its racial problems and trying to find a solution. As Rüdiger Bilden reminded his readers, many Brazilians and foreigners alike agreed that nothing positive could be expected from a country populated by a 'mongrel race' and ruled by a 'mulatto government', as the foreign stereotype of Brazil asserted.[19] The young Freyre was no exception. Together with the majority of the white elite he shared a pride in European ancestors and a deep frustration at being Brazilian.

As a result of hybridity, the country was supposed to suffer from lack of spirit, an inferiority complex and a certain sadness, which a well-known writer, Paulo Prado, considered part of the Brazilian character. His famous book of 1928, *Retrato do Brasil* ('Portrait of Brazil'), which refers to the 'vices of our mestiço origin' and to Brazil as 'the reign of mixing', described the country as backward, full of unfulfilled promises, and one which does not develop but only grows up like a 'sick child'.

The letter Ulisses Freyre wrote in 1916 to his young brother Gilberto is representative of a general feeling among the white elite of the time. 'Our greatest problem is race ... if things continue as they are now, at the end of five generations, at the maximum, we'll be a country of *mestiços*: not of White and Indian; but African and White'.

Deeply pessimistic about the future of the country, Freyre felt an embarrassment about the physical aspect of a great number of his compatriots that grew deeper while abroad. Once in New York he saw the crew of a Brazilian ship and as he confessed to his readers in 1933, he was shocked and even horrified by their mongrel aspect – it seemed he was facing 'caricatures of men'.[20] The fate of Brazil was gloomier than that of the United States, he thought, since no real effort was being made to counter this growing process of mongrelization. Among the Latin American countries, Argentina alone was offering a healthy solution, Freyre commented from Texas to his readers in Pernambuco in October 1920. The 'high tide of Caucasians' who were arriving there in great numbers could easily counteract the relatively small presence of coloured people. In the 'near future' the Argentinian population 'will be practically white', of a race 'physically and morally beautiful', which would put the country on the right road to modernity and progress. Unfortunately Brazil was not following Argentina's example, he lamented.

Arriving in New York, Freyre immersed himself in the question of race and mixture. The North American aims of 'regenerating the world' and 'promoting the improvement of the species' were described with enthusiasm to his readers, and he clearly showed that he shared the prevailing opinion about the importance of eugenics for the solution of the so-called problem of race. He referred with enthusiasm to the 'remarkable woman' Margaret Sanger (the founder of the Birth Control Movement) and her book *Woman and the New Race*, where she discussed efficient eugenic methods for the development of a 'bigger American race'. [21]

Visiting Ellis Island, Freyre was dazzled by what he saw at this famous point of entry to the United States, where thousands of immigrants a day were arriving in September 1920. He described with great admiration the efficiency with which the officials sorted out the immigrants of 'better stock', discriminating between good and bad 'acquisitions' to the country. They select only the 'elements capable of collaborating in the progress' of the nation, those who will 'maintain the high American pattern of efficiency and physical and moral health', he commented with admiration. In this 'people refinery', as he called the island, he was also deeply impressed by the power of absorption of American society which showed its talent to transform and assimilate the immigrant from the very start. He described the efficient 'process of social digestion' through which the immigrants he observed began losing their past in front of his eyes, and were put on the road to Americanization, from which 'even the Jews', he says, 'seem to be unable to escape'. [22]

In other words, the young Freyre was swimming with the tide in the early 1920s, and it would take some years for him to break with the powerful racist paradigm. To find the path that would eventually lead him to *CGS*, he had to digest those racist ideas and become aware that they were prejudices disguised as science. Furthermore, he had to see that the work of his Columbia teacher Franz Boas and others about the power of culture not only undermined that pseudo-science but also opened up new possibilities for thinking about race and mixing and their relation to the development of a society.

This digestion proved to be slow and far from straightforward. Freyre's view about race fluctuated a great deal and made him walk in a zigzag path for some time, shifting from praising the physical and mental capacity of the blacks to sympathy for the Ku Klux Klan. As his friend from the American South, Simkins, put it, knowing the United States 'from the inside' and having the ability to understand the national ethos, Freyre was 'sufficiently tolerant with the native impulses to justify the behaviour of the Second Ku-Klux Klan and the Dixie demagogues'.

The texts he published well into the 1920s, long after he had returned to Recife, reveal that the powerful racist paradigm still informed much of Freyre's thinking and observation, and that only occasionally was he capable of glimpsing the importance of Boas' critique of the idea that each race possessed an essential nature. Indeed, we might say that precisely because he had been immersed in a culture in which views opposed to the ones that he would champion years later were so widespread and popular, the period of his temporary enthusiasm deserves to be taken seriously. It is as if the young Freyre had to know and admire racism in one of its most articulate and extreme forms in order to free himself from it.

Observing Freyre's early trajectory, one is reminded of an earlier Latin American intellectual, José Martí, the Cuban essayist, poet and campaigner for independence who also lived in the United States and for whom the North American experience was equally significant. During the years he spent there (1889–95), Martí, who was a great admirer of the country's democratic traditions and of 'the poet of democracy', Walt Whitman, witnessed the alarming expansion of the most brutal form of racism, in which lynching African-Americans was becoming normal. The openness and determination with which he put forward his pioneering anti-racist views can be explained, at least in part, by this experience, which deeply affected him.[23]

Freyre's American period, two and half decades later, although briefer than Martí's, was perhaps an even more overwhelming experience, since 'scientific racism' and the eugenics movement were in their heyday and had become an 'obsession for policymakers', with the support of many respected biologists, psychologists and anthropologists.[24] But gradually, with the help of ideas he had discovered abroad and as the bitter experiences he had had, especially in the United States, sank in and counteracted the paradigm he had admired, Freyre started to think about race from an innovative viewpoint.

It is at this moment that some Victorians whom Freyre had discovered while abroad would be especially important for him. These essayists, critics and artists, who could be categorized broadly as 'anti-Victorian Victorians' – because they questioned many of the values of the world they lived in – would play a role in Freyre's process of reconciliation with his provincial homeland, a necessary prelude to the decisive changes in his ideas about race. As Chesterton once put it, 'the whole object of travel is not to set foot on foreign land; it is at last to set foot on one's own country as a foreign land … the only way to go to England is to go away from it'. In similar fashion, Freyre was able to see his Recife clearly only after travelling far away from it.[25]

Coincidentally, Borges' view of the importance of his travels for the making of his education and his self-discovery was put in terms with which Freyre would certainly have agreed. Referring to his return from Europe, the Argentinian writer says: 'It was more than a homecoming; it was a rediscovery. I was able to see Buenos Aires keenly and eagerly because I had been away from it for a long time. Had I never gone abroad, I wonder whether I would ever have seen it with the peculiar shock and glow that it now gave me.'[26]

The young Freyre learned most from literature: from *fin-de-siècle* aesthetes, including Pater, Wilde and Yeats, as well as the novels of Thomas Hardy and George Gissing, the essays of G. K. Chesterton and the life and work of Lafcadio Hearn, the Greek-Irish author whom Freyre described as an Englishman. For instance, reading Hardy at the same time as studying social science, Freyre viewed him as a kind of anthropologist or sociologist, a student of rural life in 'Wessex' whose interest, nevertheless, was not circumscribed, since his art gave local and regional themes a universal dimension. Even more significant for Freyre's future was his discovery of John Ruskin and William Morris, authors to whom he referred very early as 'writers- entrées'. Different from the 'writers-hors-d'oeuvre' – like G. B. Shaw, Oscar Wilde and Nietzsche – whose 'literature of negation and contradiction' undermines our 'most cherished intellectual, moral and aesthetic values' and stimulates people to use their own judgement, the 'writers-entrées' are more positive and offer alternative values, commented Freyre to the readers of *DP*.[27]

Ruskin and Morris, for instance, besides questioning the 'industrialism and the stupid democracy of the nineteenth century', offered a guide for action. Theirs was a 'literature of action', Freyre concluded. He had read some essays of Ruskin at Baylor, but the book that was really important for his intellectual development was the *Stones of Venice* – a study that was at least equally important to Marcel Proust – in which Freyre could see that Ruskin's art criticism had much more than an aesthetic dimension and was intimately connected to his social ideals. At Oxford he read a biography of Ruskin's disciple Morris that told the story of his path from art to socialism. Morris's devotion to beauty and tradition were described as essential to his view of the evils of the modern world and the means to minimize them. Above all, what most impressed Freyre's imagination was the idea put forward by these Victorian 'rebels', that the pre-capitalist Gothic world could serve as an inspiration for the modern one; in other words, that one could find sources of innovation by returning to the past.

In short, Freyre was an omnivorous reader who absorbed ideas from many sources. The traveller-writer Bruce Chatwin once described him as an intellectual 'sponge'.[28] The comparison is as accurate as it is vivid, but needs to be complemented by another more dynamic metaphor, which implies a greater degree of creativity. Like a sponge, Freyre absorbed a good deal from many sources, but like an oyster, he had a great capacity to adapt or transform ideas, thus making them his own. Referring later on to the way he absorbed, tropicalized and brazilianized other people's ideas, Freyre himself said with his characteristic humour that in his work 'milk from many cows could be found', but that 'the cheese was of his own making.'

To sum up, the years that Freyre spent outside Brazil were important for his development not only because they enabled him to discover new intellectual worlds but also because they encouraged him to take his distance from his own culture. One is reminded of a story by one of Freyre's favourite authors, Lafcadio Hearn, *Kokoro*, about a young ex-samurai who returns to Japan from a stay in Europe with an increased respect for Japanese culture. The author comments that 'Foreign civilization had taught him to understand, as he could never otherwise have understood, the worth and the beauty of his own.'[29]

The Return of the Native

The 'return of the native', to use the words of Thomas Hardy which Freyre adopted when referring to his own homecoming, took place in March 1923.[30] Re-adapting himself to Brazil and returning to Recife, which he now viewed as even more provincial than before, was something of a culture shock. He had come back 'greedy for local colour', but was faced with a city which was losing its social and architectural character. The Brazilian frenzy to 'modernize', 'Europeanize' and 'Americanize' the country, he commented to the readers of the the *DP*, made him feel a foreigner in his own land.

Freyre suffered at first from what he called 'acedia', a state of depression from which he was rescued by a few newly met friends who, on the one side, eagerly accepted his role of a reporter and interpreter of foreign practices and ideas, and, on the other, were prepared to help him discover the 'worth and beauty' of his own region. Thanks to these friends, Freyre was able to re-root himself in the soil of the North-East in spite of the hostile reception he met from some local intellectuals who considered him a conceited young man full of snobbery and pedantry. To his friends, whom he once described as 'my coterie', he represented a breath of fresh air, being able to articulate their vague ideas about the inauthenticity of Brazilian culture and the need to search for something more genuine. Familiar with the latest European and North American trends, he was better able than most of his fellow countrymen to denounce the taste of the time for aping foreign ideas, fashions and habits; in other words, to denounce their 'provincialism of openness' – to use the inspired expression of the Swedish anthropologist Ulf Hannerz – that is, the uncritical readiness to embrace and mimic whatever came from abroad.[31]

Indeed, Freyre was soon playing a leading part in the regionalist movement, in what has been called the 'invention' of the North-East, formerly known as the 'North'. Already in 1888 Joaquim Nabuco had spoken about the 'two Brazils', the formerly prosperous North with an economy based on sugar and the newly prospering South with an economy based on coffee. Some Northerners were already dreaming of autonomy, in protest against what they considered to be discrimination by the government in favour of the South.[32]

The state of Pernambuco, once relatively rich and powerful, was in decline in the last years of the Old Republic (1889–1930). In the 1920s, there developed a concern with the distinctive culture of the North-East (especially the states of Pernambuco and Bahia), more africanized than the rest of Brazil, since it was to these sugar-planting states that the majority of African slaves had been brought. Northeasterners were turning to their traditions in search of a sense of pride that could liberate them from their inferiority complex. The regionalist movement, which started in Recife, was in part at least the expression of collective nostalgia for the world Pernambucans had lost.

It was in this context, in 1924, that Freyre helped found the Regionalist Centre of the North-East, bringing together a group of writers, artists and scholars who defined themselves against a certain kind of modernism. For them, the rejection of the past was not a necessary step on the road to modernization – a process that could perfectly well take into account authentic Brazilian or local traditions in architecture, cuisine, patriarchal values and so on. In 1925, Freyre edited the *Livro do Nordeste*, commemorating the centenary of the *DP* with a volume of essays on the history and traditions of the region, aiming at an 'economic-social introspection' into the North-East. It was for this volume that, at Freyre's request, Manuel Bandeira wrote his now famous poem, 'Evocation of Recife', describing the sights and sounds of the city of his childhood. Freyre also organized a Regionalist Congress in 1926.[33]

Freyre's friends in Recife, who mostly belonged to the same generation, born at the turn of the century, shared his regional and regionalist interests. With his fluency, his charisma, his wide reading and – ironically enough – his European style (including the tweed jacket he wore even in the heat of a Pernambucan summer), Freyre became the natural leader of the group. The 'clan', as one might call them, included the writer José Lins do Rego and the painter Cícero Dias, who were still at the beginning of their careers and would join the cause of rooting their various arts in Brazilian traditions and of working for the much needed replacement of the country's dominant 'cultural humility' by 'creative pride'.[34]

Lins, whose family owned a plantation, would later become one of Brazil's outstanding novelists. The series of novels that he labelled 'the sugar-cane cycle', provided 'characters' for the work of Freyre. It gave names and faces to his interpretation of Brazil, illustrating through fiction the role of the patriarchal system in Brazilian history and narrating the drama of its decadence.[35] Freyre himself would later describe Lins as the sociologist of the end of patriarchy in the North-East.

Dias, another son of a plantation owner, specialized in regional themes, including a painting of 1926–8 that showed Recife at the centre of the world. In this group Freyre proudly played the role of mentor and cultural mediator. To his friends he stressed the need to look into the country's history and geography in order to produce authentic novels, poems or paintings. As the members of Freyre's 'coterie' testify, his recommended reading was accepted as law and it was through him that they became acquainted with a number of artists, critics and novelists, specially British, virtually unknown to the Brazilians at that time.

It was Freyre, for instance, who recommended Lins to read Lafcadio Hearn, Walter Pater and, with special insistence, Thomas Hardy, even sending him some of his novels; 'all England was being revealed to me', wrote Lins, referring to the poets and novelists to whom Freyre introduced him. 'You have made a person of me ... by being in contact with you my brain was formed ... if mental slavery exists, I am your slave', the young Lins told his new friend, with the most eloquent gratitude. [36]

Tradition and Modernity

Freyre's clan in Recife might be compared with the group surrounding another master, the writer Mário de Andrade, in São Paulo, also in the 1920s.[37] Both leaders were sometimes described maliciously as popes, the pope of Apipucos and the pope of Futurism. Mário's group is associated with modernism, and especially with the famous 'Week of Modern Art', a week of lectures in the municipal theatre in São Paulo in 1922. The participants included the painters Tarsila do Amaral and Anita Malfatti, the writer Oswald de Andrade and the poet, journalist and artist Menotti Del Picchia.

This 'group of five' (including Mário) was a little older than Freyre and his clan, their dates of birth ranging from the late 1880s to the early 1890s. They are now generally associated with a break with the past, with a desire to make Brazil part of an international Modernist movement, looking towards Paris in particular, while Freyre and his clan are associated with the ideas of 'region and tradition' (the title of a volume of Freyre's essays, published in 1941).

The cities in which the two groups lived symbolized this contrast. Tradition was represented by Recife, a once prosperous city that had gone into economic decline together with the sugar industry that had enriched it, and modernity by São Paulo, a city in rapid expansion (with only 28,000 inhabitants in 1875 but 240,000 by 1900). Members of one group not infrequently criticized the other. On one side, Lins do Rego mocked the modernists of São Paulo for their dismissal of traditions and regions; on the other Oswald criticized Freyre for his nostalgia.

All the same, any sharp contrast between the two leaders and between the traditionalism and regionalism of one group and the Modernism and internationalism of the other is a false one.[38] The young Freyre showed considerable sympathy for Modernism – and also for modernity, as long as it respected the past. For their part, the modernists of São Paulo did not wish to make a sharp break with tradition. They wanted to create a distinctively Brazilian form of Modernism, and this meant drawing on local traditions (colonial, Indian or African), rather than abandoning them altogether.

In this case too one might speak of the 'return of the native' syndrome, nicely symbolized by Chesterton's epigram about going abroad in order to discover his native England. Oswald's famous 'Cannibal Manifesto' of 1928, proclaiming a 'Carib Revolution', quoted the praises of primitivism by Montaigne and Rousseau. Again, it was in Paris, where Tarsila moved in avant-garde circles, that the group learned the enthusiasm for 'primitive' and African art that encouraged their discovery of Brazil.

In 1924, for instance, Mário, Oswald, Tarsila and other members of the group made a pilgrimage to the state of Minas Gerais to see its famous colonial baroque architecture and sculpture, including the work of the mulatto Aleijadinho, who was virtually unknown at this time but is now famous. In 1927, Mário made an expedition to the North-East and to the Amazon, in order to study the popular culture of these regions. He would later participate in Freyre's Afro-Brazilian Congress of 1934 (to be discussed later) and give a paper on the Pernambucan *maracatu*, a cross between a dance and a parade.

It was also Mário who drew up the plan for an institution devoted to the preservation of the cultural heritage, SPHAN (Serviço do Patrimônio Histórico e Artístico Nacional), whose founding director, Rodrigo Melo Franco de Andrade, was a friend of Freyre and even called himself his 'disciple'.[39] Another leading figure in SPHAN, who was also linked to Freyre, was the modernist architect Lúcio Costa, now best known as the designer of Brasília, but famous in his own day for his part in the rediscovery of colonial art in general and the work of Aleijadinho in particular. In Brazil, as in Mexico and other Latin American countries, the supporters of Modernism were not infrequently the same people as the defenders of local traditions. They wanted their modern designs to have a national or local colouring.

In short, the São Paulo group and the Recife group were not as different as is often supposed. Some Brazilian intellectuals, among them the poets Manuel Bandeira (who became a close friend of Freyre's) and Carlos Drummond de Andrade, were on good terms with both. The differences between them were matters of degree rather than differences of kind. The relations between the groups reflected a mixture of common interests, differences of opinion, personal sympathies and personal rivalries.

The irony that the regionalism of both groups was inspired by foreign models is worth noting. What drew Freyre to the work of the right-wing novelist Maurice Barrès was his emphasis on the need for roots. Again, on his visit to Paris, Freyre had met and been impressed by another right-wing thinker, Charles Maurras, remembered later as a Catholic Monarchist who believed that Jews, Protestants and Masons were all conspiring against France. For Freyre, on the other hand, Maurras was essentially 'the theorist of a flexible regionalist federalism'. It was also in the course of his visit to France that a friend of Oliveira Lima's, the retired general and diplomat, Clement de Grandprey, who had visited Pernambuco, asked Freyre a question about the vernacular architecture of the region. Freyre was impressed by the fact that Grandprey had been impressed. He would later devote considerable time, as we shall see, to the study of the shanties or *mucambos* of Recife.[40]

However, as suggested earlier, it was to the British writers he so much admired that Freyre's regionalism owes most, since they were the main interlocutors for the most fruitful dialogue he had during his formative years. Thomas Hardy is, of course, the most obvious inspiration, and it is not surprising that Freyre strongly suggested the reading of Hardy's novels to the young Lins do Rego. As he wrote in an article of 1925, no writer was more English than Hardy in his themes and his roots. Nevertheless, as a regionalist novelist he was able to produce the most 'universally human' English novels of the previous fifty years.

Equally important were W. B. Yeats and William Morris, whom Freyre transformed, so to speak, into regionalist authors. Both Yeats's nationalist concerns and Morris's campaign against the evils of modern capitalist society served as a rich inspiration for Freyre's regionalist campaign. Deeply concerned with the liberation of his country from political and cultural domination by England, Yeats appealed to the Irish past, searching in Irish traditions and myths for the means of resisting British imperialism. Freyre was greatly impressed by Yeats's achievement in valorizing Irish culture and his acknowledgement of the importance for the development of his style and mental tools of his long acquaintance with simple fishermen from Sligo.

On the other hand, Morris's medievalism was inspiring for Freyre because it revealed the possibility of looking back to the Brazilian colonial past in order to go forward. As Freyre noted in a biography of Morris that he read while he was in Oxford, the British critic looked back to the pre-capitalist Gothic world because he saw there 'the New World he wanted to create'; in other words, 'he was worried about the future, even when he seemed absorbed in the past.'

The Society for the Protection of Ancient Buildings, founded by Morris in 1877 as one of the means to regenerate the industrial world, was especially appealing to Freyre. The British reformer had founded it mainly as a means to 'awaken a feeling that our ancient buildings are not mere ecclesiastical toys but monuments of national growth and hope', as Freyre told his newspaper readers, quoting Morris – in English! In Recife, Freyre would therefore take Morris as a model in his campaign to educate the public in the importance of the past and the traditions of his region, as a basis for new creations and development – a campaign which, he insisted, should spread to other regions of the country, since, as he put it, 'the good Brazilianism is the one which puts together various regionalisms'.[41]

In short, Freyre read many writers with Brazilian spectacles, one might even say Pernambucan spectacles. Creatively appropriating ideas from foreign critics, he was able to adapt to Brazilian reality the project of a modernity reconciled with local and regional traditions engendered in different latitudes. That was probably what he had in mind when he described himself later as a 'Morris from the periphery' (*Morris de subúrbio*).

As for Freyre's own writing, the scholarly fruit of these years of regionalist activity was the essay 'Vida Social no Nordeste' ('Social Life in the North-East'; henceforth VSN) of 1925. This text may be viewed as an expanded, richer version of his master's dissertation, using similar sources but developing the themes of house, family and childhood and adding other topics.[42]

Thus Freyre describes the houses of sugar-planters, filled with an abundance of silverware and porcelain from China, Japan and India, as expressing a sense of dominance. Turning to the family, he notes the frequent sexual relations between upper-class white men and their servants, blacks or mulattas. He points out that girls were already little women at the age of nine or ten and mothers at fourteen. Their brothers were 'boys virtually without boyhood'. Slipping into the first person, he comments that 'we were all born like that boy in Sudermann's novel, with an air of precocious old age.' Precocity included sexual precocity, thanks to what Freyre calls 'contamination' from the black and mulatto servants.

As for nostalgia, Freyre comments on what he calls 'the superiority of the interiors of the past to those of today' and expresses his regret (as he would do again and again in later life) for 'the disappearance ... of the traditional furniture made out of jacaranda', described as 'rustic' but 'honest'. Slaves, as he suggests once again, were driven less hard in those days than factory workers later. There was more sociability. The essay ends with reflections on the history of funerals, contrasting the traditional procession with the hurried burials of 'today'.[43]

What is new and impressive in VSN is the attention that the author pays to 'sensuous history'. For example, Freyre evokes the street life of old Recife, 'the acrid smell of sugar', the shouts of the salesmen, 'the clacking sandals of the friars begging alms'. Re-entering the Big House, he draws attention to the loud voices of ladies who spent much of their time shouting at slaves from a distance.[44]

However, as to Freyre's praise of miscegenation, one of the hallmarks of his future major work, there was still no sign that he disagreed with the mainstream ideas about the pathological implications of race mixing. At this time, he still viewed African blood as a stain on Brazil and an obstacle to its development.

For the next four years, Freyre would write nearly nothing, having fallen into what he described then to a friend as a 'Rimbaud mood'. It seemed that he had given up all attempts at a literary career, despite his early promise, and that, like the French poet, he would divert his life to another route – in his case, a political career, since between 1926 and 1930 he was cabinet secretary to the Governor of Pernambuco, Estácio Coimbra. As if dominated by torpor and apathy, his self-esteem was low and his will to proceed with the regionalist campaign was severely weakened. What he did achieve was something for the city, preserving trees, building playgrounds and founding museums as well as editing a leading newspaper, *A Província*.

What seems to explain his 'Rimbaud mood' was his ambiguous feeling about the racist paradigm that had been informing much of this thinking, writing and observations. Suspecting that there was more in favour of Brazilian social reality than the stereotype of a country of mongrels allowed, Freyre decided that he would 'only read and study'. It is as if he had realized that he had to prepare himself by reading more widely, especially on the anthropology of Brazil, in order to try to think about his country in different terms.

At the end of this process, Freyre would have developed his regionalist project so as to incorporate the mixed composition of the Brazilian population into the traditions which should be valued, both as a great source of creative energy and innovation and as part of the country's local and national identity.

Circumstances helped. Freyre's years in local government came to an abrupt end for political reasons. In 1930, a revolt of junior army officers replaced the President of Brazil, Washington Luís, with Getúlio Vargas.[45] Following the revolution, Freyre lost his job along with his patron Estácio Coimbra and followed him into exile in Portugal. Living in poverty in Lisbon, he returned full time to the world of scholarship, initially taking up the project on the history of childhood in Brazil – the 'secret project', as he sometimes called it – that he had been thinking about intermittently since the early 1920s.

Gradually, however, the theme of the house began to supersede that of the child in the new interpretation of the history of the country he was thinking about. As the story by Pater, 'The Child in the House', had brilliantly shown, it was a much broader theme that would allow Freyre to make a much more inclusive study, embracing the material and the spiritual, the public and the private, children and adults, men and women, masters and slaves.[46] This study will be the focus of the following chapter.

3 Masters and Slaves

Although Gilberto Freyre was both prolific in his writings and broad in his interests, he is most often remembered for a single book, published in 1933 when the author was thirty-three years old. The book has been described as 'the most important work of Brazilian culture', one that provoked a 'revolution' in the country, so it clearly deserves a chapter to itself.[1] It is at once a poetic evocation of a past society, an important discussion of the theories of hybridity and consensus and an original contribution to the debate over Brazilian identity. Known in English (since the publication of a translation in 1946) as *The Masters and the Slaves*, the book's original title was *Casa Grande e Senzala*, literally 'The Big House and the Slave Quarters'.

On his way into exile in 1930, Freyre had the opportunity to see a little of Senegal and took notes of what impressed him on this first visit to Africa.[2] Once in Lisbon, Freyre began to study colonial Brazil, but he turned his attention from the history of the child to the history of the house. This turn was the culmination of a long process, since he had read Pater in the early 1920s, and been deeply impressed by the story of Florean Deleal, the character in 'The Child in the House' who realized how much the way in which he related to the world had been shaped by the house in which he had grown up. Florian's first ambition was to make a 'mental journey', so as to trace the 'story of his spirit', or, as Pater put it more generically, that 'process of brain-building by which we are, each one of us, what we are'.

The result of this journey, when as if in a dream he saw himself as a child, was the discovery that his childhood experiences in his 'old house', even 'small accidents', had determined the person he had become. All the tiny details of the house in which he had been brought up, from the 'perfume of the little flowers of the lime trees' to the 'angle at which the sun in the morning fell on the pillow' had 'indelibly' affected him and become 'a part of the texture of his mind'.

Above all, what Florean recognized was how 'forcible a motive with all of us' is the 'sense of home', an instinct so intense and powerful that much of our imagination, feelings, sensibility, fears and thoughts are firmly rooted in our 'early habitation'. Becoming 'a sort of material shrine or sanctuary of sentiment', the house where we all grow up, says the narrator – be it the place with the 'closely-drawn white curtain and the shaded lamp' of the Englishman or the folding tent of the 'wandering Arab' – imposes itself as a 'system of visible symbolism, interweaving itself in all our thoughts and passions'.

Echoing Pater, another favourite writer of Freyre's youth, George Gissing, also stressed in *The Private Papers of Henry Ryecroft* his discovery that many of his passions, imagination, tastes and habits were the result of his childhood home experiences. To this author, who also talked highly of 'home' as 'the illumining word', simple things like the sight of a schoolbook, a sound or the perfume or touch of a flower were enough, as they were for Proust's Marcel, to take him back to the past.

We might say, therefore, that what took shape in Freyre's exile was mainly a change of focus, with the house, in its many dimensions, becoming more prominent, while the child moved into the background. This shift may have been triggered by the destruction of Freyre's family house in Recife in the aftermath of the revolution of 1930, when Gétulio Vargas seized power. Coincidentally, the Irishman George Moore, to whom the young Freyre felt 'fraternally close' and whose *Confessions of a Young Man* he greatly appreciated, also experienced the sacking and burning of his childhood house, Moore Hall.[3] In similar fashion, behind the central place of the Big House in the twentieth-century Anglo-Irish novel lies the painful memory of destruction. Elizabeth Bowen's *The Last September* (1929), for instance, ends with the burning of three houses. These houses are symbols of the families who live in them and their burning or 'execution' symbolizes the end of the Anglo-Irish ascendancy.

The Brazilian historian Carlos Guilherme Mota once described Freyre as a 'North-Eastern Lampedusa', in the sense of a writer who evoked an aristocratic past with nostalgia.[4] In fact, the parallels between the two writers go further than this. In the case of the Prince of Lampedusa, the loss of his family palace in Palermo, destroyed during a bombardment in 1943, was one motive for his writing that famous evocation of aristocratic life, *The Leopard* (1958). Freyre had a similar experience, which may have sensitized him to the importance of the house not only in Pater but also in *The Decline of the West* by Oswald Spengler (to which CGS refers) and in the study of Greece by Alfred Zimmern, who used the expression 'Big House', as we have seen, to stand for the system of patriarchy.[5]

The opportunity for Freyre to write the book occurred in 1931, thanks to an invitation from a historian of Latin America, Percy Martin, who taught at Stanford University and had visited Freyre in Recife in 1926. As Freyre recalled much later,

> The idea took form at the University of Stanford, in California, which had invited me to give two courses on Brazil, one for undergraduates and the other for doctoral students. So I had to produce a synthesis about Brazil for first-class American students, since Stanford is the most selective of American students socially and intellectually. That was where *CGS* was born.[6]

To understand how the book came to take the shape it did, we need, at least briefly, to place or replace it in context, or rather in a number of contexts, historiographical, cultural and political.

CGS is among other things an attempt at a cure for what its author once called the 'anxiety of social introspection', the search for Brazilian identity underlying a series of essays written at this time by Paulo Prado, Caio Prado Junior, Sérgio Buarque and others. The book may be viewed as a major contribution to an ongoing discussion over the interpretation of Brazil, examining what made the country different from Europe, from North America and also from Spanish America.[7] This discussion had important political implications at a time when immigration policies were under discussion. One of the first reviewers of *CGS*, the anthropologist Roquette-Pinto, pointed to the book's relevance to this public debate.

Readers also need to remember that *CGS* was written in the early years of the regime of President Vargas, between the revolution of 1930 which brought him to power and the establishment of the dictatorial 'New State' (*Estado Novo*) in 1937. A major political question in Brazil in the early 1930s was that of the relative power of the central government and the governments of the different states. Vargas put the nation before the region in his cultural policies as well as his views about federalism. In his time, the expanding syncretic cult of Umbanda was coming to be seen as a national tradition, combining contributions from the three races, like Brazilian culture in general as presented by Freyre. Although its author was a cultural regionalist, as we have seen, *CGS* may be read as an attempt to mediate between regionalists and centralists, emphasizing what the North-East contributed to the culture of Brazil.

The study that is now to be found in the bookshops – the fortieth Brazilian edition appeared in 2000, in time for the author's centenary – is something of a palimpsest. The text itself was modified by the author over the years in small but significant ways.[8] The notes were expanded to refer to later studies and to reply to critics. Some illustrations were dropped, while others were added.[9] Most important of all, as a strategy for shaping the expectations of readers, was the production of new prefaces, so many of them that Freyre admitted that 'some said that the author was a preface-maniac.'[10] For the first English edition, Freyre wrote a preface that seems to be addressed to tourists rather than scholars, while the French and Italian editions were introduced by prefaces written by two leading academic historians, Lucien Febvre and Fernand Braudel.

The account of *CGS* that follows is organized around six main themes: the house and the plantation; patriarchal society; the history of the child; sex and gender; race, culture and hybridity; and harmony and conflict.

The House and the Plantation

Like its author, *CGS* is many-sided, concerned with the 'Big House' (as they used to say both in Ireland and in the American South), in both the literal and the metaphorical senses of the term.

Freyre's interest in architecture, especially vernacular architecture, or more widely still, in streets and cities, went back a long way. He had learned from Ruskin to see buildings as the expression of a culture. As we have seen, he had taken Morris's Society for the Protection of Ancient Buildings as a model in his 1920s campaign to educate the Pernambucan public about the importance of the past and the traditions of his region. He was also studying contemporary urban problems.

Following the precedents of Freyre's earlier essays but developing the theme in much greater detail, *CGS* described the materials, the style, the plan and the furnishings of the Big Houses of the seventeenth and eighteenth centuries, emphasising their 'fat' or 'horizontal' architecture, 'enormous kitchens, vast dining-rooms, numerous bedrooms for children and guests' and so on (despite the book's title, the author had little to say about the slave quarters, the *senzala*).[11] The description was illustrated with a number of photographs and drawings, including a charming sketch by his friend, the artist Cícero Dias, of the layout of a particular house, Engenho Noruega, a house that Freyre considered to be typical of its kind.[12]

Since the early 1920s, as was pointed out earlier, Freyre had been attracted by Ruskin's idea that that a society's state of social health is revealed by its architecture, or as he put it to his newspaper readers, that by insisting on plagiarizing 'post cards from Rio and Switzerland', the new Recife was losing its character and making its inhabitants feel like foreigners in their own land. Inevitably, 'their life, their moral, their taste' was affected by the new urban landscape. In *CGS*, even if the author does not say this in so many words, it is implied that the architecture of the Big House shaped the behaviour of the people who lived in it, the masters no less than the slaves, as well as embodying the dominant values of the local culture.[13]

Freyre's book was concerned not only with the Big House in itself but also with the house as the symbol of the sugar plantation of which it was the centre. Yet *CGS* was not a monograph on the history of sugar plantations, of the kind that the American historian Stuart Schwartz later produced for the neighbouring state of Bahia. It was something much more ambitious than that. The secondary literature cited in the book's footnotes includes articles and monographs on topics as diverse as weather, nutrition, physiology and neurology. The author concentrated on the history, sociology and anthropology of what he called a patriarchal, slave-owning and hybrid society in the North-East of Brazil, presenting it as a means to the better understanding of Brazil as a whole.

Freyre stressed the many functions of the Big House. Besides a residence it was a 'fortress, chapel, school, workshop' and other things besides. It represented 'an economic, social, political system', a system of production, transport, religion, politics and so on.[14] The point was that in this period of Brazil's history, the landowners or sugar planters, the *senhores de engenho*, as they were called at the time, in Pernambuco and elsewhere, were virtually independent of the central government. They also owned their workers, the slaves, who were forbidden to leave the plantation. For these two reasons, *CGS*, like Freyre's earlier historical studies, described the society of the North-East as 'feudal' or 'semi-feudal', with slaves in place of the medieval serfs.

Patriarchal Society

However, the term Freyre uses most often to describe colonial society is not 'feudal' but 'patriarchal'. The book is essentially a contribution to the history of the family. The contrast between this approach to Brazil and that of the British social historians such as G. M. Trevelyan or Asa Briggs to their own country, focusing on social class, surely tells us something important about differences between the two cultures. It is true that Freyre admired Trevelyan's *English Social History* (1942), while Briggs took Freyre as one of his models both for his *Social History of England* (1983) and his *Victorian Things* (1988), attracted by his 'poetical approach to place', his acute sensibility to smells, colours and noises and his concern with material culture. All the same, the differences between the British and the Brazilian styles of social history are striking.

The family was not only the topic that Freyre found most interesting, but also, so he claimed, the key to understanding the distinctive characteristics of Brazil's social development. The subtitle of the first edition of *CGS* was 'the formation of the Brazilian family under the regime of a patriarchal economy', changed in later editions to 'Introduction to the history of patriarchal society in Brazil'; by contrast, the English translation bore the subtitle 'A Study in the Development of Brazilian Civilization', perhaps to widen the book's appeal.

What does Freyre mean by 'patriarchy'? It is, as he explained later, a system of social relations 'between men and women, mistresses and slaves, adults and children, old and young', supported by what he sometimes calls a 'mystique'.[15] The essential point is the view of all the inhabitants of the estate as if they were a huge family ruled by the paterfamilias: an extended family that included the workers on the plantation as well as the servants in the Big House, all of them slaves and sleeping in the slave quarters, the *senzala* that is both juxtaposed and opposed to the *Casa Grande* in the book's title.

The master, Freyre suggested, treated his wife and children as his subjects, owing him obedience. He wrote about the 'tyranny' of fathers and husbands. As for the female slaves living on the estate, the author described them as the planter's 'harem'. He emphasized what he called the 'cohesion' of the family and its extension to include the dead, who were buried in the chapel, 'under the same roof as the living'. 'After all, the saints and the dead were part of the family'.[16] He also noted and praised the tradition of hospitality to travellers that made the Big Houses into the tropical equivalent of medieval monasteries.

The History of the Child

CGS paid special attention to children (white, black and Amerindian), to their clothes, their games and their toys, and above all to their relationships with adults. The idea of writing the book, as we have seen, and as the author explained to his readers in the introduction to the second edition, grew out of an earlier project on the history of childhood in Brazil – a whole generation before professional historians began to take the subject seriously.[17] In any case, like a good Freudian, Freyre believed that to understand the behaviour of a social group, in this case the planters, it was necessary to know how its members were brought up.

Two points about children – at least upper-class children – received particular emphasis in this book. In the first place, what adults expected from boys and girls was very different. Boys were supposed to be active, to spend their time outside the house and to learn how to give orders. Girls, on the other hand, were supposed to be passive and to stay indoors (there was a saying that 'women should leave home only twice; to get married and to be buried').[18] 'They were denied anything that might look like independence.' In the presence of adults girls were expected to remain silent or at most to speak quietly, with a 'humble air'.

In the second place, *CGS* emphasized the idea of the prematurely old child. This theme can be found in Freyre's writings from the early 1920s onwards. It is also present in the work of the German novelist Sudermann, which Freyre knew well, although he protested, as we have seen, that he had had the idea of the psychology of the prematurely old boy before he read this book. In colonial Brazil, *CGS* suggested, childhood was brutally short and boys of ten were already 'obliged to behave like adults', dressed like miniature adults and expected to treat their mothers and fathers with formal respect. As for girls, they married young and aged quickly. 'Nearly all the travellers who visited us in the days of slavery were in the habit of contrasting the charming freshness of our little girls with the wanness of countenance and the negligence of body of our matrons above the age of eighteen.'[19]

The display of affection that both boys and girls failed to receive from their parents they obtained, in compensation, from their slave nannies. The nannies gave the master's children suck, nursed them, fed them (masticating the food to make it suitable for infant mouths), told them stories and searched for lice in their hair, a practice known as *cafuné* (a term derived from one of the languages most commonly spoken in Angola, the homeland of many North-Eastern slaves).

The children of the masters and the slaves were often playmates. White boys rode on the backs of the slave boys (the *muleques*), for example, acting out the domination that they would later exercise in reality but at the same time building close relationships that would often last for life. There was certainly hierarchy on the plantation but there was not much distance.

Gender and Sexuality

For the most part, *CGS* is concerned with the world of men, but Freyre stands out from the majority of historians of his time in paying considerable attention to women as well. He has a good deal to say not only about the upper-class women of the Big House, described as living in 'oriental semi-reclusion', but also about the female slaves and the Amerindians. Earlier writers on Brazilian history had emphasized the civilizing mission of the Portuguese in the tropics, but Freyre, somewhat mischievously, suggests that the Amerindian women helped civilize the Portuguese by encouraging them to bathe more often. Freyre also discusses female clothes, the activities of women in the kitchen, making the sweets for which Pernambuco is still famous, and the sexual division of labour among the Indians in which it was the women who carried the heavy loads.[20] The book has also much to say about sex.[21] Indeed, as late as 1932, its working title was *Sexual and Family Life in the Brazil of the Slavocrats* ('Vida sexual e da família no Brasil escravocrata').[22] Suggesting that 'the atmosphere in which Brazilian life began was one of a kind of sexual intoxication', Freyre went on to discuss masturbation, sodomy, syphilis, prostitution, sadism and masochism, dirty stories, the 'almost aphrodisiac' designs on the tiles in churches and convents and the sexual symbolism of sweets. 'Even in the names of convent sweets and cakes, made by the seraphic hands of nuns, there is to be perceived at times an aphrodisiac intention, an obscene touch, confounded with the mystic – such names as nuns' sighs ... nun's belly ... angel's titbits.'[23]

It is worth noting how daring it was at this time for a historian to discuss these different forms of sexuality so openly and without moral judgements. Prepared to engage in sexual experiments himself, as we have seen, Freyre refused to condemn others who had done so in the past. He was still practising this daring and open approach to sex when he was in his seventies. The autobiography in the form of a diary that he published in 1975 included a discussion of the homosexual experience he had had at Oxford in the 1920s, an experience that he described as not only sensual but also 'lyrical'.

His publisher and friend, José Olympio, persuaded him to omit this passage, but in the course of justifying his original decision, Freyre explained his frankness. There was nothing to be ashamed of, he argued, in speaking about divergences from 'so-called sexual normality'. On the contrary, in line with Walter Pater's defence of a perpetual search for variety of experience as a philosophy of life, he defended the Oxford episode, rejecting any implication of vulgarity. Describing himself as an 'experimenter' who wished to live intensely, he even pitied those who, 'prejudiced by a kind of puritanism', narrow their experience of life and fail to experience love 'in its plenitude and in its diversity of expressions'.[24]

The author also emphasized the sexual precocity of the Brazilian boy and the white adult's sexual preference for *mulatas*. The last point takes us to one of the central themes of *CGS*: miscegenation. Freyre both described and celebrated sexual intercourse between the races, especially between whites and blacks. As he put it in a celebrated (or notorious) passage, 'from the very first moment of contact the Portuguese mingled enjoyably (*gostosamente*) with coloured women and multiplied themselves in *mestizo* children.'[25] As such passages remind us, this pioneering study of both sex and gender was written mainly from a male as well as a white viewpoint. Not entirely, though: with his customary capacity for shifting perspectives, the author also notes that 'The furious passions of the Portuguese must have been vented upon victims who did not always share his sexual tastes' and might involve sadism.[26]

Race, Culture and Hybridity

At the very beginning of *CGS*, early in the preface to the first edition, Freyre expressed his debt to the anthropologist Franz Boas, from whom he learned, as we have seen, to 'consider the difference between race and culture a fundamental one'. This passage has sometimes been misunderstood to mean that he reduced all so-called 'racial' differences to cultural ones, so that some writers on Freyre have found it necessary to insist that he never really abandoned race as an explanatory category.[27]

As we have already noted, Freyre had once shared the international interest shown by many on the Right and on the Left in the sinister pseudo-science of eugenics (and also in its opposite, 'cacogenics', as he called it) and admired the officially sanctioned programmes in the United States for the improvement of the species, programmes that were closely related to the so-called 'science of race'.

It is evident that for a while at least, like so many respectable people at that time, Freyre had been thinking and observing according to the prevalent racist paradigm and that he was convinced that the superiority of one race and the inferiority of another were unchangeable facts proved by science. Although he abandoned those views, turned them upside down and began thinking and observing from a different perspective, in which culture superseded race, he continued to use the concepts and language of eugenics, although mainly in a descriptive sense and sometimes mischievously, as when he wrote of the clergy as 'among the most select and eugenic elements in the formation of Brazil'.[28] In short, like an archaeological stratum or an inevitable straitjacket of the time, the language Freyre uses bears witness to the period he was writing in.

In any case, to say that Freyre does not free himself from the race category is to forget the apparently inevitability of its use, which should not be confused with beliefs in superiority and inferiority. The pretensions of 'scientific' racism have long been discredited, but to criticize racism is virtually impossible without using the language of race, without saying that the idea of a hierarchy of races had no foundation and that different races should be treated as equal, or without saying that interbreeding between races is good or neutral rather than a bad thing. There are still many institutes that use the terms 'race relations' in their title. Their aim is generally 'racial justice', to be achieved by the study of 'racial discrimination' or 'racial inequality'. Like 'culture', 'race' is a category that no one can define in a satisfactory way, yet it seems that no one can do without it.

All the same, the contrast between Freyre's new view and the one that the 'science of race' put forward is obvious. Instead of equating the mixture of races with deterioration, Freyre associated such mixture with the improvement of the species. One example is his argument that both the whites and the blacks in Brazil often came from 'the best stock' and that as a result of their sexual intercourse and 'genetic concourse', the mixed elements of the population showed great intellectual and physical gifts.

Freyre also studied biology and paid special attention to the ongoing debate over the possible inheritance of acquired characteristics and over the question whether nature or culture explained the mental differences between whites and blacks, but in *CGS* he often stressed the great difficulty of separating the two factors and arriving at a definite solution. What we know about this issue is, as Freyre put it cautiously, 'almost nothing: only enough to alert us against the prejudices of the system and the exaggerations of the theory'.

In short, by the time that Freyre wrote his masterpiece, there were only a few souvenirs of his previous flirtation with 'scientific racism', in the form of references in the bibliography to people such as Madison Grant, Charles Davenport or Lothrop Stoddard: nothing, therefore, that could undermine the fact that in *CGS* the emphasis falls not on race but on culture and society. On 'sexual depravity', for instance, Freyre comments that it is absurd to hold Brazilian Indians or Africans responsible rather than 'the social system in which they both functioned passively and mechanically'.[29] Even the body is presented as a social construct, shaped by diet, forms of labour, fashion ('the idealization of the plump woman as a type of beauty') and so on.[30]

The society that Freyre was concerned to describe and analyse was not only a patriarchal but also a 'hybrid' one, a mixture of three peoples and their cultures, the result of what Freyre liked to call their 'interpenetration'. The book is organized around these peoples with one chapter on the Portuguese colonizers, two on the African slaves and another on the Amerindians, who were rarely to be found on the plantations (after 1600, at least), but provided an important ingredient in the mixture that became Brazil.

In its day, the single most important statement made in *CGS* was its praise of miscegenation (*miscigenação, mestiçagem*), since to make this assertion was to turn the conventional wisdom upside down. The orthodox view in the 1930s was still the one that had been expressed by Count Gobineau (who visited Brazil in 1870) among others, to the effect that miscegenation led to physical degeneration. This was the justification for official policies of 'whitening' Brazil by encouraging migration from Europe, especially from Germany and Italy, from the 1880s to 1914.[31]

Freyre himself had earlier praised the vigorous policy of the government of Argentina for bringing into the country a 'great wave of Caucasians' – from 1853 to 1910 the foreign white population had grown from 3,200 to 2,300,000 – that was quickly and efficiently working for the disappearance of the 'inferior races'. However, he discovered, as we noted, that the whitening solution actually created a bigger problem. According to the eugenicist's rhetoric of racial purity and to the 'science of race' which gave respectability to prejudice, the white race was not homogeneous. Following Ripley's *The Races of Europe* and the work of other ethnologists, Madison Grant had been working successfully to popularize the idea that there was a clear hierarchy separating the representatives of the white race 'par excellence', the Nordic, from the representatives of the two other white sub-races, the Alpine and Mediterranean. Any mixture of these three sub-races was thought to be as undesirable as that of any other racial mixture, since it destroyed racial purity and would result in an inferior stock.

For this reason, Grant equated the southern Italians who were arriving in the United States in large numbers to the Roman slaves who outnumbered their masters and contributed greatly to the decline of the Roman Republic. By the same token, he was not impressed by the healing power of the great wave of Caucasians arriving in Argentina; these could not contribute to the country's great future because they were of the Mediterranean race, a type that is, as he put it, 'suspiciously swarthy'.[32]

The wide diffusion of this view was revealed by the intense anti-immigrant campaign of the early 1920s, aiming at counteracting the threat represented by the new wave of southern and eastern European immigrants arriving in the United States. The resulting Immigration Restriction Act of 1924 favoured the older, Nordic stocks over the newer ones and excluded the Japanese altogether. The discussions in the United States about the Latin American racial question were inevitably affected by the increasing popularity of these ideas about the inequality of the white races. So, while the belief that a massive white immigration was the solution for the Latin American 'problem' of race prevailed for decades, this solution was increasingly discredited after 1920.[33]

In short, we might say that once the encouragement of white immigrants – a policy that Freyre and many others at the time had supported
– was transformed from a solution into a problem by the most popular
works on race he came across in the United States, Freyre embarked upon
a project which would, conversely, transform what was a problem – racial
mixture – into a solution, emphasizing both the historical importance and
the value of cultural hybridity. The fourth chapter of *CGS* opens with the
famous affirmation, still shocking for many readers in 1933, that 'Every Brazilian, even the light-skinned fair one, carries about with him on his soul,
when not on soul and body alike ... the shadow, or at least the birthmark,
of the native or the Black'.[34]

Those readers would have been even more shocked had they known
that Freyre's valorization of hybridity was extended to sex and gender.
He praised the American poet Walt Whitman because he 'did not limit
himself as a poet to being of a class, of a race, or even of a sex'. In his 'semi-
novel' *Dona Sinhá e o Filho Padre*, Freyre approached the homoerotic
relationship of the two main characters, Paulo and José Maria, with great
sensibility and understanding, remarking that many men are mestiços 'not
only in race but also in gender, not only in ideas but in feelings as well. And
as such they realized themselves as humans, sometimes more than people
who are supposedly pure in race, sex, class, ideas and feelings'.[35]

Freyre illustrated his argument about the importance of the interpenetration of cultures with examples from housing, for instance, from music,
from cooking and from language. In the case of vernacular architecture,
he notes how the indigenous Indian straw hut or *palhoça* was combined
with the African cabin or *mucambo*. In music, he drew attention first to
the mixture of styles between Catholic hymns and indigenous songs, and
later to the African influence on the popular music of Brazil. The system
of Brazilian food, the *regime alimentar*, was described as owing something
to the Indians, while the cuisine of the North-East was greatly indebted to
African traditions, including the use of palm oil (*dende*) and bananas as
well as the famous *doces*, Portuguese dishes being 'modified by the season-
ing or the culinary techniques of the Blacks'.

Hybridities were also audible in language, in the Portuguese of
Brazil, especially that of Pernambuco, about which Freyre wrote some
remarkable pages at a time when socio-linguistics scarcely existed, noting
how the reciprocal influence of the languages of the masters and mistresses
and those of their slaves produced something new. 'It was from an interpenetration of the two tendencies that our national language resulted.'
Expanding a point he had made more ambivalently a few years before
about 'the corrupting, sometimes deliciously corrupting influence' of the

Africans, Freyre described the fluidity of Portuguese in African mouths, the softening or *amolecimento* that they brought to the language.[36] This example is one of the most vivid illustrations of a *Leitmotif* that recurs in Freyre's work, the contrast between hard and soft, rigid and flexible. It is also a memorable instance of his emphasis on two-way influence, on what the Cuban sociologist Fernando Ortiz would soon be describing as 'transculturation'.[37]

Although Freyre generally contrasted race with 'culture' or 'civilization', he did not neglect economic and social factors. Indeed, he placed such a great emphasis on these factors (great for his time at least) that some of his first readers accused him of materialism or Marxism, an association which, either as praise or criticism, would be relatively common until the early 1950s, as we shall see. His main point, reiterated throughout his book, is that the behaviour of the Africans and the Indians should be explained not by innate factors but by 'the social and economic system'. Brazilian culture was shaped for better or worse by slavery, by the regime of great estates and also by monoculture, the concentration, wherever the soil permitted this, on sugar production to the virtual exclusion of other crops.

What was the place of the Portuguese colonizers in this system? Freyre devoted a chapter to the subject, emphasizing what he called 'the remarkable predisposition of the Portuguese for the hybrid, slave-owning colonization of the tropics'. So far as hybridity is concerned, the *miscibilidade* of the Portuguese – in other words, their propensity to mix – is explained in terms of their geographical position, between Europe and Africa, and of their past, the tradition of interaction with Moors, Jews and Africans that went back a long way and helped to make them relatively flexible and adaptable to new conditions, softening or smoothing the asperities or rigidities that remain apparent in the case of other Europeans. It should be added, though, that Freyre claimed that the Portuguese of his own time had lost that plasticity and lived parasitically on their imperial past, a point that we shall discuss in more detail in a later chapter.

Harmony and Conflict

At first sight Freyre seems to be offering a view of the Brazilian past as unusually harmonious, and he has often been read in this way. He claimed that 'of all American societies, the Brazilian was the one that constituted itself most harmoniously so far as race relations are concerned.' Indeed, the author of *CGS* has become notorious for his optimistic vision of colonial history, in particular his claim that the slaveholding regime in Brazil was relatively benign, relatively gentle.[38] He suggested that the masters and mistresses of the Big House were socially and emotionally close to their slaves as a result of the way in which they were brought up, with black nurses and black playmates. In adulthood, sexual intercourse between master and slaves reduced the social distance between the Big House and the *senzala*, softening or 'sweetening' social relations and creating what the author called 'zones of fraternization'. 'Fraternization' is a favourite term of his and a recurrent theme in *CGS*, adding to the impression that Freyre saw social relations in plantation society through rose-tinted spectacles.

However, brothers do not always live in harmony. In any case, on a more careful reading of *CGS*, the author's concern with antagonisms and conflicts becomes impossible to deny. He described Brazil as 'a field for the conflict of the most violent antagonisms', illustrating his point with reference to 'explosions of race hatred' or 'cultural earthquakes', slave revolts like the one that shook Bahia in 1835.[39] On more than one occasion he referred to the 'shock' of encounters between cultures. He not infrequently used the term 'sadism' to describe the relations between some masters – and mistresses – and their slaves.[40]

In a passage of central importance for the interpretation of the whole book, Freyre underlined the place of antagonisms and the equilibrium of antagonisms in the formation of Brazil.

> Economic and cultural antagonisms. Antagonisms between European culture and native culture. Between European and African. Between the African and the native. Between an agrarian and a pastoral economy, between that of the agrarian and that of the mining regions. Between Catholics and heretic. Jesuits and landowners. *Bandeirantes* and planters. The Paulista [from São Paulo] and the *emboaba* [from Portugal]. The Pernambucan and the *mascate* [Portuguese peddler]. Great landowners and pariahs. Graduates and illiterates. But predominant over all these antagonisms was the most general and the deepest one: between master and slave.[41]

Two points are worth bearing in mind when trying to understand and assess Freyre's apparently rosy view of Brazilian society in general and the slave regime in particular. The first is that the harmony, consensus or benignity that he identifies in the Brazilian system is only claimed to be a relative one – relative, that is, to the slave regimes that existed in the Caribbean, for instance, or in the Southern states before the American Civil War. The comparison recurs in his pages and owes something to his own observation of race relations in the American South during his time in Waco in 1918–19 and during his visit to Simkins in South Carolina in 1926.

The second point to remember is that Freyre often describes this apparent harmony or consensus more precisely as an 'equilibrium of antagonisms'. The phrase was coined by Thomas Carlyle to describe the English gift for political compromise as illustrated by the actions of the ruling class in the early nineteenth century. As a tool of sociological analysis, the concept goes back to Herbert Spencer, where it plays a central role in his ideas about evolution, in the cosmos, in society and in mental life. Discussing intellectual conflicts, for instance, he suggested that neither side is 'completely right' or 'completely wrong' and that 'truth generally lies in the co-ordination of antagonistic opinions'. Turning to society, he described the adjustment of population and resources, the interplay of supply and demand and the alternation of conservatism and reform as so many examples of what he called 'equilibration', the progress towards a more or less stable equilibrium.[42]

The idea of antagonisms in equilibrium is also prominent in the work of a follower of Spencer, Freyre's former professor Franklin Giddings. In his *Theory of History* (1920), Giddings suggested that civilization originated in a struggle between the forces of the old and the new in which neither won a complete victory. In his copy of the book, Freyre wrote the significant word 'equilibration' in the margin at this point.[43]

The idea of the equilibrium of social as well as intellectual antagonisms is central to Freyre's thought, from an early essay on the emperor Dom Pedro (1926) to *O&P* (1959) and beyond, where the survival of antagonisms, and not their overcoming, is gradually emphasized. Dom Pedro, for instance, is criticized for wanting to conciliate oppositions instead of managing them or keeping them in equilibrium. Carried along by the 'fear of the coexistence of antagonisms in Brazilian political life', Freyre argues, the emperor sacrificed 'healthy divergences' or 'the clash of healthy antagonisms', so failing to exercise the role of the 'co-ordinator of necessary divergences' for which he was fitted.

In this respect Freyre's view of social equilibrium is distant from and indeed more subtle than the affirmations of harmony and consensus to be found in the social theory of Emile Durkheim. However, his view also differs from that of Spencer and his school in some respects. Instead of being an instrument of scientific analysis based on the models of physics and chemistry, as it was for them, the concept was for him fundamentally descriptive and normative. In fact, we might say that Freyre used this notion of equilibrium as a kind of metaphor for attempts at compromise between antagonistic forces. For him, therefore, far from being a neutral tool of objective analysis, 'equilibrium' was a positive value and also a very Brazilian one. Emperor Dom Pedro, for instance, so he argued, failed in his government because he had failed to realize that his actions were 'out of harmony with the traditions of our country'. In this sense Freyre may be said to have 'tropicalized' Spencer.

Freyre's version of the idea is expressed with particular clarity and force at the end of the first chapter of *CGS*, quoted above, which noted the number of antagonisms between master and slave that coexisted with or underlay the many everyday acts of fraternization. The title of the book, bringing together both the Big House and the slave quarters, is surely intended to remind the reader of the conflict as well as the complementarity in the relations between masters and slaves.

After this account of the book's major themes, the pages that follow will offer an assessment of *CGS* from a number of angles, emphasizing the variety of its viewpoints, the many disciplines on which it draws, its sources and methods and its value as a work of literature.

Insiders and Outsiders

CGS is a book written from multiple viewpoints, an approach that its author had appreciated ever since he read Nietzsche and that he tried to emulate while travelling in Europe a few years earlier as a 'scholar gypsy', as we have seen. The author was extremely conscious of the co-existence of different points of view, those of the Church and the laity, for instance, the view from the veranda of the Big House and the view from below, or the respective standpoints of insiders and outsiders. One of his most perceptive critics, the anthropologist Darcy Ribeiro, described the strength of the book as precisely its combination of these two perspectives, a combination made possible by the career of its author at home and abroad and by his two identities, 'the Pernambucan and the Englishman'. Freyre himself noted that his time abroad allowed him to see Brazil 'with the eyes of an outsider' (*com olhos de exógamo*).[44]

In the first place, the view from within. The French cultural theorist Michel de Certeau once suggested that when we read historians, we should always ask ourselves the question, 'Where are they speaking from?' From what location, at what moment and from what social position do they observe the past?[45] In Freyre's case we cannot afford to forget that he came from the world he was describing, or at least from its fringes. He was born in Pernambuco just twelve years after the abolition of slavery in Brazil in 1888. Two of his four grandparents, to whom *CGS* was dedicated, had lived in the world of the plantations. Indeed, Freyre had used their testimonies as sources for his master's thesis on social life in mid-nineteenth-century Brazil, discussed earlier.

Freyre's nanny, Dadade (short for Felicidade – which, ironically enough, means 'happiness'), was a former slave about whom he liked to reminisce in later life. His Rocha Wanderley ancestors owned a plantation, called Agua Preta ('Black Water'), in Serinhaém, and the names 'Wanderley' and 'Serinhaém', together with anecdotes about family history, recur in the book, as they do later in the author's work. These were magical names for him, like that of Balbec for Proust. In the first edition of *CGS*, immediately after the title-page, we find a photograph of an unknown nineteenth-century lady of the Wanderley family, placed as if she were presiding over the book.

CGS has often been described as informed by a deep nostalgia for the patriarchal world that Brazilians had lost. Freyre was and deliberately presented himself as a Proustian historian, concerned like his friend the painter Cícero Dias to evoke lost sensations and social relationships. When he writes about the standardization of the products of the toy industry 'according to American and German patterns' and the consequent disappearance of traditional Brazilian toys, we can feel his sense of loss, as we can when reading a note added to a later edition of the book lamenting the replacement of narrow streets by wide avenues.[46]

Particularly revealing of the author's attitude to the colonial past is Freyre's recurrent employment of the word 'we', in much the same way that G. M. Trevelyan, one of Freyre's favourite English historians, used to do, as if differences between genders, regions and social classes were unimportant. He refers, for instance, to 'the amount that remains in us from our *tupi* and *tapuya* [Amerindian] ancestors'. 'We almost all of us bear the mark' of African influence, he writes elsewhere. Or again, 'that viscous lustfulness in which we all feel ourselves ensnared as soon as we reach adolescence' (*a pegajenta luxúria en que nos sentimos todos prender, mal atingida a adolescência*). Yet again: 'We were the sadists.' [47]

On the other hand, as if to compensate for this limited perspective, Freyre was also able to look at Brazilian culture, society and history with the 'distant eye' of the anthropologist or the foreigner. *CGS* makes constant references to anthropology. The book cites famous names such as Edward Tylor, Bronisław Malinowski and, above all, Franz Boas, Freyre's 'master', as he liked to call him in later life. The distinction between race and culture made by Boas is cited again and again from the preface onwards. Freyre also uses and acknowledges the work of E. A. Westermarck on marriage and moral ideas, Melville Herskovits (who had studied with Boas) on culture areas, Alexander Goldenweiser on diffusionism, race and culture, George Pitt-Rivers on the clash of cultures, Robert Lowie (confirming the views of Boas on the importance of culture rather than heredity) and Lucien Lévy-Bruhl on primitive mentality.

Freyre adopted a number of concepts from anthropology. He was careful to point out, in the first footnote to the second chapter of the first edition of *CGS*, that he was using the term 'culture' in its anthropological or sociological sense, to mean 'that combination of styles, methods and material values that together with moral values characterize a people or a society'. He sometimes drew on 'my own observations', as in the case of 'the practices and rites of the African sects in Pernambuco' which sometimes follow Muslim customs such as removing one's shoes before participating in the ceremonies.[48]

Particularly close to anthropology was Freyre's chapter on the Indian. It involved the historical reconstruction of the culture, or rather the cultures of the Tupí and other indigenous peoples (the Bororo, for instance, and the Nambikwara), by combining evidence from the descriptions given by early European travellers to Brazil with that offered by recent anthropologists, notably Roquette-Pinto, with whom Freyre's friend Rüdiger Bilden was well acquainted (Lévi-Strauss only arrived in Brazil in 1935). Among the indigenous practices to which Freyre gave particular attention was that of the *couvade*, the custom of visiting and congratulating the father after the arrival of a baby as if he were the one who had given birth.

In short, by combining the view of an insider with that of an outsider, Freyre developed anthropological eyes which he turned on the colonizers as well as the colonized. As a result, he produced a study of Brazil that makes a fine example of what Pierre Bourdieu would later call reflexive anthropology.

Multidisciplinarity

Anthropology was only one of the many disciplines on which Freyre drew in this book. It was indeed appropriate that the English honorary degree that he received in the 1960s should have come from the militantly interdisciplinary University of Sussex, and that the historian Asa Briggs, presenting him for the degree, should have described him as a 'Sussex man'.

Although he preferred the anthropological approach, with its emphasis on direct observation and the details of everyday life, Freyre was more involved with sociology, a subject on which he was to write a textbook. He presented *CGS* in the preface to the first edition as a study in both 'genetic sociology and social history'. Among the authors cited in his essay are Max Weber on Protestantism, capitalism and the economic role of the Jews; William Thomas (a 'master' whom Freyre once described as second only to Weber) on sex and society; Pitirim Sorokin on social mobility; and the Cuban Fernando Ortiz (not yet famous) on black sorcerers.

Franklin Giddings, 'our old master at the University of Columbia', as Freyre calls him, is cited in a footnote explaining his phrase 'consciousness of kind' (or as we now say, sense of identity). Indeed, as Freyre later admitted, his debt to Giddings in this book, especially whenever he discussed the equilibrium of antagonisms, was at least as great as the debt to Boas. Much later in life, adjusting his accounts and confessing his debts to the mentors presiding over his long and successful intellectual life, Freyre acknowledged with regret that throughout his career he had not been fair in leaving Giddings 'in the shade'.[49]

Freyre regularly used technical terms from sociology: 'sub-culture', for instance, social 'cohesion', or 'mobility', or the idea of a 'complex' (the *couvade* complex, tobacco complex and so on, a sociological term without the pathological associations that it has in psychoanalysis). His repeated preference for economic and social explanations over racial ones, like his presentation of the Big House as the centre of a social 'system', reveals the sociologist in him at a time when historians, in Brazil as in Europe or the United States, were generally concerned with politics rather than society and with explanations in terms of events rather than structures. At the same time, his openness to sociological insights from non-sociologists is revealed by remarks like the following about Lafcadio Hearn. Referring to Hearn's observations of the mixed population of the French West Indies, Freyre praised him for being able to see much more 'as a simple writer, than many sociologists'.[50]

Still more unusual for its period was Freyre's bold attempt to combine history with psychology, especially but not exclusively the psychoanalysis of Sigmund Freud, who is cited in a footnote to his third chapter (Freud, incidentally, had been accused of writing pornography, just as Freyre would be). Freyre regularly uses terms such as 'libido', 'obsession', 'sadism' and 'masochism', in order to analyse the importance of sexual swearwords and stories, for instance, the symbolism of sweets, and above all the relationships between masters and slaves. Adapting some of the ideas of William McDougall on the 'group mind' (later taken up by Carl Gustav Jung) to the context of the tropics, he described the Indians as 'introverts' and the Africans as 'extroverts'.[51]

In one of the central arguments of *CGS*, following Freud and disciples of Freud such as Havelock Ellis, Stanley Hall, Albert Moll and Oscar Pfister, Freyre emphasized the importance of childhood for the development of adults, the psychological importance of sucking at the breast and the sexual life of children. His analysis of the *couvade*, mentioned above, hesitated between an anthropological interpretation and a psychological one (in terms of bisexuality).

By comparison with sociology, anthropology and psychology, Freyre drew rarely on the work of economists or geographers; *CGS* does make occasional references to the importance of the environment, but the author's interest in ecology developed a little later, as we shall see. On the other hand, the author did make considerable use of what might be called 'hard' science, including physical anthropology, physiology, nutrition, hygiene and climatology. CGS refers to articles from such journals as the *Eugenics Review*, *Brasil Médico*, the *Boletim Sanitário* and the *Transactions of the American Gynecological Society*. CGS also reveals an impressive acquaintance with discussions about race questions among the international scientific community, especially as to the inheritance of acquired characteristics. These studies included a famous monograph by Boas, *Changes in the Bodily Form of the Descendants of Immigrants* (1910).

The expertise of his cousin Ulisses Pernambucano, a doctor and a psychiatrist, was doubtless of assistance in this area, but even more important – indeed, paramount for Freyre's new interpretation of Brazil – was his acquaintance with the work of the anthropologist Roquette-Pinto, which provided him not only with information about the anthropology of Brazil, but also with the wider scientific knowledge and references that he lacked.[52]

Well informed about the newest research at home and abroad, Roquette-Pinto, like a Brazilian Franz Boas, led what one might call a campaign against the 'hasty eugenicists' who, basing themselves on very questionable evidence from a still immature science, were proposing harsh measures for the 'improvement of the species' around the world. It was through Roquette, for instance, that Freyre became acquainted with the work of dissident scientists like the biologist H. S. Jennings, who insisted, against the prevailing trend, that there was a lot of pseudo-science backing both the eugenics movement and the American anti-immigration campaign.

Preaching caution and scientific humility by various means – among them books, newspaper articles, conference papers and radio programmes – Roquette-Pinto in Brazil, like Boas in the United States, criticized the unscientific base of many of the notions of the so-called 'science of race'. On the questions of race and heredity, Roquette-Pinto insisted, it was 'scientific dilettantism' and 'prejudices' that prevailed. As he put it, 'in the explanations of the Abbé [Mendel] there is, in fact, too much metaphysics', while the works of people such as Gobineau, Chamberlain and Keyserling, which sing the 'Teutonic hymn', are nothing but 'diffuse, loquacious and exhibitionist volumes, drawing their information from cheap encyclopaedias, lacking a critical spirit and full of prejudice'.

So it was with caution and moderation that Roquette-Pinto approached the difficult question of miscegenation. The so-called 'degeneration' of the race that miscegenation inevitably causes, he warned the public, is an assertion made without proper rigorous scientific experiments. There is a lot of uncertainty surrounding this issue and the 'objective documented study of this question' is only beginning, he claimed in the 1920s. But what is certain, he added, is that those mixed people who are taken as 'degenerate' are, in many cases, nothing but 'sick men', who, instead of being examples of racial inferiority bear witness, in fact, to poor social conditions. In short, they are not the result of 'pathological causes', a concept that should be avoided, but a problem to be tackled by 'sanitary and educational policies'.

For those like Freyre who had been impressed by the eloquence and authority of eugenicists like Madison Grant, the ideas of Roquette-Pinto represented a breath of fresh air. The air was also tropical, for as Freyre would admit a few years after writing *CGS*, Roquette-Pinto studied the problem of race 'from the Brazilian point of view and within the parameters of Brazilian development'.

Roquette clearly opposed the widely diffused views of the Swiss scientist Louis Agassiz, who was frequently quoted by those who wanted to support their condemnation of miscegenation. Lothrop Stoddard, for instance, in *The Rising Tide of Colour*, had appealed to the authority of Agassiz to convince those people who denied the disastrous consequences of allowing people of different races to mix.

> Let anyone who doubts the evil of this mixture of races, and is inclined from mistaken philanthropy to break down all barriers between them, come to Brazil. He cannot deny the deterioration consequent upon the amalgamation of races, more widespread here than in any country in the world, and which is rapidly effacing the best qualities of the white man, the Negro and the Indian, leaving a mongrel nondescript deficient in physical and mental energy.[53]

This comment by Agassiz is used by Roquette-Pinto as an illustration of prejudices with an air of science. 'Agassiz was born in Switzerland, but when he wrote this he was a professor in the United States, a country where Negros were lynched as easily as one kills mosquitoes.'

We can say, then, that the most important legacy of Roquette-Pinto to Freyre was the way he changed the focus of the Brazilian problem, dismissing the whitening of the population as a solution for the backwardness of the country. Mixing ceased to be important because in his view, the main problems of Brazil were not racial but social and environmental. The difficulty was that there was a good deal of 'disguised or manifest prejudice' in the discussions about the most pressing national questions. His constant refrain – obsessively repeated in the various media to which he had access, including the educational radio he founded in 1923 – was that 'the national problem was not to whiten the mixed population of Brazil. Our problem is the kind of education that they receive here, whether they are light or dark ... anthropology proves that men, in Brazil, need to be educated, not replaced.'

Sources and Methods

From a historian's point of view, one of the most remarkable features of CGS is the wide variety of the primary sources on which its author draws. In the first place, he was able to consult some of the family archives – wills, inventories, letters, recipes (important for his pages on regional cuisine) and so on – preserved, though sometimes mouldering away, either in the Big Houses themselves, often semi-ruinous, or in the library of the State of Pernambuco. The contents of one family archive, that of the owners of Engenho Noruega, made a particularly important contribution to the book. Other documents of the period were already in print, notably the letters of the Jesuits and the denunciations of individuals to the Inquisition, together with their subsequent interrogations or confessions.

Freyre's great regret was the relative lack in colonial Brazil of the personal documents such as diaries and journals so abundant in the Protestant world. In Brazil, unfortunately, one could only find a 'shabby version of Mr Pepys' (*Pepys de meia-tigela*), he lamented, suggesting that in a Catholic country, it was not the diary but the confessional that 'absorbed the secrets'.[54] For a view of the plantation from within he had to rely on his own memories of Engenho Ramos, 'the first plantation that I knew and one which I will always view with special emotion'; on those of his grandparents and his friends (notably the painter Cícero Dias and the novelist José Lins do Rego, both of them brought up on *engenhos*); and on some more or less systematic oral history, including an interview in 1932 with an ex-slave, Luiz Mulatinho, who was then a hundred years old.

To these witnesses from a later period Freyre added the testimony of fiction – the novels of Machado de Assis, for instance, as evidence for family customs – and also that of folklore, especially the folksongs he regularly quoted as evidence of popular attitudes, the view from below. Discussing African influences on Brazilian culture, for instance, and returning to his favourite theme of the child, Freyre notes how, like the language, 'Portuguese lullabies were modified in the mouth of the black nurse, who altered the words and adapted them to regional conditions' – changing 'fountain' into 'creek', for instance – and 'associating them with her own beliefs and those of the Indians'.[55]

The type of source on which Freyre drew most heavily was one that historians, with the exception of his friend Bilden, were not yet in the habit of taking seriously. It was the travelogue, the description of Brazilian customs by a visitor to the country. Freyre had long been interested in this form of literature, as we have seen, and now he was able to draw on the testimonies of travellers to compose his historical anthropology of the colonial period, since the visitors were, in a sense, amateur ethnographers. 'For a knowledge of the social history of Brazil', he wrote, 'no source is more dependable than the travel books written by foreigners', although it was necessary to use them with care and distinguish the 'honest' witnesses – Henry Coster, for instance, Maria Graham or Richard Burton – from the superficial and prejudiced ones.[56]

A number of important points made in CGS are based on the evidence of travelogues. For example, Freyre calls the sixteenth-century French Protestant Jean de Léry as a witness to both the frequency of bathing by the Indians and to the surprised reaction of the Europeans; and Léry and the German Hans von Staden as witnesses to women's work. Again, the Englishman Coster testifies to the custom of allowing the children of the plantation owners to play with the children of the slaves.[57]

Freyre also paid more attention to visual sources than historians customarily did in the 1930s. As he remarked in his original preface, 'the iconography of slavery and patriarchal life' can be found in the works of leading artists from the Dutchman Franz Post in the seventeenth century to the Frenchman Jean-Baptiste Debret in the nineteenth, foreigners whose travelogues were written with a brush.[58] Besides its decorations by Cícero Dias, the first edition of CGS included five photographs of Big Houses, two of town houses, five of planter families, two of traditional furniture, one of a black woman wearing a distinctive head-dress and five prints of work on the plantation.

The use of relatively unexploited sources raises important questions about Freyre's methods as a historian. If 'methods' mean systematic and rigorous procedures, then it must be admitted that Freyre was unmethodical or even anti-methodical.[59] He was well aware of this, and wrote on occasion of his 'non-methods' as well as his 'impressionism'. He repeatedly referred to CGS, despite its five hundred pages, as an 'essay', in order to emphasize the personal and provisional quality of his interpretation, qualities which he prized in essays, as we have seen.

In a broader sense of the term we can describe impressionism as Freyre's method, since it was a deliberate choice, linked to his ambition to write a sensuous history. The vivid images and descriptions of sounds that we have noted in Freyre's early work recur in CGS, including the 'creaking of a canvas cot' accompanying the sexual initiation of young white men by black or mulatto women; the 'squeaking hammock, with the master copulating in it'; or the loud voices of the ladies of the Big Houses, accustomed as they were to shouting orders to slaves.

In later life, Freyre liked to compare his historical method to that of St Ignatius Loyola in his *Spiritual Exercises*, since Ignatius recommended the use of all five senses in the practice of meditation. To the vivid visual and aural images of *CGS* may be added his description of the smell of sweat, especially the sweat of blacks; the taste of the famous sweets of Pernambuco, a *Leitmotif* in the author's writings; and the feel of the fingers of the slaves when they gave their masters and mistresses *cafuné*, searching their heads for lice and massaging them at the same time. The sensation of fingernails gently scratching the scalp was often remembered with pleasure.

'Pointillism' might be a more exact term than impressionism to refer to the way in which Freyre constructed his portrait of patriarchal society out of a multitude of small but revealing observations, 'intimate details' or 'significant details' as he liked to call them, placing himself, like the Italian micro-historian Carlo Ginzburg more recently, in the tradition of Sherlock Holmes and Sigmund Freud. No wonder then that a Brazilian social historian recently described Freyre as a pioneer in micro-history who was able to shift back and forth between different scales of observation, between the close-up and the big picture.[60]

The significant details include anecdotes, which play an important role in *CGS*: the tradition of the planter who killed two slaves and buried them in the foundations of his house, for instance, or the child who envied the funeral of his playmate and died soon after, or the planter whose sexual arousal required sniffing the underwear of his black mistress.[61] This use of anecdotes was criticized by a number of reviewers as an unscholarly procedure, so it is worth emphasizing the fact that these stories are not repeated in *CGS* as if they were true – they are introduced by phrases like 'it is said that' or 'according to tradition' – but because they are revealing. What they are supposed to reveal are the attitudes or mentalities characteristic of a particular culture. Freyre appreciated the epigram of the English historian Edward Augustus Freeman, 'a false anecdote may be good history', and would have agreed with Kenneth Burke's praise of the 'representative anecdote' a few years later.[62]

It should therefore be clear that Freyre was not a methodical writer. He usually preferred to follow his impressions and intuitions. He was tempted to speculate, and frequently yielded to the temptation, as in the case of his discussions of the influence of African or Indian or Jewish influences on the culture of Brazil. An extreme case of this kind of speculation is the attribution to Sephardic influence of the Brazilian 'mania for spectacles' as a status symbol, 'an outward mark of learning or of intellectual and scientific attainment'.[63] All the same, Freyre could be methodical when he wanted to, and at times it is possible to speak of his methods in a fairly precise sense of the term. As he emphasized later in response to criticisms, he employed the complementary notions of *casa grande* and *senzala* as 'ideal types' in the sense that Max Weber employed that expression, in other words as sociological abstractions or models derived from a number of different examples rather than as literal descriptions of particular realities.[64]

The great French historian Marc Bloch emphasized the importance of two historical methods that he considered to be neglected by the scholars of his day. Although he seems to have discovered Bloch's work only later, Freyre was already employing both these recommended methods in *CGS*: the comparative and the regressive.

The so-called 'regressive method' was recommended by Bloch for the study of medieval agriculture. His argument was that historians should proceed from what is better known, the later period, to what is less known. Scholars should not assume, according to Bloch, that the same agrarian system persisted over the centuries, but they should call on their knowledge of the better-documented later period to interpret the fragments of evidence surviving from earlier times.

In *CGS*, the chapter on the historical anthropology of Indian cultures reveals the author employing this regressive method in a relatively systematic and rigorous way, combining the detailed accounts offered by recent anthropologists such as Roquette-Pinto or the Swiss Alfred Métraux with the fragmentary testimonies of colonial travellers. Elsewhere, Freyre followed the same approach in an informal way, the present, especially in remote regions, being scrutinized for traces of the past. For example, Freyre attributed to the influence of Amerindian culture 'the custom, which is very Brazilian, especially in the interior of the country and in the *sertão*, of keeping the women and children out of the sight of strangers'.[65]

'Even today' (*ainda hoje*) is a recurrent phrase in *CGS*, with reference to the surprisingly joyful funerals of children, for instance, to figures of animals as toys (interpreted as a survival of Amerindian customs), to the sensuality of traditional church festivals (interpreted as an African survival), to Muslim traditions in the Brazilian rituals of *candomblé* (a religious cult that had arrived in the North-East with the slaves from West Africa) and so on. Again, he made frequent use of nineteenth-century sources – fiction, photographs, travelogues and so on – in a book that was supposedly concerned with the period 1500–1800.

As for comparisons, including contrasts, they recur in *CGS*. They are not casual but essential to the argument, in particular to the claim that the Portuguese possessed qualities that made them particularly suitable for the enterprise of colonizing the New World. A few are distant comparisons, the most famous of these being the reference to Brazil as 'a kind of American Russia', a large country with slavery in the place of serfdom. His discussion of the diffusion of disease takes the author as far afield as India, China and Japan.

Most of Freyre's comparisons, however, are what Bloch called 'neighbourly' comparisons between societies that are not far apart in space, or have historical connections, or are at any rate similar in structure. He made regular reference, for instance, to the plantation societies of the Caribbean, such as Jamaica and Cuba. He contrasted Brazil more than once with Spanish America, beginning with the very first paragraphs of *CGS*, describing how the 'lords of the plantation ... always spoke up boldly to the representatives of the crown', while their equivalents in Spanish America 'were inert in the dominant shadow of the cathedrals and the palaces of the viceroys'. Again, following the anthropologist Melville Herskovits, Freyre compared and contrasted the 'moral and material values' of America with those of Africa, especially the culture areas in Africa from which the Brazilian slaves were taken.

Most frequent of all are the comparisons that were always at the back of his mind between the plantation society of the North-East of Brazil and that of the South of the United States before the Civil War. The region was one that Freyre knew at first hand, and he was struck by a number of parallels with Brazil ('almost the same type of aristocrat and Big House'), as well as by certain differences between the two societies, pointing to these differences in order to reinforce his arguments about the special qualities of the Portuguese colonizers.

Freyre's treatment of these similarities and differences in *CGS* was considerably more subtle and nuanced than it had been in his earlier writings. When he was still under the spell of the 'good old days' of the American South and of Brazilian plantation society, Freyre had already drawn analogies between the two regions. They were, however, of a different kind, revealing a very different standpoint from his book of 1933. He had longed, for instance, for this 'delicious thing which was the American South before the Civil War', with its traditions and its true aristocracy and its 'southern dignity'; all those values which were destroyed by the arrogant industrialism of the north. In the same way, he had once referred with nostalgia to the plantation society in Brazil which had been deeply affected by the arrival of the 'absentee factory owners' who completely subverted the old patriarchal order. The old days had been a time when the country was peaceful and the slaves were faithful to their masters.[66]

Still dazzled by the American segregationist solution for the problem of race, Freyre even wrote a newspaper article in 1926 praising Benjamin Tillman, an important political figure of the Old South who had been responsible for measures to ensure that blacks could not occupy key positions in the state of South Carolina – or as Tillman put it, measures that would prevent the conversion of the South into a mulatto state (for him, nothing could be worse than miscegenation, especially for the 'most noble of the races', the Caucasian). The occasion for Freyre's verdict was the recent publication of a book by his old friend Simkins, a book that aimed at studying Tillman's role in the history of the progress of democracy – 'white democracy' – in South Carolina and praised his political wisdom.

Referring to the 'post bellum South' as a most interesting period, Freyre explained to his readers that that was the time when the South started organizing associations aimed at reacting against the humiliating 'government of blacks' that the arrogant industrialist North was imposing on them. That was when the Ku Klux Klan was created, as 'a kind of war-like Freemasonry at the same time militant and mystic', he says; and that was also the time that a new type of leader like Tillman was needed for the economic reconstruction of the South. His actions were aimed at giving the new white farmer the pride and training that he lacked. And for this he had 'personality', he 'possessed boldness'. It is true that he was not a great man, Freyre admits, but he had a 'realistic sense of the problem' and his view was not tainted by 'any sentimentality' (no wonder that he was praised later by the author of the book as someone who appreciated 'race discrimination as a constructive force in American nationalism').

As an example of Tillman's boldness and objectivity, Freyre mentions the way in which he had reacted to the execution of a Black deputy. The man was shot, and Tillman watched this act 'with the calm of someone watching a shooting-match. He was convinced of the need to expel the nigger from government; that was his realistic sense of the problem. And this view was not qualified by the slightest sentimentalism.'

This is where Freyre extrapolated from South Carolina to Brazil. Without defending his violence, but not really repudiating his racism either, he presented Tillman as a model leader for the remaining plantation owners in Pernambuco – as if his support for race segregation did not disqualify him for the role. Aiming at invigorating the 'small white farmer' who had replaced the old aristocracy and was needed for the economic reconstruction of the South, Tillman had worked to give the new group the education and confidence that they lacked. His example should be followed in Pernambuco, claimed Freyre, where the 'rest of the plantation owners' would also profit from someone who would help them to organize themselves against the 'absentee factory owners' and against exploitation by demagogues.

It was after writing this review that Freyre fell into what he called, in a letter to his old mentor Armstrong, a 'Rimbaud mood' and, like the brilliant French poet who had abandoned his promising career at a very early age, he did not write, except under a pseudonym, for a number of years. It is as if he had, all of a sudden, become deeply shocked by the extreme racist position he had just advocated and realized that he should not continue along this dark track. So, in the hope of finding new tools for thinking about Brazil, he decided to abandon writing for studying, and became immersed in a new type of reading: Brazilian ethnography and anthropology.[67] That was the occasion when he discovered in his own country the rich and stimulating work of Roquette-Pinto, who would lead him back to the ideas of Franz Boas.

CGS as Literature

When Freyre called CGS an 'essay', he was not simply trying to disarm potential critics of his scholarship by stressing the provisional nature of his findings. He identified himself, as we have seen, not as an academic sociologist or historian but as a writer. Style was important for him and it was part of the substance of his book, which is, apart from its importance as social history or historical sociology, one of the great works of twentieth-century Brazilian literature.[68]

In a much discussed study of four great nineteenth-century historians, published a generation ago, the American scholar Hayden White claimed that each of them, whether consciously or unconsciously, modelled his narrative or 'plot' on that of a leading literary genre. Thus Jules Michelet wrote his histories in the form of romance, Leopold von Ranke in that of comedy, Alexis de Tocqueville in that of tragedy and Jacob Burckhardt in that of satire.[69] White also emphasized the predilection of these historians for particular figures of speech – metaphor in Michelet, metonymy in Ranke, synecdoche in Tocqueville and irony in Burckhardt.

In Freyre's case the model is surely comedy, or more exactly tragicomedy, a story about conflict and suffering that produces a harmonious resolution. A central theme of the book is the way in which the violent actions of the Portuguese colonizers and plantation owners, taking and sometimes raping indigenous and African women, led to a miscegenation which would lead in its turn to a situation of relative racial harmony. In other words, the reader is offered a complex story about unintended consequences and not the simple story about good colonizers that the author has often been accused of writing. As for figures of rhetoric, although *CGS* is full of metaphors, as we shall see, as well as suffused, like the author's other books, with irony, the dominant figure is surely synecdoche, the part standing for the whole and the Big House for the plantation system and even for the patriarchal civilization of colonial Brazil.

The organization of *CGS* deserves attention. Following a general introduction, successive chapters are devoted to the three major groups out of whom Brazil was formed: the Indian, the European and the African (following the chronological order of their arrival in South America). Within each chapter, however, the principle of organization is less obvious. The two final chapters on the Africans follow, despite digressions, a kind of chrono-logic, that of the life of an individual from the cradle to the grave. Other chapters appear to be organized by nothing more than free association. The chapter on the Portuguese colonizer, for instance, moves from diet to the influence of Africa in the *sertão*, to syphilis and finally to sadism. This problem of organization is not, of course, confined to *CGS*. It is one that has always been difficult for works of social and cultural history to resolve since they lack the equivalent of political events on which to string their beads.

In any case, it is not the organization of *CGS* but its language that captivates most readers. Today, after generations of informalization, it takes an effort to remember that Freyre's easy, semi-colloquial style was unusual for its day in a printed book, especially a work of scholarship, and that it shocked some conservative readers. Regretting as he did what he called 'the enormous void that exists between the written and the spoken language', Freyre did his very best to bridge it.[70] The result was something of a mixture. Parts of *CGS* are written in an academic mode, discussing the arguments of scholars and scientists about nutrition, interbreeding, geology, agriculture, medicine and so on. The more memorable passages, on the other hand, are extremely personal and immediate, like the references to 'us' and 'today' that were cited earlier.

Freyre often wrote as he spoke, vividly and informally. When he wished to stress the lack of a middle group between masters and slaves, for example, he wrote of 'a thin and insignificant remnant of free men sandwiched in between' (*uma rala e insignificante lambujem de gente livre sanduichada entre os extremos antagônicos*).[71] When he wanted to discuss the colonists' propensity for interbreeding, he described them as 'mixing themselves enjoyably with coloured women at the first encounter and multiplying themselves in children of mixed race' (*misturando-se gostosa-*

mente com mulheres de cor logo ao primeiro contato e multiplicando-se em filhos mestiços).

Freyre was not afraid of using rare words or terms of his own coinage, and he was particularly fond of unusual adverbs such as *aristocratamente, patriarcalmente, jesuiticamente, mussulmanamente,* in other words in the manner of aristocrats, patriarchs, Jesuits or Muslims. He experimented with word order. Following the model of his admired Walter Pater, he began the sentence with whatever he wanted to emphasize, so that 'in Brazil, the names of almost all animals and birds remained Tupi names' comes out as *Tupis ficaram no Brasil os nomes de quase todos os animais e pássaros.*[72]

A number of the early reviewers of CGS drew attention to the novelty of its style, whether they praised it as 'a language adapted to our epoch' or denounced it as a sacrifice to 'the modern idol of verbal slovenliness'.[73] On one side, the novelist José Lins do Rego drew attention to the rhythm and the melody of Freyre's prose, while another member of Freyre's clan, Otávio Tarquínio de Sousa, described his style as 'without a shadow of pedantry, without an academic air, without an overcoat'. On the other hand, Alfonso Arinos de Mello Franco regretted the use of undignified language and compared the use of a colloquial style in a serious book to a man turning up for a formal dinner dressed for tennis. This criticism may not have displeased Freyre, since he once expressed his appreciation for a description of Walt Whitman's poems as written in a 'shirt-sleeve style'.[74]

Freyre studied prose rhythm just as he studied verse – he annotated his copy of George Saintsbury's history of English prose rhythm – and he was a master of controlled repetitions and echo effects. To achieve these effects he was prepared to dispense with orthodox rules for composition and produce sentences of one, two or three words, often without verbs. Here is a not untypical short passage:

> In the age of slavery, many Brazilian boys were brought up entirely by nurses. Rare was the one who was not suckled by a black nurse. Who did not learn to speak more easily with the slave than with his father and mother. Who did not grow up with slave boys. Playing with slave boys. Learning bad ways with them and with the pantry-girls. And losing his virginity early. Physical virginity. Mental virginity.
>
> (*Muito menino brasileiro do tempo da escravidão foi criado inteiramente pelas mucamas. Raro o que não foi amamentado por negra. Que não aprendeu a falar mais com a escrava do que com o pai e a mãe. Que não cresceu entre muleques. Brincando com muleques. Aprendendo safadeza com eles e com as negras da copa. E cedo perdendo a virgindade. Virgindade do corpo. Virgindade de espírito*).[75]

Freyre's frequent lists produced a similar musical effect: the list of dishes sold in the street by slaves, for instance, the calf's feet, corn cakes (*pamonhas*), beans in *dendê* oil, rice with coconut (*arroz de coco*), beans with coconut (*feijão de coco*), sponge-cake (*pão-de-ló*), sugar-cane roll (*rolete de cana*), and so on.[76] Freyre's writings appeal to the eye as well as to the ear. His interest in the 'imagism' of Yeats, Lowell and other poets left many traces on his prose as well as his poems.[77] It produced vivid vignettes like the contrast between the plantation owners in the saddle, 'silver stirrups and all', and the same planters inside the Big House, 'so many barefooted Franciscans, clad in cotton nightgowns and at times in nothing but their drawers'. Elsewhere the same planters are portrayed in their hammocks after meals 'as they lay there picking their teeth, smoking a cigar, belching loudly, emitting wind, and allowing themselves to be fanned or searched for lice'.[78]

The paragraphs of *CGS* are rich in metaphors, some of them disconcertingly original. 'The Church', remarks the author, 'was a species of disinfectant chamber at the service of the colony's moral health, a hospital where souls remained in quarantine.' Again, the lazy planters in their hammocks are described as 'letting themselves be extracted from their house like jam from a spoon'.[79] As this example (among so many others), illustrates, the contrast between what is hard, rough or rigid (associated with Europe or with the United States) and what is soft, gentle, flexible or fluid (associated with the tropics, whether in Africa or Brazil) is a *Leitmotif* in this book, as indeed it is in Freyre's work as a whole.

Having described *CGS* from a number of angles, it is time to place or replace it in a broader cultural context, both national and international.

Traditions

CGS both belongs to and subverts a Brazilian tradition of interpreting Brazil. As a history of the colonial period, it may be viewed as a response to the suggestion made by the nineteenth-century German naturalist Carl von Martius in his essay 'How the history of Brazil should be written'. Martius suggested that this history should take the form of the story of the encounter, interaction, mixture and 'fusion' of three races, 'the copper or American, the white or Caucasian, and the black or Ethiopian'. Again, the claim that the slaveholding regime in Brazil was relatively benign was an elaboration of an argument put forward in the nineteenth century by one of Freyre's heroes, the North-Eastern statesman Joaquim Nabuco.

As an account of the successes of the colonizers, *CGS* both follows and develops the work of Adolfo Varnhagen, whose *General History of*

Brazil (1854–7) emphasized the civilizing influence of the Portuguese. Indeed, one recent scholar has gone so far as to describe *CGS* as a simple repetition of Varnhagen's eulogy of Portuguese colonization.[80] However, it would be more exact to say that Freyre praises Portuguese colonization for different reasons from Varnhagen's, emphasizing the adaptability of the colonizers to local conditions. In his discussion of civilization, as we have seen, Freyre inverted the Western commonplace and described indigenous and African women as people with a 'civilizing mission' (*missão civilizadora*) – that of civilizing the Portuguese.

As an analyst of Brazilian national identity, Freyre has his place in a tradition that goes back at least as far as the literary critic Sílvio Romero, whose introduction to his *History of Brazilian Literature* (1888) was concerned with national character. In a manner inspired by the French critic Hippolyte Taine, who viewed literature as the product of three factors, 'race, milieu and moment', Romero discussed the tropical environment and the mixture of races, arguing that this 'mixture' or 'fusion' was both inevitable and positive.[81]

However, the greatest of Freyre's predecessors was surely the journalist Euclides da Cunha, whose study *The Backlands* (1902), told the story of a revolt against the new Brazilian Republic in the 1890s, placing this story in its regional context, that of the desert (*sertão*) of the interior of the North-East. Like *CGS*, *The Backlands* is a contribution to history and sociology that is also a work of literature, with much to say about the physical environment. On the other hand, as an interpretation of Brazil that stressed the difference between superior and inferior races and the unfortunate consequences of interbreeding (qualified by a certain admiration for the cross between Europeans and Amerindians), *The Backlands* was the classic text against which Freyre could define his own position.[82]

As a social history of Brazil, on the other hand, *CGS* owed more to the work of Capistrano de Abreu, whose *Chapters of Colonial History* (1907) was concerned with some of the same main themes, notably the Big House, the role of domestic slaves as mediators between the plantation owners and their workers and the importance of interbreeding – which Capistrano, like Euclides, approved of in the case of Europeans and Amerindians, but not in the case of Europeans and Africans.[83]

In its comparative approach, *CGS* followed the work of Freyre's old mentor, Manuel Oliveira Lima, whose *Evolution of Brazil* (1914) compared and contrasted Brazilian history with that of both Spanish and 'Anglo-Saxon' America. Oliveira Lima also gave a lecture at the Institute of Politics in Williamstown in 1922 in which he contrasted race relations in the United States and Brazil to the advantage of the latter. Oliveira Lima noted the lack of racial conflict as a happy consequence of Brazilian miscegenation. He described the Brazilian solution to the race problem as 'wiser' and 'more humane' than segregation. His views were reported in the *New York Times* under the headline 'Dr Lima in favour of racial mixture'. On the other hand, unlike the Freyre of the 1930s, he saw mixture not as good in itself but as a means to the 'whitening' of Brazil.[84]

Closest to *CGS* in time are three of its competitors, books that offer explanations of the distinctive characteristics of Brazilian culture. It is surely no accident that three new interpretations of the nature of the nation, Paulo Prado's *Retrato do Brasil* ('Portrait of Brazil'; 1928), Caio Prado Jr's *Evolucão Política do Brasil* ('Political Evolution of Brazil'; 1933), and Sérgio Buarque's *Raízes do Brasil* ('Roots of Brazil'; 1936) should have appeared at much the same time as *CGS*.

Buarque's reference to 'roots' says it all. In retrospect, these books, like the foundation of SPHAN in order to preserve colonial architecture or the composition of the *Bachianas Brasileiras* by Heitor Villa-Lobos, combining themes from classical music with Brazilian popular tradition, all appear to be responses to a crisis of national identity provoked by a new wave of immigration. The immigrants, nearly three million of them in the period 1880–1914, came for the most part from Italy, Germany, the Ottoman Empire and Japan, escaping from the economic problems of their own countries at the very time that Brazil needed people to work on the growing coffee plantations. A sharper awareness of problems of identity may also have been stimulated, as it was in other Latin American countries from Mexico to Argentina, by the centenary of national independence, which was celebrated in Brazil in 1922.

Paulo Prado, who was born in 1869, belonged to an earlier generation than Freyre. A member of the so-called 'coffee aristocracy' of São Paulo – he served as president of the Coffee Council – Prado is best known today as a patron of modernist literature and art but he was also a writer and an amateur historian, a friend of Capistrano. There are obvious similarities between his portrait of Brazil and Freyre's: the ambition to interpret a whole country, the essay form, the impressionist manner ('This portrait was made like an impressionist painting') and the emphasis on sex and hybridity. The two men became friends. Prado gave him the diary of the French engineer Vauthier that Freyre edited, while part of *S&M* was written in Prado's country house.[85]

In other ways, though, *CGS* is diametrically opposed to the *Retrato do Brasil*. Prado gave his *Portrait* the subtitle 'an essay on Brazilian sadness', and opened it with the remark that 'in a radiant land live three sad races'. The sadness of Brazilians was something of a commonplace, remarked on by Prado's friend and mentor, the historian Capistrano, as well as by the poet Olavo Bilac, who wrote about 'the loving flower of three sad races' (*flor amorosa de tres raças tristes*). CGS refers to this in passing, while the title of Claude Lévi-Strauss's memoirs, *Tristes Tropiques* (1955) is another allusion to this tradition of interpretation.[86] Paulo Prado himself described his book as optimistic, 'the optimism of a doctor who wants to cure, or that of the surgeon'. It certainly offered a diagnosis of a pathological state – sickness as well as sadness – and a recital of failure that drew attention to the country's anarchy, backwardness, corruption, decadence and laziness.[87] If we approach Paulo Prado from the perspective of Hayden White, we might say that Prado, like Tocqueville, emplotted his interpretation of Brazil as tragedy. We hear the voice of the businessman from the South, concerned with obstacles to economic progress, very different in its tone from the North-Easterner evoking the traditions of his region. And so, like the work of Euclides, *Portrait of Brazil* provided Freyre with a foil, an interpretation against which to define his own.

Caio Prado, who came from the same large and wealthy family as Paulo, belonged to Freyre's generation. He might be described as a patrician Marxist who stressed economic factors in Brazil's 'evolution'. His *Political Evolution of Brazil* (1933) was published too late for Freyre to use in his own study, though the footnotes to later editions of CGS carry on a debate with Caio's ideas about the family and monoculture in Brazilian history, especially in his later and more famous study *Formação do Brasil Contemporâneo* ('The Formation of Contemporary Brazil'; 1942).

As for Sérgio Buarque de Holanda, he and Freyre had become friends in the 1920s. Both were precocious intellectuals, men of letters and scholars combined, writing well for a wide public. Both read Wilde, Hardy, Proust and Joyce with enthusiasm. Both were lifelong journalists, beginning at an early age. Both lived abroad (Sérgio in Germany), and on their return tried to introduce foreign ideas to a Brazilian public. Like Freyre, Sérgio was on the margin of academic life, at least until 1958, when he defended a thesis at the University of São Paulo, only to have it criticized, as Freyre's work was criticized, for its 'fluidity' or 'lack of precision' and for its style – a literary essay rather than an academic dissertation.[88]

Sérgio's *Roots of Brazil* was published in a series that Freyre edited. Like CGS it discussed patriarchy, used travellers as a major source, and contrasted adventure with routine. Both men were interested in Max Weber, in his use of 'ideal types' or sociological models as well as his contrast between Catholic and Protestant cultures. Sérgio, who came from São Paulo, was more interested in the Indians than Freyre and less in the

African slaves. He discussed the Jesuits with the sympathy that Freyre reserved for the Franciscans. Sérgio was also more critical of Brazil both in the past and in the present, attempting to identify in the colonial history of the country the obstacles to its modernization and democratization. More specialized studies of Brazil also offered Freyre inspiration as well as information. He was indebted to Roquette-Pinto not only for general ideas, about race, for instance, but also for his monographs on the Indians of Brazil, as he was to the writings of Raimundo Nina Rodriguez, a professor of medicine in Salvador, on the African element in Brazilian culture. He also owed a great deal to his many discussions with his friend Rüdiger Bilden over more than a decade, and to Bilden's published and unpublished work on slavery in nineteenth-century Brazil. In fact he cited Bilden in *CGS* even more often than he cited his 'master' Franz Boas.[89]

Bilden was more interested than Freyre in economic issues such as the productivity of the slave system, and his view of Brazil and its lack of 'discipline' and 'efficient labour' was less sympathetic and, one might say, more Germanic. All the same, the overlap between the interests of the two young scholars was considerable. Reporting to the Carnegie Foundation in 1924 on the progress of his work, Bilden was already emphasizing the seclusion of women, venereal disease, 'idleness as the badge of freedom' and 'the influence of domestic slavery' on the 'the mental, moral and cultural development of the children of the slave owners'. Like Freyre, Bilden used the accounts of travellers as one of his main sources, viewed the plantation as 'a self-sufficing economic unit' and emphasized 'the humane treatment of slaves in Brazil'. On the other hand, Bilden was the first to draw attention to the contrast between the British and the Portuguese colonial systems and also to the deep influence of domestic slavery on Brazilian private life. Perhaps most important of all, it was the now forgotten interlocutor who, as Freyre acknowledged in the notes to *CGS*, first emphasized that 'the evils attributed by some critics to the racial composition of the country should rather be blamed on slavery'.[90]

Foreign Models

Exemplifying a common paradox, Freyre's account of what was most specific to Brazilian culture, what was most authentically – or as he would say, 'tellurically' –Brazilian, followed foreign models in important respects.

For example, historians of the American South helped Freyre formulate his view of plantation culture in Brazil. As we have seen, he noted the parallels between the two slave-owning societies on a number of occasions. One of his friends, Francis Simkins, was a historian of South

Carolina, and it was with him (and Bilden) that Freyre visited the Deep South in 1926. *CGS* bears traces of the visit, among them a reference to the Afro-American food prepared in Mrs Simkins' kitchen. It was Simkins who gave his friend a book by Francis Gaines, *The Southern Plantation* (1925), in which Freyre marked the discussion of 'the mansion' as 'the focal point of the whole plantation pattern'. Freyre also owned Arthur W. Calhoun's *A Social History of the American Family* (1917) and turned down the pages on 'childhood in the colonial south' and on 'negro sex and family relations'.

Among historians of the South, however, Freyre's greatest debt was surely to Ulrich B. Phillips, a Georgian who published a study called *American Negro Slaves* (1918), including a detailed description of 'the "big house", as the darkies loved to call it'. Later accused of romanticizing the South and of encouraging what American historians call the 'Plantation Legend', Phillips described the rule of the planters as 'benevolent in intent and on the whole beneficent in effect', emphasized 'harmony' and 'adjustment', in plantation society and linked this to the fact that white and black children were playmates. His work is cited more than once in *CGS*, and later in *Brazil: an Interpretation*, where Freyre quotes Phillips on the lack of 'impersonality and indifference' in the paternalist plantation system, and comments, 'how true for Brazil'.[91]

Another major thesis in *CGS* has its parallels in studies of the United States and elsewhere. The anthropologist Melville Herskovits, who studied under Franz Boas and later became an acquaintance of Freyre's, was arguing in the 1930s that Africans retained much of their culture after they had been enslaved and transported to the Americas – to Haiti, for instance, to Surinam and to the United States.

In short, Freyre was not alone in his views of the virtues of miscegenation, the importance of African cultural survivals in the Americas or the benevolent aspect of the patriarchal plantation system. He formed these views in dialogue with both friends and books. Besides Walter Pater, the philosopher Oswald Spengler and the economic historian Gustav Schmoller (both of them cited in *CGS*) helped Freyre to become aware of the historical significance of the house. Lafcadio Hearn encouraged him to see miscegenation in a positive light. G. K. Chesterton and other English writers offered a model for his definition of national identity in terms of hybridity. The study of ancient Greece by Alfred Zimmern argued that 'The slaves at Athens were so well treated, had become so integral a part of the life of the city, that they were indistinguishable in appearance from citizens.' It is true that Zimmern contrasted slavery in Athens and on 'a tropical plantation', but the idea was there for Freyre to appropriate and adapt.[92]

Freyre's development thus illustrates the importance of what linguists call the 'convergence' of similar stimuli coming from different sources, forming ideas and later reinforcing them. It is probably fruitless to debate whether he learned more from one author or another in the course of his wide reading. Freyre's intellectual trajectory offers a vivid example of what Freud called 'overdetermination', suggesting that a single phenomenon, a hysterical symptom for instance, is the result not of one cause but of a number of factors.

In any case, to note the sources of Freyre's ideas, as the preceding paragraphs have done, is not to deny the originality of *CGS* but to try to define that originality more precisely. Many, if not all, new ideas, when analysed closely, turn out to be creative adaptations of older ones.

In Freyre's case, he was often thinking about Brazil while he was reading about other countries or visiting other places. On a visit to Virginia in 1926, he described what he saw as 'Big Houses that are relatives of the Brazilian ones'. A manuscript of his, written in 1933 or thereabouts, is entitled 'An American book that makes one think about Brazil'. The marginal notes he scribbled in books tell the same story. Reading Hearn on the West Indies, for instance, he noted 'as in Bahia', or 'as in Brazil'.

To employ a favourite later phrase of his, what Freyre did was to 'tropicalize' the ideas of Chesterton, Phillips and others, arguing that miscegenation or the Big House, for instance, were particularly characteristic of Brazil rather than of Britain or the American South, and that they formed part of the 'plantation complex'. By means of this tropicalization, he helped give Brazilians a new sense of their collective identity.

Imagining Brazil

It may be illuminating to juxtapose *CGS* not only to other essays in the interpretation of Brazil, such as the work of the Prados, but also to contemporary works of the imagination. In the South as well as the Northeast, the works of leading artists and writers of the 1920s and 1930s, from the paintings of mulattos by Cândido Portinari to Mário de Andrade's fantastic novel *Macunaíma* (1928), reveal a similar preoccupation with miscegenation and national identity. Mário, for instance, asserted that 'The Brazilian has no character because he has neither a culture of his own or a consciousness of tradition', symbolizing this lack by the protean protagonist of his novel, a tropical 'man without qualities' who is born black but turns white in the course of the story.[93]

Even more striking are the parallels between *CGS* and the North-Eastern fiction of the time. Freyre's study was published at the time of the rise of the regional novel of the North-East, which, as we have seen, he did a good deal to encourage. Leading examples of the regional novel include José Américo de Almeida, *A bagaceira* (1928), set on a sugar plantation; *Os Quinze* (1930), by Rachel de Queiroz, a spare but vivid evocation of the great drought of 1915 in Ceará; Jorge Amado's *Cacau* (1933), set on a cocoa plantation and described by Roger Bastide as a work of sociology rather than literature; and above all, the cycle of novels by Freyre's friend and disciple Lins do Rego. His *Menino do Engenho* ('Plantation Boy'; 1932), describing a childhood spent in a Big House, is a fictionalization of some themes central to *CGS*.

Much of the later work of Jorge Amado may be seen as a translation into fiction of themes that are central in *CGS*, notably sex, miscegenation and African-American traditions. A younger member of Freyre's generation, born in 1912, Amado was another North-Easterner (he came from Ilhéus, in the state of Bahia). He became a friend of Freyre soon after the publication of *CGS* and gave a talk about popular literature at the famous Afro-Brazilian conference in Recife that Freyre organized in 1934.

Himself an upper-class white intellectual, born on a plantation, Amado took the side of the people and joined the Communist Party. In his many novels, he not only dramatized social problems but also celebrated the food, the drink, the women, the festivals, the religion and the popular wisdom of the African or mulatto culture of the North-East. His sensuous – and sensual – novels may be regarded as fictional equivalents of Freyre's sensuous history. Like Freyre, he had a good ear for the local vernacular, just as he had a good eye for women's curves. If Freyre had more to say about the sweets of Pernambuco, while Amado sang the praises of the spicy *acarajé* and *moqueca* of Bahia, the two writers shared an enthusiasm for the North-Eastern cuisine.

It has been said that 'Jorge Amado's *Gabriela* could not have been written before the *Masters and the Slaves*'.[94] Even closer to *CGS*, however, is *Tent of Miracles* (1969), romancing the debate over *mestiçagem*, playing with Freyre's ideas and attributing some of them to a poor mulatto from Bahia, Pedro Arcanjo (based on Manuel Querino, a writer to whom *CGS* referred more than once). Arcanjo and his creator both employ the phrase 'racial democracy', which we will discuss later. Amado also remarked that 'There is only one solution for the racial problem, the mixture of blood. No other solution exists, only this one which is born from love.'[95]

'Born a Classic': the Reception of CGS

CGS was an immediate success. From the Brazilian capital, Rio de Janeiro, Freyre's friends sent him enthusiastic news about the success of the book and the stir it was causing. Friends reported that the book was becoming known in Rio as the '*Ulysses*' of Pernambuco. Roquette-Pinto dedicated the 'educational hour' of the Radio-Sociedade to a talk about the book, which he classified as a 'monumental oeuvre', reading whole passages to the audience. It was he who declared that the book was 'born a classic'.

Among the witnesses to the impact of CGS are the writer José Monteiro Lobato, who compared it to 'Halley's comet' and declared that what the author had done was 'to reveal ourselves to ourselves'; Jorge Amado, who described the book as 'a revolution in our literature, in our cultural life, in our national development'; the critic Antonio Candido, who viewed this 'great book' as an earthquake that 'shook a whole generation' with its frank discussion of sex, dazzling its readers with its concern with 'humble facts' and its emphasis on the African heritage and thus changing the view that Brazilians had of their culture; and Freyre's disciple Edson Nery, for whom reading CGS was like a psychoanalysis, liberating him from 'the complex of national guilt inculcated by abolitionist rhetoric, and the sense of inferiority on account of the underdevelopment attributed to miscegenation.'[96]

From the first, CGS was read as a work of literature as well as of social science. The journalist Assis Chateaubriand praised it as 'a notable work of literature'. The poet Manuel Bandeira drew attention to its poetic qualities. Rodrigo de Andrade agreed, describing it as 'a work of intense poetry'.[97] The novelist José Lins do Rego noted its 'lyricism' and the powerful images of this 'great work of prose', which revealed an essayist of the type of Walter Pater or John Henry Newman.[98]

Freyre's contribution not only to the analysis but also to the making of Brazilian identity has often been noted. It was this more than anything that made him famous in his own country in the 1930s. For the success of CGS was not confined to the literati. The booksellers seemed to have been surprised by the high number of sales, while the general public was sufficiently interested to take part in celebrations like the ball organized by the French Embassy in February 1935 on the theme of 'Casa Grande e Senzala', at which everyone attending was required to dress as a character inspired by the book.[99]

CGS became famous well beyond the confines of the academic world. As early as 1934, when the question of establishing quotas for immigrants was discussed during the debate on the new constitution some op-

ponents of the quotas quoted Freyre's work to justify their arguments.[100]
A hotel called 'Casa Grande e Senzala' opened in Recife in 1972, built in
traditional style with the staff dressed as slaves and the menu including
the sweets of the region, so often mentioned in the book. A 'translation' of
the text into the form of a comic book, entitled *Casa Grande e Senzala em
quadrinhos*, appeared in 1981. A postage stamp in honour of Freyre was issued in 1983 for the book's fiftieth anniversary, also marked by an interview
with the author in the popular weekly *Veja*. The book was also used as a
theme for Carnival floats and parades. It was put on the stage in 1980.[101]
There were two abortive projects to turn it into a film, one to be directed
by Joaquim Pedro de Andrade, the other by Roberto Rossellini. CGS was
in fact adapted for television as a mini-series in 2000, though the thirteen
episodes originally planned were reduced to four. [102]

CGS clearly told the Brazilian public 'something that it wanted to
hear'. Its emphasis on Brazil's African heritage came at a time that African
food (*feijoada*), African sport (*capoeira*) and African religion (*candomblé*),
formerly rejected by upper-class Brazilians, were being redefined as part
of the national culture, while Carnival and football were becoming africanized.[103] Of course a celebration of racial mixing was not what everyone
wanted to hear in 1933, just when Hitler came to power. As one early reviewer pointed out, CGS would have been burned if it had been published
in Germany. A book by Franz Boas – in its German translation, entitled
Kultur und Rasse – was indeed burned in public in Kiel in 1933.

However, Freyre's book generally received a warm reception abroad,
especially in France, the United States and Latin America. Soon after the
book was published, Alfonso Reyes, the Mexican Ambassador to Brazil at
that time, showed great interest in making Freyre known in Mexico and
New York. Incidentally, Borges also developed a friendship with Reyes,
having met him in Buenos Aires in the early 1930s and having been helped
by him when he was a young author. The friendship was based on many
affinities, including an interest in English literature.

The Swiss anthropologist Alfred Métraux wrote to Freyre in 1940
calling CGS a masterpiece. The American anthropologist Melville Herskovits described it as a 'classical study', while the historian Percy Martin
called it 'one of the best sociological treatises that has ever appeared on
Brazil'.[104] Another American historian, Frank Tannenbaum, described
the history of Brazil as divided into 'Two parts: that before and that after
Gilberto Freyre' because he had 'succeeded in changing Brazil's image of
itself'.[105]

The Cuban sociologist Fernando Ortiz praised the book and noted
the need for an equivalent study of Cuba. A study of this kind was eventu-

ally published in 1964 by the economic historian Manuel Moreno Fraginals, who has more to say than Freyre about the techniques of producing sugar, but wanted like him 'to follow the trails which start with sugar and surface in the founding of a university chair, in a decree on tithes, in a characteristic style of town mansion or in the dire effects of deforestation and soil erosion'.[106]

In France, the critic Roland Barthes praised the author's concern with the history of the body and material culture. He noted Freyre's 'concern for *histoire totale* of the kind practiced in France by Bloch, Febvre and Braudel', and both Febvre and Braudel agreed with this description.[107] Lucien Febvre wrote a preface for the French translation of *CGS*. As for Fernand Braudel, he had already discovered *CGS* while he was teaching in Brazil, at the University of São Paulo, in the later 1930s. In a long review essay, published in France while he was in a German camp for prisoners of war, Braudel described the book a masterpiece by a 'born writer' and praised the author's 'acute intelligence'. 'The crucial miracle is to have known how to join an exact, careful historical narrative to a fine and flawless sociology.'[108]

It was not only French scholars who appreciated Freyre's work. Eric Hobsbawm read *CGS* with approval after it was translated into English.[109] Asa Briggs offered Freyre an honorary degree from the University of Sussex in 1965. In the preface to his *Social History of England* (1983), Briggs recognized his 'immense debt' to two historians, Freyre and the great French medievalist Georges Duby, names that are not often juxtaposed.

CGS has been translated at least nine times. A Spanish translation was published in Argentina in 1942. An English translation was published in the United States in 1946, and its second edition had reached its sixth printing by 1970. There followed translations into French, German, Italian, Polish, Hungarian and, most recently, since the year 2000, into Romanian and Japanese. On the publication of the Hungarian translation in 1985, the work was described on the Hungarian radio as 'monumental' and 'one of the major works of twentieth-century sociology and anthropology'.[110]

The Critics

On the other hand, some reviewers were extremely critical of *CGS*. The book was attacked from both the Right and the Left.[111] A common charge was what an American review in *Books Abroad* called the book's 'excessive emphasis' on 'sexual irregularities' between whites and blacks. Some critics went so far as to call *CGS* 'pornographic'.[112] Others drew attention to what has been called Freyre's 'anti-Semitic perspective', an accusation that continues to be debated. There is little doubt that here and elsewhere, Freyre saw the Jews – as he did the 'orientals' – in a stereotyped way and that he sometimes used offensive language about them, including metaphors like 'birds of prey'. On the other hand, the place that he gives them in his historical sociology of Brazil is an essentially positive one. The Jews are included among the adaptable, 'plastic' Portuguese who helped create a mixed society and culture in the New World.[113]

Objections were also made to the author's sentimentality, to his nostalgic tone, and to what the anthropologist Darcy Ribeiro later described as Freyre's stress on the picturesque (*pitoresquismo*).[114] Other critics dismissed *CGS* as excessively anecdotal. The book was also faulted for its exaggerated generalizations. Conversely, some reviewers regretted the absence of general conclusions. *CGS* does indeed end abruptly and unexpectedly with a quotation from a paper read by a physician to the Medical Society of Rio de Janeiro about the prevalence of worms among the illnesses of the poor in that city – an ending, incidentally, that belies the author's reputation for painting too rosy a picture of Brazilian history.[115] The literary style, admired by some readers, was condemned by others as too informal, as we have seen, while the book has been compared to a city that expanded without a plan because of the way in which the author jumps from one subject to another.[116]

As an intervention in the great debate on the interpretation of Brazil, *CGS* was inevitably criticized from almost every possible point of view. Some readers believed the author to be a Marxist, but Marxists rejected him as a reactionary.[117] Some critics faulted Freyre for his lack of attention to economic factors, others for his excessive materialism. Some thought he said too little about religion, others that he was excessively critical of the missionary methods of the Jesuits. Critics also drew attention to the author's neglect of politics – though he certainly discussed what Foucault would call 'micropolitics', the distribution of power within the family and the *engenho*. His positive view of miscegenation was rejected on occasion as 'a new kind of racism: mulatto racism'.[118]

Even as an interpretation of the history of the family or the history of the plantation in the North-East, *CGS* has attracted criticism. So far as the family is concerned, the comment that Freyre neglected the existence of matriarchs is worth noting. The highly professional studies of sugar plantations in Bahia by Stuart Schwartz and Bert Barickman, largely based on archival sources, also throw some of the weaknesses of Freyre's book into relief, among them his lack of concern with smallholders, a point already noted by Braudel.[119]

Three criticisms in particular have recurred in discussions of the book from 1933 to the present. One is that Freyre's description of colonial Brazil is too static – a criticism that has also been levelled against ethnographies and also against other portraits of an age, such as Jacob Burckhardt's and Johan Huizinga's. The limits of the period 1500–1800, with which the book is supposed to be concerned, are not respected (Freyre often digresses into the nineteenth century) and changes within the period are rarely discussed, although the author would soon make up for this omission in the second volume of his trilogy, published in 1936. The need to draw on nineteenth-century sources in order to reconstruct the social history of the colonial period has not always been sufficiently appreciated by the critics, though it is equally true that the author, in 1933 at least, did not fully appreciate the risks of the regressive method.

A second major criticism of *CGS* is that it is too regionalist, or even 'Pernambucocentric'. According to the critics, the interpretation of Brazil put forward in the book is based almost entirely on evidence from one region, the North-East, especially from the state of Pernambuco and even, according to one of the sharpest reviewers, from a single sugar plantation, Engenho Noruega.[120]

In its simplest form this critique fails to engage with Freyre's argument that the history of other regions of Brazil, not only Minas Gerais but also São Paulo and Rio Grande do Sul, were shaped by the patriarchalism that first developed on the sugar plantations of the North-East and was later extended to the coffee plantations and cattle ranches of the South. In a more qualified form, however, the critique is a cogent one. Writing a book that is at once a history of the North-East and a sociology of Brazil, the author does not always keep these contrary tendencies in equilibrium.

In the third place, most serious of all, *CGS* has been criticized for offering an idealized picture of colonial Brazil. The description of the patriarchal system as a benign one has been one major focus of this criticism and the author has been accused of producing myth rather than history. The Marxist Rodolfo Ghioldi, for instance, attacked Freyre's work in general and *CGS* in particular for its failure to see 'the tragedy of slavery' and wrote of the need 'to demolish the fable of gentle slavery in Brazil' (*acabar con la fabula acerca de la dulzura de la esclavitud en Brasil*).[121]

Accusing Freyre of oversimplification, the critics have themselves often simplified his argument, omitting his references to conflict and to the sadism of particular planters or their wives or children. Where the author wrote 'equilibrium of antagonisms', the critics sometimes read unqualified 'equilibrium' or social harmony. All the same, the virtual absence from the book of references to slave resistance –whether in the form of going slow, sabotage, flight or revolt – encourages this simple interpretation.[122]

CGS has been criticized as a social history written from the veranda of the Big House. In a discussion at the University of São Paulo in 1968, the poet Décio Pignatari declared that 'Freyre sees the tropics from the point of view of the big house. We see things from the slave quarters.'[123] It is somewhat ironic that this criticism makes use of a phrase used by Freyre himself – about women – as well as being made about an admirer of Malinowski, who famously told his fellow-anthropologists to get down from the veranda and try to understand 'the native's point of view'.[124] In the case of the chapter on the Indians, the criticism does not apply. In the case of the slaves, on the other hand, the view from below appears relatively rarely (and is based mainly on folksongs), while the better documented view from above is dominant.

A particularly learned and vociferous Marxist critic of CGS in the 1950s was Gláucio Veiga, a lawyer who was also Professor of Sociology and Political Science in Recife. Encouraged by the Communist Party, and combining a solid foundation in social theory with the typical irreverence and arrogance of youth, Veiga denounced the 'patriarchal sociology' of CGS in a series of violently polemical articles in the *Jornal do Comercio* (mainly though not exclusively in 1952), treating the book as a work of literature but not of science, written by a 'feudal lord of the Pernambucan intelligentsia' and a lover of the Big House. Even Freyre's critique of the *usina* or sugar factory was criticized in its turn. The *usina*, as Veiga explained from the Leninist point of view (which he later repudiated) represented a historical moment of progress in the transition from feudalism to industrial capitalism. Its rise spelt the decline and fragmentation of the traditional plantation. 'In attacking the *usina* … Gilberto did not turn Marxist, much less Communist. On the contrary, he was fighting for the re-establishment of the feudal or parafeudal order of patriarchy.'[125]

Freyre's Response

Sensitive as he always was to criticisms, Freyre responded in the prefaces he wrote for later editions of CGS, as well as in the notes that grew with successive editions, producing the palimpsest that most of us read today.

Freyre wrote no fewer than thirteen prefaces – including a 'quasi-preface' – for the Brazilian editions of his book alone, as well as more than one for versions in English.[126] Already in 1934, in his preface to the second edition, the author defended himself against the charges that the book was disorganized, that it lacked a conclusion, that the language was too colloquial and so on. Later, he referred, sometimes with sarcasm, to the misunderstandings and misinterpretations of some of his critics, although he also singled out a few of these critics for praise. He defended himself repeatedly against the charge of regionalism, sometimes stressing the sociological rather than the geographical aspect of the book and sometimes promising to correct the overemphasis on the North-East in later volumes.

In essence, however, as the author pointed out in the preface to the fourth edition, he made no essential changes in his text. Some mistakes were corrected, though. Following the suggestion of friends, an index of subjects and one of names were added to the second edition. The bibliography was regularly updated. Some of the illustrations were redrawn. Certain phrases in the text were added, subtracted or modified. A reference to the polarity between the Apollonian and the Dionysian, for instance, a contrast that would become dear to Freyre, as we shall see, was added to the discussion of Africans and Indians, complete with a reference to Ruth Benedict's *Patterns of Culture* (1935), which made considerable use of these terms.[127]

What the author did expand, on a sometimes massive scale, were the notes, some of which turned into mini-essays or as the author would say, 'quasi-essays'. Like the prefaces, these notes were mainly devoted to defending Freyre's position against critiques not only of *CGS* but also of some of the author's later works. Besides a whole series of notes about the missionary activities of the Jesuits, for instance, we find lengthy replies to articles by the literary critic Sérgio Milliet and the historian Sérgio Buarque de Holanda on the question of what Freyre called the Portuguese colonizer's 'distaste' (*desamor*) for agricultural labour.[128] Considerable space was devoted to later writers who support the main arguments of the book, and in some of the later prefaces, to lists of the famous foreigners who praised it.

Concessions to critics are relatively rare, but one of them is particularly worth noting. This is the reference to 'para-patriarchal, semi-patriarchal and even anti-patriarchal' forms of family in colonial Brazil, responding to studies published in the 1940s by the American sociologist Donald Pierson and others. As for the suggestion that the author neglected matriarchy, this was answered in his next volume, *Sobrados e Mucambos*, with its reference to the 'simulation of matriarchy', when women took the place of men within a fundamentally patriarchal system.[129]

To sum up. Despite its length, *CGS* was written as an interpretative essay, not as a general history of colonial Brazil. It is not appropriate to criticize it for lack of 'coverage'. It is not even appropriate to criticize the author for failing to substantiate all his assertions. Only a much longer book or series of books could have done this. What Freyre did provide, and in very good measure, was a series of fertile hypotheses about Brazilian history which provoked debate in 1933 and have continued to do so ever since.

Conclusions and Comparisons

It is time to conclude and to attempt to assess the author's achievement in his most famous book, as a contribution to intimate history, consensus history and the definition of national identity.

Viewed as a work of social and cultural history, CGS is an impressionistic, intuitive and extremely personal portrait of an age.[130] It may have broken with professional academic history in the style of Leopold von Ranke, but it did not break with an alternative historiographical tradition that runs from Voltaire to Burckhardt, Huizinga and beyond. It is a vivid, sensuous and poetic evocation of a place and a period, full of 'local colour' (as the author noted in the preface), concentrating on what we now call 'the history of private life', while Freyre referred to it as 'intimate history'.

The slogan 'intimate history' came from the work of the brothers Goncourt, who are not often taken seriously as historians. They have often been dismissed as amateurs and as popularizers who were writing simply to entertain. However, they had ideas of their own about the writing of history, ideas that contradicted the orthodoxy of their day. In the preface to their study of the mistresses of Louis XV, published in 1860, the brothers argued for a 'new' or 'social' history that they called *histoire intime*, a history of private life that would do justice to 'woman, that great unrecognized historical actor' and draw on a wide variety of sources, such as newspapers, novels and paintings.[131] Both the concern with women and the use of newspapers mark Freyre's work too, as we have seen.

CGS is also the major Brazilian example of what North American historians call 'consensus history'. In the first half of the twentieth century, the interpretation of the history of the United States was dominated by the so-called 'Progressive' school, including Frederick Jackson Turner, Charles and Mary Beard and Vernon L. Parrington, who emphasized political and economic conflict. After the Second World War, a new school emerged, including Richard Hofstadter and Daniel Boorstin and stressing consensus and a common culture. As one member of the group put it, 'community is just as real as conflict'.

Freyre wrote a generation earlier than these scholars and his kind of consensus was defined against race conflict rather than class conflict. All the same, his emphasis on a more or less homogeneous or at any rate a shared culture, as in Boorstin's case, supported his view of harmony. His position is even closer to that of Hofstadter, who treated conflict and consensus as complementary ideas rather than as pure opposites and criticized the Progressives for missing the complexity of history.[132]

CGS was also, as we have seen, a major contribution to the debate about Brazilian identity – or lack of identity, as some Brazilians had seen it – a way of re-imagining the community. Discussions of national identity were not confined to Brazil at this time. Far from it. In the United States, for instance, the rise of an interdisciplinary doctoral programme in American Studies at Harvard in the 1930s – a model widely followed elsewhere – expressed a concern with national identity at a time when it seemed to be threatened, as in Brazil, by new waves of immigration. The way in which this interdisciplinary programme was taught has more than a little in common with the way in which Freyre approached Brazil, from the concern with social consensus to the interest in myth and symbol (in the work of Henry Nash Smith for example, which would later inspire Sérgio Buarque's discussion of sixteenth-century views of Brazil as paradise). This first approach to American Studies would later be criticized, like the work of Freyre, for placing too little emphasis on cultural diversity.[133] A degree of blindness to diversity and conflict might be described an an occupational hazard of studies of national identity.

In Spain too, the problem of identity was much discussed in the first half of the twentieth century, by writers such as Unamuno, Ganivet and Ortega y Gasset, whose work Freyre knew well.[134] Still closer to *CGS* in its interpretation of the history of a nation in terms of the interaction between three cultures is Américo Castro's famous study of Spain, originally entitled *España en su Historia* ('Spain in its History'; 1948), discussing the contribution of Christians, Muslims and Jews to the making of Spanish identity, the 'intermingling' or 'interlacing' of three peoples. For example, the Christians took over words, objects, practices and institutions from the Muslims who had lived in the Iberian peninsula for nearly eight hundred years. Castro was actually born in Brazil, raising the possibility that his early years there may have encouraged him to view Spanish history in this way.

In any case, when Freyre discovered Castro's work, he was enthusiastic, noting the similarity between the author's approach and his own, as his notes on the book show – on more than one occasion writing 'Casa Grande e Senzala' in the margin (in similar fashion he turned down the page discussing the symbiosis of Spanish and Muslim culture in a study by Claudio Sánchez-Albornoz).[135] Castro placed more emphasis than Freyre on conflict and especially on the self-definition of each of the three groups against the others. All the same, the parallels between these independent studies of the role of cultural encounters in the making of a nation leap to the eye.

In Latin America too, there were many discussions of national identity at this time. In the same year as *CGS*, for instance, the Argentinian poet Ezequiel Martínez Estrada published his *Radiografía de la Pampa* ('X-Ray of the Pampa'; 1933), a pessimistic book closer to Paulo Prado's vision than to Freyre's. A few years later came the best-known contribution to the genre, *El laberinto de la soledad* ('The Labyrinth of Solitude'; 1950) by another poet, the Mexican Otávio Paz, equally pessimistic in its emphasis on loneliness and on Mexican suspicion, vulnerability and obsessions with betrayal and death.

Some of these discussions of the problem of Latin American identity proposed miscegenation as a solution. In Mexico, for instance, Manuel Gamio, a student of Franz Boas, had called for a 'fusion of races' and also of cultures in his *Forjando la Patria* ('Forging the Nation'; 1916). In *La raza cósmica* ('The Cosmic Race'; 1929), José Vasconcelos (most famous as the Mexican Minister of Education who commissioned murals from Diego Rivera) described the mestizo as the essence of the Mexican nation and the chosen race of the future (a view that he was later to repudiate).[136] Whether or not Freyre knew the work of Vasconcelos at this time – he was to cite it much later – what he produced was a very different kind of book. Vasconcelos wrote a rather abstract meditation on the philosophy of history, Freyre a concrete historical ethnography. The persuasiveness of *CGS* is linked to the author's gift for pointing to significant details and describing them in vivid images.[137]

A final point concerns the parallels between the writer of *CGS* and his subject. Describing and celebrating the hybridity of Brazilians and their culture, Freyre was writing a hybrid book – part literature, part history, part sociology – as well as drawing ideas from many sources into a personal synthesis. He exemplified at the same time that he analysed the Brazilian gift for creative adaptation or tropicalization. This hybrid or tropicalizing approach would be carried on and carried further in Freyre's later contributions to both history and theory, to be discussed in later chapters of this book.

4   A Public Intellectual

As we have seen, *CGS* was a contribution to the analysis not only of Brazil's past but also of its present, undermining racism and taking a stand in contemporary debates over immigration and national identity. Following the publication of this book, the author's career would continue for more than half a century, from 1933 to 1987, divided between three main activities: public life, the writing of history and the formulation of social theory. Freyre's achievement as a historian and as a theorist will be discussed in the following chapters. What we offer here is a brief sketch of his activities as a journalist, as a cultural critic and in politics: in short, as a public intellectual (the greatest Latin American intellectual according to one of his contemporaries, Juan Marichal, Professor of Spanish at Harvard).

The Role of Public Intellectual

What is an intellectual? A whole library of books has been written to answer this question. According to the French historian Jacques Le Goff, intellectuals are people who master knowledge and spread ideas, and the role already existed in the Middle Ages. For another French historian, Christophe Charle, the role only came into existence towards the end of the nineteenth century, at the time of the 'Dreyfus Affair'. [1] When the Jewish artillery officer Alfred Dreyfus was found guilty of espionage in 1894, his innocence was defended by a group that included the novelists Emile Zola and Anatole France and the mathematician Henri Poincaré. The term 'intellectual' came into use at this time – in French and soon afterwards in Spanish – to refer to the group and to others like them: writers, thinkers and scholars who concern themselves with public issues.

In the early twentieth century, a number of leading public intellectuals of this kind were active in the West and beyond. In the case of India, one might take the example of a man Freyre once met and long admired, Rabindranath Tagore, whose concerns included deforestation (he organized a 'festival of tree-planting' in 1928). In the case of Europe, some of the best-known names are those of men who were primarily or at any rate originally philosophers. In Italy there was Benedetto Croce; in Spain, José Ortega y Gasset; in Britain, Bertrand Russell; and in France, Jean-Paul Sartre, who by the 1950s had acquired the reputation of *the* intellectual *par excellence*. All four wrote essays and articles for a wide public and were active as both cultural and political critics. Russell, for example, was imprisoned for his opposition to the First World War, and supported the Campaign for Nuclear Disarmament half a century later.

An intellectual has been neatly defined as 'someone who involves himself in what is not his business' (*quelqu'un qui se mêle de ce qui ne le regarde pas*). With more nuances, the role has been described as involving 'constant movement between the poles of specialized cultural achievement and general "speaking out"'. The balance between the two roles varies with the individual and also with the culture. It was argued in the 1930s by Alfonso Reyes, himself a good example of the species, that Latin American intellectuals were 'necessarily less specialized' than European ones.[2]

There was and is no consensus about the way in which this role should be performed. Sartre's view emphasized political commitment (*engagement*), while the sociologist Karl Mannheim, who lived much of his life in exile from his native Budapest, emphasized the detachment and freedom from social ties of 'free-floating' thinkers. For Edward Said, the Palestinian-American critic who considered himself to be 'out of place' everywhere, one of the marks of intellectuals is precisely the condition of exile (literal or metaphorical), a condition that encourages them to see the world from unconventional and unorthodox angles.[3]

Whether we define the intellectual as an outsider or as someone who speaks up publicly for his ideas (and even his doubts), one might say that Freyre soon showed his attraction towards the role. When he was only seventeen, in the speech he gave on leaving school, he stated very clearly that his ambition – contrary to that of the affected, verbose and pompous graduates, 'this plague of locusts', as he put it, who aimed at shining in high positions but are useless to the nation – was that of action. Without a 'social objective', knowledge is 'the greatest futility', said the young student to his colleagues and teachers; it is, in fact, 'nothing if we cannot dissolve it in action'.

As mentioned above, one of the incentives for Freyre to study abroad was that provincial Recife did not seem either to his family or himself to be the ideal environment for acquiring the education that would allow him to contribute to the country's much needed development. 'Uncle Sam is not only the banker, but the schoolmaster of the world', remarked the young student soon after arriving at Baylor, and some of the 'cream' of the youths from abroad who were studying in the United States would probably play an active role on their return to their own countries.

Extremely revealing about this concern with action are the marks that he made on the lines given to Lewis Davenant, a character in George Moore's *Coming of Gabrielle*, a play that Freyre read while he was in Oxford. An educated man living in the provinces, Davenant confesses to his beloved Gabrielle that he cannot accept the idea of being a simple author, that is, 'an intellectual abstraction represented by seventeen volumes'.[4] Years later, Freyre would defend himself from the critics who thought he should confine himself to academic issues, insisting that pure 'academic dignity' was not worth 'a snail'. He simply could not content himself with being a 'pure intellectual' because it was for him unthinkable not to want 'to participate in the conflicts of my time and my people'.[5] Back in 1918, it was with avid and insatiable curiosity and enthusiasm for knowledge and experience that he left his home town.

As if he knew the danger of falling into the trap of provincialism, when your worldview is shaped by the limited perspective of a margin that is given universal importance, the young Freyre left Recife determined to acquire greater knowledge, to widen his horizons and to see life from the standpoint of an 'experimenter', as he later described himself.

It is therefore not too far-fetched to say that the experience of living in exile was essential for this intellectual who did so much to reveal Brazil to the Brazilians. His voluntary exile of 1918–23, followed by the forced exile of 1930–31 (when fleeing from the political persecution following the revolution of 1930 he went to Portugal and the United States), shaped his outlook forever and made him a sort of permanent exile for his entire adult life. In spite of the inevitable ties that bound him, like everyone else, to specific social and ideological groups, Freyre never could and never wanted to free himself entirely from a sense of detachment, from the feeling of not belonging completely to his natural environment and to any sort of institution, from seeing his and other worlds with critical distance and from more than one angle. In order to keep his independence, he avoided becoming either a full-time academic or a 'writer-civil servant' like the poet Carlos Drummond de Andrade and others who occupied posts in the administration in the age of Vargas.[6]

Francis Simkins, his American friend from the Old South, was impressed by Freyre's ability to be a 'nationalist' and at the same time to avoid indulging in 'laughable exaggerations' about the good of the country. With his 'intelligent humour' and wit, as Simkins put it, Freyre could both appreciate and laugh at Brazilian and American manners and customs alike,

contrasting and counterpoising them to each other. In fact he did this to
great effect in his journalism.

The Journalist

What made Freyre work as a journalist for most of his life? Part of the
answer can be found in his will to make a difference in the world and his
belief that the periodical press could be a useful ally in this enterprise. A
great admirer of what he called the 'journalist-writers' of late nineteenth-
century Brazil, he realized that those 'hybrids' who wanted to intervene
in the national life were capable, thanks to their talent, form and style, of
influencing the public through this 'less majestic activity' to a much higher
degree than the writers who limited themselves to publishing books.[7]

One of Freyre's early nineteenth-century heroes was Miguel do
Sacramento Lopes Gama, a priest, educator, politician and man of letters
from the North-East of Brazil who devoted most of his life to journalism,
making criticisms of society and fighting, as he put it, 'against private and
public vices' in a witty, vibrant and, when he thought it necessary, aggressive way. His periodical O Carapuceiro (1832–47), which has been praised
for the lucidity and exactness of its observations and social portraits, was,
in fact, one of the richest sources for Freyre's major works.[8]

As a journalist, Freyre began young, as we have seen, writing for DP
as soon as he arrived in the United States in 1918.[9] Already conscious about
the difficulties of talking about the 'other', he referred to the danger of 'superficial views' (ligeireza de opinião) and to the need to see things from more
than one angle, taking into account the 'eclecticism of moral opinions'.[10] In
an equilibrium that was quite remarkable for such a young man, Freyre's
admiration for the different achievements of the United States, which he
often praised when writing his articles 'From the Other America', did not
blind him to the evils of galloping Puritanism, 'narrow Americanism' and
the 'tentacles of the Almighty Mr. Dollar', which, as he put it, lay behind the
widespread mania for evaluating everything by its price.

Above all, with great acuity and insight, he referred to the 'roaring
spirit' of America as a cultural trait which should be denounced for the
threats it represented to the world. It consisted, as the young journalist explained, of that American arrogance and self-indulgence that allowed the
country to be 'lyrically' convinced that in everything – government, art,
literature, morality, sport – 'they were a league and half ahead of the world'.
A lead, which, they thought gave them the right, so Freyre argued, to limit
the sovereignty of other countries, if that would promote and safeguard
their national interests.

From 1926 to 1930, Freyre edited *A Provincia*, a Recife paper owned by his patron Estácio Coimbra, as well as writing for it under various pseudonyms. Other members of his 'clan' (José Lins do Rego, Manuel Bandeira and Cícero Dias) also contributed to it. Later on, he became for a brief period the editor of *DP*, at the invitation of its new owner, Francisco de Assis Chateaubriand, otherwise known as 'Chatô' or 'the king of Brazil', a leading figure in the world of journalism.[11] As editor, Freyre tried to simplify the style of journalists, eliminating clichés and what he called 'precious language' (*preciosismos*). He even put up a notice prohibiting 'Byzantinisms', pedantic words such as 'esteemed' (*estimável*) or 'onomastic' (*onomástico*). His aim, as he later recalled, was to encourage 'a form of journalism that was not so much a passive reflection of the metropolitan style as the expression of the life and preoccupations of regional cultures.'[12]

Freyre continued to write for newspapers and magazines for most of his life. Between 1921 and 1925 he wrote at least seventy-six articles for the papers, while during his editorship of *A Província* he wrote scores of articles for that journal (the number is impossible to calculate because he not only used pseudonyms, but shared some of these pseudonyms with other writers). After 1930 he wrote less for the papers – he was working on *CGS* and *S&M* – resuming regular contributions in 1938. For the next thirty years Freyre produced articles at the impressive rate, given his other activities, of more than one a week. The *DP* was his favourite journal, for which he wrote well over 150 articles in the course of nearly seventy years, from 1918 to the year of his death, 1987. He was also a regular writer for other Pernambuco newspapers, the *Correio da Manhã* (between 1938 and 1942) and the *Jornal do Commercio* (from 1942 onwards).[13]

Freyre also published on occasion for newspapers with a national readership, among them the *Jornal* of Rio, the *Estado de São Paulo* and the *Folha de São Paulo*, as well as foreign papers such as *La Nación* in Argentina and *The Reporter* in the United States. From the late 1940s onwards, he also made regular contributions to the most important Brazilian weekly of the time (owned, like the *DP* and the *Jornal*, by Chatô), the *Cruzeiro*. By 1960, when Freyre gave up writing for it – after having produced more than sixty articles – this magazine was selling a million copies a week.

Together with his royalties from books and his fees for lectures, the proceeds of journalism made an important contribution to Freyre's income, allowing him to support his family (his wife, Magdalena, whom he married in 1941, and his children Fernando and Sonia) without compromising his position as an independent man of letters, who lived, as he once said, 'from writing and for writing' (*de escrever e para escrever*). He was fortunate that his career coincided with the expansion of the market for books and journals in Brazil and that his publisher, José Olympio, was one of the most successful. Olympio, whom Freyre described as 'a minister, independent of governments', published most of the literary classics of his day, as well as Freyre and Sérgio Buarque and also books by the then dictator Vargas and his followers. According to the poet Drummond de Andrade, his bookshop was a centre where writers and artists met, including Freyre himself and his friend José Lins do Rego.[14]

Freyre's way of making a living cannot be disentangled from his decision to embrace the intellectual's role of outsider. To accept a permanent position, which might have paid better, seems not to have been an option for a man who sometimes held temporary posts but deliberately avoided a normal professional career. Unacademic rather than anti-academic, Freyre was always ready to praise intellectuals who were not confined to their narrow specialities or comfortably established in their ivory towers. Talking about the English intellectuals from Oxford and Cambridge in the 1940s, he wrote that they very rarely 'let themselves be stuck to their academic gowns', like a 'second skin' that deprived them of humanity. Cardinal Newman was cited as an early example of an intellectual who was both a specialist and a man who spoke to all sects and parties of the nation.[15]

To use Said's words, Freyre opted to be more of an 'amateur' than a professional, refusing to be confined to a narrow speciality or to undergo the pressures and constraints of a profession. A strict scientific speciality, he once remarked, requires the specialist to feel 'no emotion at all in front of the facts'; but Brazil is a 'demoralizer of over-rigid professional canons'.[16]

The relative freedom that Freyre gained with this choice came at the cost of some deprivation. His income seems to have been always uncertain and precarious, his wife Magdalena being the one who would always try to talk the DP into paying higher fees for her husband's articles, while Freyre himself was always struggling to be paid better royalties for his publications. The house in Apipucos, of which he was so proud and which became emblematic in the public imagination as the 'Master's Big House' was, in fact, bought and enlarged over many years only with great effort. For quite a long time, Freyre, his wife and the two children had to sleep in one bedroom, the only one in the house. Dona Magdalena's notorious skill at making ends meet and in managing the 'hard-won pennies' (*suados tostões*) that her husband earned as an independent intellectual, was indeed a necessary one. [17]

That this independence was for Freyre the supreme value of an intellectual is attested by the moving passage in which he praises William

Morris for the choices he had made at the cost of being always restless and not completely contented. The English 'rebel' had chosen not to establish himself 'in any profession or philosophy', Freyre writes to his newspaper readers, and he had never realized that 'in this incapacity to take up a conventional career or profession lay one of the signs of his genius: a plural genius, with an extraordinary variety of aspects, that demanded everything from him without favouring him with the sweet advantages that make men happy and tranquil.' If we remember that Freyre once referred to himself as 'a Morris from the periphery', we may say that, despite his relative poverty, he identified himself with the wealthy 'Victorian rebel'.[18]

Like the generalist or 'one man band' he was, Freyre wrote articles on a wide variety of subjects, from football to photography, from cigars to circuses and from comics to *caipirinha*, the Brazilian cocktail that he characteristically celebrated for its mixture. As a commentator put it, the articles he wrote for DP after he returned from his five years abroad, were, 'in a way, a social history of Recife'.[19] In fact they were more than that. The earlier series 'From the Other America', which the young Freyre started sending in 1918, when he arrived in Texas, together with the ones he continued publishing after his return home in 1923, are representative of the very broad scope of Freyre's journalistic activities, which would remain his mark over the decades. A mixture of chronicles, literary and social criticism and the impressions of an attentive traveller and observer of social habits, Freyre's early contribution to the press is not only a rich source for his formative years, but also reveals the wide spectrum of interests and concerns of the mature writer of the trilogy on the formation of Brazilian society.

Extremely revealing of Freyre's early concern with multiple approaches and of the importance he gave to emotion is the text by the American critic, journalist and biographer Francis Hackett that he copied into his notebook as early as 1920 or 1921, as if to remind himself of the qualities he should develop for a future career. 'A critic should be a linguist, a philologist, a psychologist, a man who knows literary and aesthetic ideas as well as history, social and economic and political; but all of it is cold inanimation unless the flame of sympathy is touched to it. Criticism is an art limited by the capacity of the critic for emotion.'

The reception that Freyre had in his home town as a young journalist seems to have been in line from the start with his ambition to have some effect on the world around him. In 1926, while visiting him in Recife, his friend from Columbia, Rüdiger Bilden, wrote to a common friend, impressed with what Freyre was achieving, in spite of being so young and still having a lot to learn: 'he does really fine work as arbiter of good taste and champion of culture against cheap modernization.' [20]

Freyre often wrote in the newspapers about famous figures in Brazilian history, among them Rui Barbosa, the statesman who supported the abolition of slavery; the Baron of Rio Branco, a leading diplomat; the Baron of Mauá, a businessman and banker; the aviator Santos Dumont; and the president-dictator Getúlio Vargas. Continuing to be an anglophile, Freyre also wrote a number of articles on English culture that ranged from Florence Nightingale to Winston Churchill. His articles on literature, for instance, were often concerned with English, Scottish or Irish writers, among them Walter Scott, Robert Browning, George Meredith, W. B. Yeats and James Joyce, who were virtually unknown to the Brazilian reading public at this time.

Freyre also discussed the work of Brazilian writers, including the journalist-sociologist Euclides da Cunha and the novelist João Guimarães Rosa, whom he praised for his Joycean experiments with language.[21] On the publication of the first part of Erico Veríssimo's classic *O Tempo e o Vento* ('Time and the Wind'; 1949–62), a historical novel set in the South of Brazil, Freyre reviewed it. He criticized the novel for sentimentality and a narrative technique that reminded him of 'the worst Hollywood films', but he also noted 'moments of greatness' and treated the novel as a contribution to 'intimate history', as we shall see later on.[22]

As a journalist, Freyre was able to indulge his life-long passion for architecture by writing articles on Brasília, for instance, on the vernacular architecture of Recife and on the critic Lewis Mumford.[23] Mumford was one of Freyre's heroes, a fellow admirer of Ruskin and Morris whom he described as 'the master of us all in matters of urban sociology' and as a humanist able to combine sociological with aesthetic interests.[24]

Freyre's readers were also introduced to a number of foreign historians, among them Jules Michelet, Lucien Febvre, Charles Boxer and Américo Castro, while the work of Freyre's friend Sérgio Buarque de Holanda was discussed on several occasions. Other articles described and assessed leading sociologists and anthropologists, including Franz Boas, Thorstein Veblen, Bronisław Malinowski, Alfred Radcliffe-Brown and Georges Gurvitch.[25] The fact that these articles were written for mass-circulation newspapers and magazines should give us respect for both the editors and the readers of the 1940s and 1950s.

It should be added that Freyre was not only a prolific but also a brilliant journalist. One might not have expected the author of large books such as *CGS* and *O&P* to have been capable of concision, and it is true that some of his topics spill over into several consecutive articles (as many as seven of them in the case of the Baron of Rio Branco and six in that of Rui Barbosa). All the same, it is impossible not to admire the vivid descriptions, the epigrammatic style and the light touch with which the author introduces an important theme in a page or two or evokes a personality in a few deft strokes.

One example of Freyre's journalistic style will have to stand for many, but this one is too good to miss. In 1938 he published a newspaper article on Brazilian football, on the occasion of the World Cup, in which Brazil unexpectedly defeated Czechoslovakia and reached the semi-finals for the first time.[26] He described the Brazilian style of playing as 'a combination of the qualities of surprise ... cunning, lightness and at the same time of individual brilliance and spontaneity'. Observing the field with anthropological eyes, he took over from Ruth Benedict's then recent book *Patterns of Culture* (1935) the contrast between the cool rational Apollo, symbolizing the European style of play, and the warm emotional Dionysus, symbolizing the Brazilian or more exactly the mulatto style, assimilating football to *capoeira*. 'The Brazilian mulatto de-europeanized football by giving it curves ... We dance with the ball.' Today, this style is well known all over the world, but Freyre deserves the credit for describing it sixty years ago in an article that reveals his capacity for mediating between cultural worlds and introducing anthropology and football to each other. He would repeat these points over the years, bringing them up to date in the 1950s with a reference to Pelé.[27]

What marks Freyre's contribution to the press from the very beginning is precisely this effort to make connections rather than seeing things in isolation, to compare and contrast books, people, cultures, situations, experiences and ideas with others, thus offering new perspectives. His reflections on biography, for example, make a good example of this approach. An enthusiastic reader of the genre from very early in his life, he was soon writing small biographical articles himself and reviewing published biographies. Remarkable in these pieces is his comparative approach, contrasting one biography with another or distinguishing different ideas about the way to write a life history, comparisons that allow him to offer some acute reflections about the genre.

Bringing to the debate writers like Gertrude Stein, Lytton Strachey, Arthur Symons, Alfred R. Orage and Catherine Drinker Bowen, together with Brazilian ones such as Otávio Tarquínio de Sousa, Álvaro Lins and Lúcia Miguel Pereira, Freyre again and again insists on his idea of what a biography should be. Beginning with one of his first discussions of this theme, in *DP* in 1923, the young journalist insisted on the need for biographers to reveal a person 'without rouge' that hides their true colour; and to be above what the English critic Orage had called 'necrophilia', that is, 'the superstition about the "immaculateability" of the dead'. Emperor

Dom Pedro II, Freyre commented on that occasion, did not need any 'necrophilia' to remain morally great. What he needed was a true biography, which would be very different from the panegyrics that existed and which were nothing but 'caricatures' of biography, hiding any human imperfection or incoherence. From then on, Freyre would stress the fact that those who insist on picturing men as Olympian, without imperfections, weaknesses, failures, complexity and contradictions, steal from them their human dimension and run the risk of transforming them into 'monuments' or statues or, as he put it, of freezing them into cold 'marble figures'.[28]

This 'monumental' type of biography, argued Freyre, is especially common when the person whose history is written is a major national figure. In these cases, civic glorification tends to supersede all other considerations and the person studied 'stops being a man ... to become a monument, civically and perhaps artistically, perfect, but full of false points in his humanity'. Extremely revealing of the wide importance that Freyre gives to this topic is his contribution to the conference organized in Paris in 1948 by UNESCO to discuss 'Tensions Affecting International Understanding'.

Among the topics that Freyre put forward for discussion in the Paris meeting – and that he soon publicized in Brazil both in print and in conferences he gave in the Ministry of Foreign Affairs and in the Army General Staff College – was the need to revise textbooks of history and geography, and also the biographies of national heroes, since they could be the 'source or fuel that feeds the hatred among nations, the prejudices among races, the antipathies among peoples'. For a better understanding among nations and peoples, he argued, it was essential that national heroes, who are sometimes 'deformed by nationalistic myths and in the interest of a particular nation or group', be presented with their contradictions and 'from various national points of view'. Oliver Cromwell, Francisco Solano López of Paraguay, Juan Manuel de Rosas of Argentina and so many other national figures were waiting for this kind of 'transnational and inter-scientific' biography, which would reveal not only their greatness and achievements, but also their faults, weaknesses, incoherences and so on. That would be the way they could make an important contribution to avoiding the tensions that cause wars.[29] He also remarked that 'Real biography, like real history, always seems to be a study in the contradictions of human nature. When seen as contradiction, human nature never becomes easy material for propagandists to use in building up false images of perfect peoples or heroic individuals'.[30]

It seems that in the different periodicals to which Freyre contributed, either daily newspapers or weekly or fortnightly magazines of wide circulation, he was given a free hand to write on his favourite topics: about literature, about houses, about children, about himself (including the proper spelling of his name), his friends and even his cat. Children, for example, and their toys, clothes and books were the subject of articles published over three decades, from the 1920s to the 1950s. Some pieces summarized books that Freyre had already published or defended his work against his critics, while others gave his readers a foretaste of books to come. A number of these articles were weapons in Freyre's 'culture wars', since he was active for much of his life as a cultural critic, in the style of two of his role models, H. L. Mencken and Lewis Mumford: Mencken the critic of Puritanism, democracy and the misuse of language, and Mumford the critic of architecture and society.

The Cultural Critic

Although he has often been accused of nostalgia, Freyre was very much concerned with the problems of the present and the future and took a public stand on a number of cultural and social issues – literary, artistic, ecological, racial and even hygienic. The testimony of José Lins do Rego in 1924, soon after he had returned from Europe, is extremely revealing about Freyre's concerns. Referring to the impact that he, together with another intellectual of 'good sense', Jackson Figueiredo, had had on young men like Lins, he wrote in an open letter to both mentors: 'my generation is ready to remake Brazil with you.'[31]

As a literary critic, Freyre did what he could to support local talent, drawing the attention of his readers to the culture of the North-East. In 1944, for instance, Freyre reviewed novels by two friends of his: *Fogo Morto*, by José Lins do Rego (part of his famous 'sugar-cane cycle') and *Terras do Sem Fim* by Jorge Amado. Both authors were described as 'historians disguised as novelists', with an eye for 'details full of social significance.'[32] Freyre also praised the work of other North-Easterners such as the novelist Raquel Queiroz and the playwright Ariano Suassuna.

Freyre was himself an amateur painter whose work evoked the culture and the history of his native Pernambuco. He was drawn to the work of a number of artists from his region, among them his old friend Cícero Dias, the painter Lula Cardoso Ayres and the ceramic artist Francisco Brennand. He did his best to launch their careers or make them more widely known, singling out for praise their predilection for local themes, tropical colours such as green and what he called the 'regional light'. He presented Dias and Cardoso Ayres in much the same way that he presented Lins and Amado, as interpreters of regional life.[33]

Even earlier, when he was only a young journalist from the provinces, Freyre was already trying to persuade young artists to abandon the
'passively colonial' habit of reproducing motifs and conventions that were
distant from the Brazilian present and past. Instead, he suggested that
they search for sources of innovation in regional and local traditions. As
he wrote as early as 1925, Brazil lacked interpreters of both the national
and the local of the scope of a Pedro Figari in Uruguay or a Diego Rivera
in Mexico. It is in this context that Dante Gabriel Rossetti and the Pre-
Raphaelites were frequently mentioned by Freyre, in order to stress the
fact that they had revolutionized English art and subverted the conventions of the Royal Academy by looking back for inspiration to the despised
medieval traditions.[34]

Freyre's interests were not confined to high art. He concerned himself
with almost every aspect of material culture: with cuisine, clothing, housing
and furniture, defending and attempting to preserve North-Eastern traditions such as the sweets or *doces* so characteristic of that sugar-producing
region. He defended regional traditions not only as a writer, notably in the
essays that were later collected in the book *Region and Tradition* (1941),
but also as an organizer. He co-founded the *Centro Regional do Nordeste*
(1924), edited a volume of essays on the culture of the North-East, *Livro
do Nordeste* (1925), and organized the *Congresso Regionalista* (1926). Most
important of all, soon after his appreciation of Afro-Brazilian culture in
CGS, Freyre organized, together with his cousin the psychiatrist Ulisses
Pernambucano, the first Congress of Afro-Brazilian Studies (1934).[35]

The event, which was described by Freyre as 'the least solemn of con-
gresses' took place in the Teatro Santa Isabel in the centre of Recife, and
brought together writers such as Mário de Andrade and the young Jorge
Amado; priestesses (*ialorixás*) of *candomblé*; students; women cooking local dishes in the theatre lobby; a representative of the 'Black Front' (*Frente
Negra*); and scholars such as the folklorist Luis de Câmara Cascudo and
the anthropologists Edison Carneiro (another anthropologist, Melville
Herskovits, a former student of Franz Boas, was unable to come but sent
a paper). The happening provoked the anger of some conservatives, who
saw it as 'Bolshevist' and demanded that the congress be closed down.
According to Freyre's later account, some of the participants lost their jobs
or were even arrested.[36] All the same, the proceedings – papers on art,
slavery, resistance, music, dance, *maconha* and popular poetry – were published in two volumes in 1935 and 1937 and attracted considerable attention
in Brazil. A second congress was organized in Salvador in 1937 and a third
in Belo Horizonte in 1939.

Another contribution worth mentioning is Freyre's inspiration for the foundation, in the mid-1950s, of the Regional Centres for Research into Education (*Centros Regionais de Pesquisas Educacionais*), one of the most important and promising enterprises of the great Brazilian educationalist Anísio Teixeira. Like Freyre, Teixeira had studied at Columbia University in the 1920s, and, perhaps even more than him, wanted to make a difference in the world. Commenting on the importance of Freyre's regionalist ideas for the concept of these centres ('our centres', he called them, at least once), where the social sciences were joined in order to promote schools that were united in their democratic ambitions but regionally diverse, Teixeira wrote that 'much of the inspiration for what we are trying to do comes from what we have learned from you and your work'.[37]

Freyre often defended the traditional culture of the North-East on ecological grounds, saying that it was well adapted to the environment of the region. His concern with trees in particular was relatively unusual at the time and developed quite early in his career. In 1924, for instance, his Centro Regional organized a 'Tree Week' (*Semana dos arvores*). When he was working for Estácio Coimbra, Freyre encouraged the planting of local trees and plants in the streets and parks of Recife. His newspaper articles discussed ecological problems, notably one on 'The Forests of Brazil' (1935), protesting about the Vargas government's concession to Ford of a million hectares in the state of Pará, not only because it was a gift to foreign capitalists but because the forest should be preserved from the invasion of industry and agriculture alike. His book *Northeast* (to be discussed later) was not only a history but also a denunciation of the devastation of the environment by the concentration on the cultivation of a single crop, sugar-cane, and of the pollution of the river Capibaribe, which runs through Recife, by industrial waste.

Freyre was particularly interested in urban problems. In 1926, for instance, he asked an acquaintance to recommend 'the best new book about "city planning"'. In 1927, when he was working for Estácio Coimbra, one of the leading French urban planners, Alfred Agache, was invited to Recife by the governor to lecture on town planning (perhaps at Freyre's suggestion). Freyre showed Agache around the city. In the same year, he told his mentor Oliveira Lima that he planned a series of articles 'on Recife and urban problems'.[38] Although he abandoned this plan when he stopped working for *DP*, Freyre's concern for urban problems persisted. In 1937, for example, he intervened in a public debate about housing.

At this time many of the poor in Recife lived in *mucambos*, cabins or shacks made from local materials such as palm fronds and thatch, with earth floors, often raised above the swampy ground on stilts. At the end of the 1930s, 164,000 people were living in houses of this type. These shacks, like other forms of housing for the poor in Rio and São Paulo, the *cortiços* and *favelas*, had become an embarrassment to the upper classes, who viewed them as incompatible with civilization, modernity and progress.

There was a campaign for the demolition of these 'slums' not only because they were ugly but also because they were unhygienic, or to use the language of eugenics that was widespread at this time, a threat to the future of the race. [39]

At the Regionalist Congress of 1926, Freyre had already described the *mucambos* as being in harmony with nature, and had been criticized for this in a newspaper report. His response to the new challenge of the 1930s was to write a pamphlet about the *mucambos*, published by the Ministry of Education and Health on behalf of SPHAN, the new Brazilian organization for the preservation of the historical patrimony in which Freyre held for a time the post of 'Technical Assistant, Third Class'.[40] In the pamphlet he argued in favour of the preservation of this form of vernacular architecture on the grounds that it was beautiful, hygienic and well adapted to the local environment (on the other hand, Freyre considered the *favelas* of Rio de Janeiro to be insanitary and 'degrading').[41] Despite these efforts, a 'League against the *mucambo*' was founded in 1939 by the politician Agamenon Magalhães, whom Vargas had appointed as *Interventor Federal* in Pernambuco, in other words an agent of the dictator in his attempt to reduce the autonomy of the regions. Thousands of traditional dwellings were demolished and cheap new houses constructed.[42]

So far as modern architecture was concerned, Freyre expressed some ambivalence. He criticized the work of Le Corbusier, or at least its imitation in the tropics, on both aesthetic and ecological grounds, complaining about the straight lines as well as the excessive use of glass; he does not seem to have known of Le Corbusier's designs for the High Court and Assembly in tropical Chandigarh, the capital of the Punjab, which provided shady cool interiors by means of screens and pierced walls and façades that did not receive sunlight until late in the day.[43] He once described as 'a monster' the famous building for the Ministry of Education in Rio de Janeiro (designed by a team that included Le Corbusier, Lúcio Costa and Oscar Niemeyer). On the other hand, Freyre praised Costa and Niemeyer for 'tropicalizing' the modern style advocated by Le Corbusier, assimilating 'Moorish and Arabic colours', drawing on the tradition of colonial architecture and 'happily brazilianizing the excesses of the Swiss rationalist', which meant among other things replacing straight lines by curves. Freyre's preference for undulation was shared by Brazilian architects such as Affonso Reidy and the garden designer Roberto Burle Marx, who also shared Freyre's interest in ecology and spoke at his seminar on 'tropicology', to be discussed later.[44]

Again, Freyre liked the idea of building a modern city in Brasília to serve as Brazil's new capital, though he disliked the design of the city when he saw it. This project of President Kubitschek's was carried out in the later 1950s by a team led by Costa, the chief planner, and Niemeyer, the chief architect. Invited by the president to visit Brasília in 1959, Freyre criticized the design on the grounds that it was more sculpture than architecture (*arquitetura escultural*). According to him, Brasília was ill adapted to the tropical environment and there was not enough space for leisure. He also complained that social scientists had not been invited to collaborate on the project.[45] In other words, Freyre was a sharp architectural critic in the manner of his hero Lewis Mumford or later of Jane Jacobs, whose book *The Death and Life of Great American Cities* (1961) he owned and annotated.

As a cultural critic, Freyre was both negative and positive. He often wrote in defence of a Brazilian cultural heritage that he believed to be under threat. He opposed what he called 'the devastation of the forest' in Brazil, just as he opposed the cutting down of trees in Recife.[46] He was equally concerned about the devastation of Brazil's architectural patrimony. He hated the growth, or as he called it the 'swelling', of his native Recife, and urged a social policy that he called 'rurban', seeking an equilibrium between cities and the countryside.[47]

However, as we have seen, his concern with preservation did not prevent Freyre – any more than it prevented William Morris – from thinking about the problems of the present and the future. He supported some kinds of modern architecture and some forms of town planning. When he wrote about clothes, it was often to denounce garments that were inappropriate for a tropical climate. He recommended men to wear tunics and day pyjamas in hot weather, as well as attacking what he called the 'anti-ecological' clothes that had made women and children in the tropics into the 'martyrs' or the 'victims' of European fashions.[48] His essential message concerned the need to reconcile international modernity with local tradition.

The Intellectual in Politics

If we take politics in a broad, foucaultian sense, Freyre – like any intellectual who writes, publishes and speaks his views about any topical theme – entered political life very early. In a more specific sense, he wrote many articles on political topics as well as giving interviews on the problems of immigration, democracy and monoculture. On immigration, for example, his view was, at least in the 1940s, that the newcomers needed to be assimilated to the dominant culture. In other words, although Brazilian culture had originally emerged out of the mixture or fusion of Portuguese, African and Indian traditions, he had his doubts about the possible contribution of later groups such as the Italians or the Japanese. One of the reasons for his description of his native North-East as 'the most Brazilian part of Brazil' (*a parte ... mais brasileira do Brasil*), was that the new waves of immigrants had not reached that region. He was also unhappy with the continuing use by immigrants of languages other than Portuguese. By the 1970s, though, Freyre seems to have modified his position somewhat, recognizing that Italians, Syrians and others had something valuable to offer Brazilian culture, and accepting the existence of bilingualism, though not of separate Japanese-Brazilian or Italian-Brazilian sub-cultures. [49]

He was also active in politics *strictu sensu*. On different occasions, from the 1930s to the 1960s, it was rumoured that Freyre would be appointed prefect (in other words mayor) of Recife, ambassador to France or Mexico or Minister of Education, but on various occasions he claimed not to be interested in taking these posts. He was also invited to direct the Department of Social Sciences at UNESCO, but he refused the offer.[50] Whether or not he had a slight flirtation with these positions of power, what is certain is that none of these appointments materialized. Freyre's role in politics turned out to be more modest, but it was both significant and controversial.

His first appointment as an assistant to the Governor of Pernambuco, Estácio Coimbra, was accepted with a good deal of hesitation and after consulting his closest friends, who tried to dissuade him from experiencing 'the caricature of action that is the public life of Brazil', as one of them put it. In the end, the consideration that weighed most in favour of his acceptance was his hope that Coimbra would give strong support to his regionalist 'dreams', helping 'the culture and the traditions of Pernambuco to have fair expression'. In short, what counted in his decision was the possibility he saw of fulfilling his early ambition of making a difference in the world by 'dissolving' his ideas into action.

As we have seen, Freyre lost this official post following the revolution of 1930, in which Getúlio Vargas came to power. After his return to Brazil, and as the Vargas regime developed into the dictatorial *Estado Novo* of 1937, he had more than one brush with the police. In 1935 he was arrested and interrogated for signing a manifesto against the new Law of National Security. In the same period he was denounced as an 'agitator' for writing another manifesto, advocating an official inquiry into working conditions in the sugar-mills (*usinas*) of rural Pernambuco. He was once again imprisoned briefly in 1942 following his denunciation of Nazis in Recife (whom he had already provoked in 1940 in a public lecture on 'a threatened culture').[51] It was also around this time that Freyre complained in public about the pollution of the river Capibaribe.

Freyre's police file, now accessible, contains an article on 'The Topicality of William Morris', in which he reviewed a book about Morris entitled *Victorian Rebel*, praising the type of socialism which his hero professed and presenting him as the 'greatest and the best inspiration for the English socialism' which was renewing English life. 'His socialism never lost the regional note, the romantic taste for indigenous and traditional things, without the sacrifice of universality, human breadth or the boldly experimental modernism of his ideas'.[52]

Speaking in 1946 about the dictatorial Vargas regime that had just ended, Freyre recalled that in the attempt to isolate him from the rest of the country and from his friends and correspondents, the postal censorship by the police of Pernambuco had made it impossible for him to subscribe to journals or to import books. Whether in ignorance or in bad faith, as he put it, the police took everything that was 'sociology' or 'social' for Socialism, which they believed to be necessarily either 'Marxist' or 'Bolshevist'.

Freyre was actively opposed not only to the urban policy of Agamenon Magalhães, but more generally to what he called *agamenonismo*, a set of political ideas 'inspired by the fascist and racist models of Mussolini and Hitler' and leading to a police state. He later described Agamenon, when the latter was a candidate in a democratic election for Governor of Pernambuco in 1950, as 'an enemy of coloured people', hostile to Carnival and other forms of popular culture.[53] It should be added that Magalhães was a pious Catholic, whose policies were supported by the Church in Recife, especially by the Marian Fathers and the Jesuits. To all these groups, as well as the so-called *integralistas* (the green-shirted quasi-fascist party founded by Plínio Salgado), Freyre expressed his opposition. As a result, obscene graffiti were painted on the walls of his house, the work, he said, of 'people from Nazi-Jesuit centres and associations'.[54]

Thanks to this stand against the Right, Freyre was encouraged to enter politics. In 1945 he campaigned for election to the Chamber of Deputies of the Constituent Assembly, as a member of the Democratic National Union (*União Democrática Nacional* or UDN), which supported the candidature of Brigadier Eduardo Gomes as President, against General Eurico Gaspar Dutra (who had been Minister of War under Getúlio Vargas) and the Social Democratic Party (*Partido Social Democrático* or PSD). The fact that both candidates were army officers is worth noting, as well Freyre's strong support for Gomes, whom he saw as 'not a narrow man of a political sect or an economic group anxious for exclusive and absolute power'. It was during one of the public meetings in favour of the candidacy of Gomes, that a student was shot by the police – apparently by mistake, since the order, as a witness put it, was 'to "liquidate" Gilberto Freyre' – and that the offices of *DP* were occupied by the authorities. Dutra won the presidency, but Freyre was elected a deputy in the Constituent Assembly.[55]

At the time of his election campaign, Freyre was attacked as an extremist, the 'Antonio Conselheiro de Apipucos' (a reference to the messianic leader of a rural revolt of the late nineteenth century). He was also labelled a Communist, one journalist going so far as to write that 'To vote for Gilberto is to hand over the State to the agents of Moscow.' Freyre was represented in a caricature of this period as carrying a flag bearing a hammer and sickle.[56] His answer to this kind of attack was to declare that he would not feel offended to be called a Communist, because, after all 'what could be the dishonour for a man of our time to be "Communist"?' Morally, there was nothing wrong with being a Communist, and Brazil had plenty of very decent and honourable people – 'our most respectable men of intelligence and character' – who had joined either the Party or the movement in favour of a better Brazil and against the growth of fascism.

He did not support Communism – or for that matter, Evolutionism, Positivism or sociological determinism – he explained, because he could not agree with any system that dealt with human problems in a simplistic and uniform way, looking for certainties and clarities which could only be 'fictitious', when they relate to problems that are essentially complex.[57] In short, Freyre bluntly declared at this time that for these reasons he had never been a Communist, but that, on the other hand, he supported anti-anti-Communism. In the same way, his extremely sympathetic references to Luis Carlos Prestes led his words to be labelled as 'words of a communist' (*palavras de comunista*). Prestes, an engineer and army officer known as 'the Knight of Hope', had been one of the leaders of the failed 'Revolution of the Lieutenants' of 1922 and of the *Intentona Comunista* ('Communist Rising') of 1935, and would be the head of the Brazilian Communist Party for over fifty years. Freyre replied to his critics that he thought of Prestes as a lucid thinker, a man of 'deep public spirit', a truly honourable man and a 'great, although mistaken, friend of the Brazilian people'.[58]

In spite of his opponents' references to Conselheiro and the Bolsheviks, Freyre did not make fiery speeches in the Brazilian Congress, though he did speak about the redemocratization of Brazil, agrarian reform, race prejudice, museums, children's books and other topics.[59] He was not even a good Party man. On one side, he welcomed the success of the British Labour Party in the General Election of 1945, praised Stafford Cripps, the

Labour Chancellor, and described Winston Churchill as 'archaic'.[60] On the other, he wrote an article in praise of Charles Maurras, a leader of the reactionary party *Action Française*. As he once wrote about the Spanish Civil War, Freyre himself was 'difficult to classify', neither Right nor Left.[61] He often expressed strong political attitudes, but he was surely correct to describe himself as 'non-party' (*apartidário*), unlike contemporaries on the Left such as Caio Prado Jr, Sérgio Buarque and in the next generation, Antonio Candido.

All the same, to some intellectuals at the time it was obvious that Freyre was, if not a Communist, then definitely a Socialist. Gustavo Corção, a famous Catholic right-wing intellectual, recalls that once in the 1940s he heard a Dominican mentioning Freyre's name in the middle of a lecture he was giving at the Catholic Centre of Rio de Janeiro, just to lament that 'that great intelligence had slid into socialism'.[62] A phrase Freyre himself used in the 1940s to describe his position was 'democratic left', claiming that it was the political position of the great majority of the population in the North of the country.

In 1945 Freyre warmly welcomed the victory of Labour in Great Britain not only in itself but also as having an 'international significance' (*significado transnacional*). No one in the world should miss this significance, he stressed, since all 'modern peoples' would be inspired by the 'socialist-democratic revolution in Great Britain'. This revolution was not to be confused with the 'official Marxist dogma of the Second International', he explained, since far from professing atheism, it maintained a 'strong ethic and even a Christian character'.[63]

Freyre's sympathy for the English tradition of socialism frequently resurfaced, even when he was commenting on the achievements of the great Brazilian jurist Rui Barbosa, the 'champion of *Habeas Corpus*' in Brazil. As Freyre put it, unaware of the true Brazil, Barbosa had put a lot of hope into bringing *Habeas Corpus* to the country, not realizing that in many cases it was a 'useless therapy', like treating an injured leg with a simple ointment. Barbosa, Freyre argued, was an anglophile who was dazzled by the 'bourgeois liberalism of the 19th century'. Like 'a European or North American missionary amongst African tribes', he had no eyes to see the great English tradition of English Socialism – which was turning the Welfare State from dream into reality – although it might have inspired him to deal with Brazilian 'social questions', that he also did not have eyes to see.[64]

That the label of Marxist attached to Freyre was taken seriously by at least part of the public is shown by the reaction it provoked among true Marxists both inside and outside Brazil. Rodolfo Ghioldi, the head of the

Communist Party of Argentina and a member of the Comintern, who
had participated with Prestes in the Communist Revolt in Brazil in 1935,
strongly opposed his views and published a pamphlet against him with the
title *Gilberto Freyre, Reactionary Sociologist* (1951), analysing *CGS, S&M,
IB* and other works by Freyre, accusing the author of 'historical escapism',
nostalgia for feudalism, 'theoretical nihilism' and eclecticism, and finally
describing him as a Pernambucan version of T. S. Eliot (*un Eliot Pernambucano*), presumably in the sense of a former member of the avant-garde
who had turned conservative.[65]

Still more revealing of the way in which Freyre's supposed Marxism
was taken seriously is the Communist Party's effort to deny it. Determined to 'neutralize the influence of Gilbertism, which was growing in the
academic sector', the Communist Party leadership requested the young
and talented Marxist Gláucio Veiga, as we have seen, to dismantle Freyre's
work in the press, using a variety of arguments to discredit his scholarship
as well as making the point that ideas that might appear to be Marxist,
such as Freyre's attack on the capitalist owners of sugar factories, actually
served the traditional social order.[66]

Veiga, a former sergeant in the Brazilian army and a graduate of
the Recife Law School who became Professor of Sociology and Political
Science at the University of Recife and later, a celebrated Brazilian jurist,
was one of the few intellectuals in Freyre's native city with a comparable
breadth of interests to his, with publications on topics ranging from the
philosophy of Kant and the sociology of Max Scheler to Proust's *A la re-
cherche du temps perdu*. Like Ghioldi, he dismissed *CGS* and other works
by Freyre as reactionary, supporting the 'retrograde structures' of an Old
Regime. As a commentator has put it, Veiga 'hated Freyre with love'. No
wonder then that Freyre described Veiga, who later became a friend of
his, as having once been 'the most terrible anti-Gilberto in the whole
world'.[67]

As might have been expected, during his time as a deputy Freyre was
very much concerned with the problems of the North-East. In 1949 he
presented a project for the foundation of an institute for studying these
problems, to be named the Instituto Nabuco in homage to the nineteenth-
century statesman Joaquim Nabuco, who came from the North-East
himself. The Institute was planned as an interdisciplinary organization,
independent from universities, concerned with the anthropology, folklore and sociology of the region and including a museum of the everyday
culture of the North-East. Freyre was also involved with SUDENE, an institution founded to encourage the development of the North-East, both
in the age of Juscelino Kubitschek, who was President of Brazil from 1956

to 1961 and in that of Humberto Castelo Branco, who became president following the military coup of 1964.

On the international front, Freyre took part in the small two-week conference mentioned earlier on 'Tensions Affecting International Understanding', organized by Julian Huxley, Director-General of UNESCO. At this time, soon after the end of the Second World War, a good deal of effort was being put into avoiding 'aggressive and virulent nationalisms' that might lead to disaster once again. Freyre was invited together with seven other well-known social scientists from Europe and America: the sociologists George Gurvitch, Max Horkheimer and Alexander Szalai, the Norwegian philosopher Arne Naess and the psychologists Gordon Allport, John Rickman and Harry S. Sullivan (the emphasis on psychology reflected the organizers' belief that UNESCO's concern was primarily with 'man's subjective life'). The occasion was described as 'apparently the first time in world history when the people of many lands have officially turned to the social scientist to seek his aid in man's quest for enduring peace'.

It is worth noting that the social scientists invited were selected not only for their professional competence but also as people 'who felt sufficiently secure personally' not to 'waste time as a group trying to impress each other'. 'In addition to being knowledgeable, they had all gained some wisdom from experience'. It was reported that 'Four of them [including Freyre] had been in jail sometime during their lives for refusing to give up points of view they thought were right. Two of them had had to leave their mother country; two of them had been physically tortured during World War II'. [68]

From the beginning of the 1950s, Freyre came increasingly to be seen, rightly or wrongly, as a conservative. One reason for this was the fact that in 1951, he accepted an official invitation to visit Portugal and 'Overseas' (*Ultramar*, the new Portuguese name for their colonies in Goa, Angola, Moçambique, Portuguese Guinea, Cabo Verde and elsewhere). [69] The invitation was obviously a tempting one for a historian of colonial society, allowing him to visit Angola, Moçambique and Goa for the first time and to compare and contrast them with Brazil. Officially, there were no strings attached to this visit. However, the invitation emanated from the Portuguese government and indirectly from António Salazar, the Portuguese dictator. Freyre hesitated before accepting; indeed, he had refused two earlier invitations, considering them 'rather "compromising"' because they had come from the Secretariat for Information. However, the third invitation, from the Minister for Overseas, 'could not', he said, 'have been more clearly apolitical'. To have refused would have made him a supporter of political purism, as he put it, 'a purism that I have never claimed to cultivate'.

On arriving in Portugal, Freyre met Salazar and was impressed by him, as an intellectual and as an individual who knew how to listen 'with the acute intelligence of a Jesuit' and found verbose rhetoric repugnant. As the diplomat Alberto da Costa e Silva observed during his service in Lisbon, visitors from Brazil, whether intellectuals or politicians, were often dazzled by Salazar and even seduced by his manner and intelligence, irrespective of their political opinions.[70] In Freyre's case, the fact that the head of state received him at their first meeting 'with the simplicity of a teacher', showing an interest in books and having some of Freyre's own books 'at his side, including the most recent, *Quase Política*', could only have contributed to the positive view he had of Salazar. Although he criticized the system of censorship, he also wrote that the regime in Portugal was superior to others that were 'apparently more democratic'.[71]

The speeches Freyre made in Ultramar during his tour and the book that he produced describing his visit, *Aventura e Rotina* (1953) – not to mention his contributions to the celebration of the 500th anniversary of the death of Prince Henry the Navigator in 1460 – were widely interpreted as a defence of Portuguese colonialism at a moment of increasingly vocal opposition to the regime. Ironically, the man who had once organized the first conference of Afro-Brazilian studies now told the governor of Angola that the country was 'an African Portugal'.

Freyre's 'Luso-Tropicalism' – in other words the idea that the Portuguese proved more adaptable to the tropics and so more successful colonizers than their European rivals – will be discussed in more detail in Chapter 6. The point that needs to be made here is that the idea was obviously going to be exploited by the Portuguese government, which needed such an intellectual defence against the anti-colonial movements of the time: the MPLA in Angola, Frelimo in Mozambique and the PAIGC, led by Amílcar Cabral, in Guinea and Cabo Verde (before the 1950s, the Salazar regime had not accepted Freyre's positive view of miscegenation).[72] Two of Freyre's books, *Integração Portuguesa nos Trópicos* ('Portuguese Integration in the Tropics'; 1958) and *O Luso e o Trópico* ('The Portuguese and the Tropical'; 1961) were published by the government and sent out to embassies in order for representatives of Portugal abroad to make use of their ideas. Luso-Tropicalism was also a major element in courses given at the Institute for Overseas Studies (*Instituto Superior de Estudos Ultramarinos*), where future colonial administrators were trained.[73]

It was equally obvious that Freyre's ideas would be rejected by the leaders of anti-colonial movements. Cabral, for instance, wrote that 'Perhaps unconsciously confusing realities that are biological or necessary with realities that are socioeconomic and historical, Freyre transformed all of us who live in the colony-provinces of Portugal into the fortunate inhabitants of a Luso-Tropical paradise'.[74] Freyre was criticized, somewhat unfairly, for having sold himself to Salazar, though he must have realized that by accepting the invitation he could not avoid some degree of complicity with the regime.[75] As Mrs Thatcher once remarked, 'There is no such thing as a free lunch', and the same point might be made about a free trip. The man who had once described the modern Portuguese as pathetically clinging to the belief that they were a great colonial power (as we shall see in more detail in Chapter 6) allowed himself to be carried along and drifted into connivance with the propagandist use made of his statements about the Portuguese in the tropics, apparently taken in by the impression management practised by his hosts during the visit.

Freyre's view of Luso-Tropicalism, so strongly rejected by the opponents of Salazar, was cited all the same in 1995 by Mário Soares, the former Socialist Prime Minister, later President of Portugal, in a discourse concerning the national 'capacity for reconciliation and for adaptation to new situations'. Today, however, his ideas on this topic appear to have been almost forgotten in Portugal. During the celebrations of the 500th anniversary of the Portuguese discovery of Brazil, in the year 2000, his name was hardly mentioned.[76]

Still more of a break with his radical past was Freyre's support for the military regime that replaced President João Goulart following a *coup d'état* in March 1964.[77] The early 1960s were a time of social conflict in Brazil, especially in the North-East. Miguel Arraes, a Socialist, was elected Governor of Pernambuco in 1962. Francisco Julião, leader of the Peasant Leagues (*Ligas Camponeses*) that were demanding land, was also based in Pernambuco. Goulart, though a great landowner himself in Rio Grande do Sul, supported agrarian reform as well as the expropriation of foreign oil companies. 1964 might be described as Brazil's 'McCarthian moment', a decade after the rise of McCarthy in the United States, since it seems to have been the fear of Communism that provoked the generals to act, while anti-Communism was used to legitimate their regime.

Freyre supported the new government from the first day. He made a public speech in Recife stressing the perils of Communism. By this time, his original sympathy for a party and a movement that he had openly praised in the 1940s seems to have been completely eclipsed. Instead of a movement around which the most respectable Brazilians 'of intelligence and character' gathered to fight Nazi-Fascism, as he had described it in the 1940s, Communism was now taken to be essentially anti-Brazilian, and, by betraying the country's traditions and history, to constitute a threat to its economic, political and ideological independence.

It was as if Freyre had turned into an ultra-nationalist, similar to the type he had criticized in his proposals at the Paris conference of 1948, for avoiding tensions that lead to wars. At that point, he had referred to Latin-American peoples as being easily moved by fear of foreign threats, and so easily exploited by shrewd nationalistic leaders ('caudillos of a paternalistic type') who, under the guise of the defence of the nation against 'possible dangers' such as '"Red" Bolshevism', had had 'the ideal pretexts for long years of the paternalistic rule of their peoples'.[78] Now it was his turn to see 'Reds under the bed'. One wonders whether Freyre's fears, especially his sense that Brazil was under threat from the USSR, became more acute following the Cuban missile crisis of 1962.

As for the open and warm regard he had once had for 'socialism in the English style', or even 'Marxism in the English style' no traces seemed to be left of it. It was with relief and rejoicing that the Catholic intellectual Gustavo Corção recalled in 1973 that Freyre had redeemed himself, so to speak. Abroad, he defended the coup. Interviewed in Harvard, he declared the March 'revolution' to have been 'absolutely necessary': 'Goulart thought he was using the Communists, but the Communists knew they were using Goulart'.[79] He also wrote an article for *Life* magazine comparing the new president, General Humberto Castelo Branco (an old friend of his) to General De Gaulle (another friend of Freyre's, the journalist Chatô, made the same comparison).[80] Meanwhile, at home, Freyre tried to persuade the new government, as he had tried to persuade Vargas, to do something about the problems of the North-East. For his part, Castelo Branco gave a speech at SUDENE that quoted Freyre on these problems.

In assessing his position at this time it is important to avoid the temptations of hindsight. If Freyre was mistaken to see the Brazilian Communist Party of the 1960s as revolutionary, his mistake was widely shared. Again, in contrast to posterity, no one knew in 1964 what the generals would do after they had taken power. After all, the birth of the Republic had been the result of a military coup in 1889.

Even more important for interpreting Freyre's support of the military coup of 1964, so we believe, was his positive view of the Brazilian army. On many previous occasions, especially in the 1940s, he had openly spoken about the true 'Brazilianism' (*brasileirismo*) of the army's ethos, and a hostile critic had even accused him in 1947 of wanting a 'military coup'.[81] Working, for most of Brazil's history, as a coordinating, equilibrating force, the army, according to Freyre, had only occasionally resorted to violence or allied itself with a political party or particular groups or interests. Traditionally a supporter of social reform and democratic institutions, the Brazilian army was never a systematically or consciously antidemocratic or antipopular force, he noted. Canudos (where the supporters of the rebel Antonio Conselheiro were massacred in 1897) was the site of one of the mistakes committed by the Brazilian army, one of the few occasions in which it appealed to 'militarism' in a vulgar Prussian sense, that is, to the idea that every problem 'could only be solved by weapons'. For most of the time, though, in tune with the tendency to the 'equilibrium of antagonisms', a feature of Brazil that he so much stressed and admired, the army had been 'among us, a peaceful force towards the coordination of contraries'. Working in collaboration and with the same public good in mind, responsible 'civic leaders', together with 'military leaders', have been guided by this 'sense of coordination of contraries' in the direction and organization of national life.[82]

Hence Freyre welcomed the revolution of 1964 as a search for 'Brazilian solutions to Brazilian problems' and 'Brazilian situations' – solutions, as he liked to stress, that would be faithful to the 'constant features of Brazilian culture'. We might say, therefore, that his 'Brazilianism' had got out of hand at this time, and that his concern with foreign ideas and intrusions, which according to him might 'debrazilianize' the country (or give that impression to itself or on the international scene), had made of him an aggressive nationalist.

The preoccupation with the country's international reputation, which seems to have been one of the marks left on Freyre by his years abroad, was probably one of the reasons for his growing concern with 'Brazilianism'. Writing 'From the Other America' to his readers in Recife in 1922, his wounds still fresh from the difficult experience of being a young South American in the country that considered Nordics and Protestants to be the white race *par excellence*, Freyre wrote about 'patriotic lies' being totally unacceptable in history books, wherever they come from. But outside Brazil, he adds, patriotic lying is 'excusable': 'it is the safety-valve for homesickness' as well as 'the means of neutralizing the unfavourable lies of travellers, reporters and other gentlemen of superficial opinions whom one constantly meets'.[83]

Apparently he never came back to this topic, and we can say that most of the time his Brazilianism did not slip into a narrow patriotism. In fact, the social scientist who was invited by UNESCO in 1948 to discuss the tensions that cause war had plenty to say against narrow nationalism and in favour of international understanding and co-operation. However, there is evidence that like an archaeological stratum, those early experiences of feeling despised for coming from a backward and racially mixed country could resurface and lead him to justify statements that were contrary to his personal beliefs. In 1954, for instance, when the elected president Getúlio Vargas – ex-revolutionary leader, ex-interim president and ex-quasi-fascist dictator – committed suicide, Freyre, despite admitting Vargas's mistakes, praised him for his 'Brazilianism' and asked an important figure in the government to provide him with 'something' about Vargas's policies that would be 'in the interest of Brazil' to reveal to the North American audiences of the 'first order' whom he was shortly to address. He would gladly 'present those points of view' abroad, he stressed, 'even if I did not agree with them.'[84]

Speaking about the military regime of 1964, Freyre frequently referred to the armed forces as 'once again' acting in the service of 'the will of almost the whole of the nation', as acting in the sense of 'civism', not of 'militarism', and in solidarity with 'this authentically Brazilian Brazil', against the anti-Brazilian and anti-national forces represented by Communism. The suggestions Freyre made in 1972 for the program of the Arena (Aliança Renovadora Nacional), the party that supported the military regime, is revealing of his trust that the government was willing to be and capable of continuing to be the 'spokesman of national consciousness' and of developing a 'constructively revolutionary' programme without resorting to transplanting foreign ideas and organizations, alien to Brazilian reality and values.[85]

Once again, carried away by his 'Brazilianism', Freyre urged the government party to put an effort into using the modern mass media to present not only to Brazilians, but also and especially to foreigners, the 'synthetic image' of the country's 'destiny' and of its 'valid and valuable constants'. This cultural and informative diplomacy, he explained, would be a way to counterattack the 'malicious distortions' of the country's 'reality and values', and the view that some of its organizations were not original and independent but on the contrary, the 'aberrations' of democratic regimes.

In his list of the Brazilian cultural 'constants' that he believed the government was able to support, Freyre mentioned the tendency for its peoples to affirm themselves as 'a race beyond race' (uma além-raça), its appreciation of diversity, its tendency for tolerance; but – rather disconcertingly for those who expected to see a supporter of the coup putting forward purely reactionary views – he also strongly defended the need for the 'difference in socio-economic level between the populations of different regions to be attenuated' and for agrarian reforms to be made in order to correct 'socio-economic imbalances' and 'prevent the increasing marginalization of the rural population.'[86]

All the same, his original decision to support the coup of 1964 definitely pushed Freyre towards the Right. In 1972, he was still describing the military regime as 'a far better form of government than the totally corrupt, paralysed congressional form we had before 1964'.[87] Freyre had once been an enthusiast for Dom Helder Câmara, the radical priest who became Archbishop of Olinda and Recife, describing him in 1958 as a priest who was also 'an intense man of action' yet kept his distance from political parties and factions, linking the Church to the aspirations of the poor. By 1967, however, Freyre was accusing Dom Helder of being a Brazilian Kerensky and playing the Communist's game.[88] In similar fashion, asked by journalists what he thought about two leading North-Eastern intellectuals, the economist Celso Furtado and the educationalist Paulo Freire, Freyre replied that they were aiding Communism, even if that was not their intention.[89] In fact, he seems not to have hesitated to criticize or even denounce to the police certain Marxists whom he saw as a threat to the new regime.[90]

One of the actions that weighed most against him was his putting pressure, in 1964, on his old acquaintance, the Minister of the Interior, to accept the resignation of the Rector of the University of Recife, something that the government seemed to be unwilling to do. If the minister maintained in the post a person who was 'compromised by Communist infiltration' and hostile to 'non-communist students' (something he claimed to know because his son and his friends had experienced this hostility), Freyre threatened to 'make a public break with the government' that he had so strongly supported.[91]

It is not surprising, then, that 1964 marked a rupture in his relationship with a number of friends and acquaintances. This was the time of the sudden end of Freyre's long friendship with Sérgio Buarque de Holanda, a steady opponent of the military regime as well as part of the group who founded the Brazilian Labour Party (*Partido dos Trabalhadores*) in 1980. For the literary critic Antonio Candido, another member of that group and an early admirer of *CGS*, Freyre was a kind of lost leader. He admired 'that Gilberto' who had been a radical in the 1940s, but not the Gilberto of the 1960s.[92]

To be fair to the ambivalence and the complexity of Freyre's behaviour – so often ignored or denied by his critics – and of the reactions of others to it, we should also note two testimonies that go in a different direction. According to his Marxist critic Gláucio Veiga, Freyre gave refuge in the Joaquim Nabuco Foundation to many people who were persecuted by the government after 1964. As for the reaction of others, his old friend Erico Veríssimo did not break with Freyre. On the contrary, he wrote to him in 1972 to assure him that he remained his admirer, in spite of their political differences, 'especially today'. Like a classic liberal he declared: 'I recognize your right, Gilberto, to think, write and take (or refuse to take) political positions as you see fit'.[93]

When it was that Freyre realized that the coup (or 'revolution') of March 1964 had failed his expectations, it is hard to say, but in 1981 he admitted in an interview that 'the ultracentralizing State' of Brazil might be compared to 'Soviet totalitarianism' and that the military regime had 'succumbed to the pressures of economic technocrats', thus losing sight of the interests of the country as a whole. He stated quite clearly that '1964 was a great revolution that failed. The leaders of the movement had the opportunity to make a real revolution, but they did not take it. They failed because they had too much economism and too little social sensibility'.[94]

It would have been much better for his reputation – and for the country – if Freyre had spoken up more loudly and more often against the military regime after he came to adopt this view, especially as the milder regime of Castelo Branco (1964–7), turned into the harsh regime of Emílio Garrastazú Médici (1969–74) in which many more dissidents were tortured or killed.[95] With his international reputation and his authority in certain circles, he was in an ideal position from which to criticize the regime which he had supported from the start and in which he had placed so much hope. Denouncing its abuses and the betrayal of its promises would also have allowed him to admit his own fears, his illusions, his weaknesses and his failures – all things that he had so strongly and so poetically stressed as marks of humanity, present in everyone's trajectory but especially in the lives of great men.

Nevertheless, Freyre apparently never spoke out against the generals, even when it was clear that many atrocities were being committed under their rule. Like Borges, who was much less of a political animal than he was, and who did not speak out against the military regime in Argentina, to the regret of his admirers and at a great cost for him, Freyre's silence on this issue led to his being vilified. His earlier work tended either to be ignored or to be read in the light of his later attitudes and so dismissed by many people. Any reconstruction of Freyre's motives is necessarily speculative, but we might suggest that by the late 1970s he had nurtured past illusions for too long and that he shut his eyes to aspects of the present that were painful for him to see, especially since there was not much time to replace old illusions with new ones.

Alberto da Costa e Silva, discussing Freyre's visit to the Portuguese colonies, described him as having been the 'prisoner of his dream'. As a result, he praised what did not exist and was not able to see the Portuguese empire with fresh eyes. The same might be said of him in relation to the military regime. Having a rather rosy view of the army, he welcomed the new regime of 1964 wholeheartedly, and continued to support it, as if the moment for the Brazil of his dreams to become reality had finally arrived. What he dreamed of was a Brazilian Brazil that continued and even went beyond the British model of 'the art of compromise', as Freyre wrote in the preface to a new edition of *IB* published in 1977. Intoxicated with optimism, he suggested that if the British excelled in political and economic compromise, the Brazilian art of combining racial and cultural opposites and allowing their interpenetration offered 'new perspectives on the human condition'.[96]

A Conservative Revolutionary?

The early biography of Freyre presents him as a man of the Left, though not an orthodox one. Younger people on the Left, such as Antonio Candido, admired his opposition to dictatorship during the *Estado Novo* and saw him as 'a master of radical thought' (*um mestre de radicalidade*).[97] That he grew more conservative as he grew older is of course difficult to deny. However, we should not read his entire intellectual life in terms of its last phase. Freyre's political attitudes were never simple, especially in his youth. He sometimes described himself as an 'anarchist', and more often, in the same way that he characterized some Brazilians of the early Republic – Joaquim Nabuco, for instance, Rui Barbosa, the baron of Rio Branco and the bishop of Olinda, Dom Vital – as a 'conservative revolutionary'.[98]

Like Carlyle, Ruskin and Morris, all of whom were opposed to capitalism but nostalgic for some aspects of the Middle Ages, Freyre's political position originally combined elements from the Left and the Right.[99] Colonial Brazil was his equivalent of the Middle Ages. His nostalgia for aristocratic life on the traditional plantation was linked to his opposition to what he called 'the plutocracy of the factories', including the new sugar factories that were replacing the old *engenhos* in the North-East in the 1920s, a process vividly described in the novels of his friend José Lins do Rego.

Vargas too combined elements from Left and Right, and Freyre's attitude to him was appropriately ambivalent.[100] In a phrase that would later be applied to himself, he divided the history of Brazil into two phases, 'before and after Getúlio'.[101] He recognized that the man was, to use Max Weber's famous term, 'charismatic', as well as someone interested in ideas, who read his books, and even articles, 'with the intelligent attention of an illustrious reader'. The fact that Vargas read Freyre's books could only increase his admiration. In 1941 he wrote an article praising Vargas for the

government's use of sociology in the search for solutions to social problems, though he denied being a 'unqualified enthusiast' for his political
methods.[102]

The revolution of 1930, so Freyre declared in 1949, 'seems to me to
have done some good in Brazil, as well as a good deal of harm'.[103] In 1947
he distinguished the 'good side' of the Vargas regime, including social
legislation and public works in the North-East, from 'the bad side' that
he sometimes described as 'parafascist'.[104] In fact, Freyre saw in Vargas an
eloquent example of the multiple personalities that may inhabit a single
individual, a 'creative philistine' struggling with a 'bohemian', for instance,
or 'a Mr Hyde inside a Dr Jekyll'.

The same Vargas who was 'avid for power and command' placed
himself on several occasions on the side of the poor, 'against sterile conventions and powerful plutocratic groups'.[105] His 'sociological awareness
of Brazilian and American problems', so Freyre argued, made it possible to
expect from Vargas the role of promoter and leader of an inter-American
cultural policy, a movement that would be 'unionist and pluralist' at the
same time. On the other side, Vargas was also capable of a narrow patriotism and nationalism, and in their name allowed, or perhaps turned a
blind eye to, political persecutions. At one point, Freyre even seems to pity
Vargas for being 'himself a victim of the dictatorship'. By 1942, he claims,
Getúlio had been reduced to 'a simple and pitiful fragment of a leader, at
most a semi-leader', the real bosses being Agamenon Magalhães and the
chief of police, Filinto Müller. In 1952 Freyre said that he both approved
and disapproved of the Estado Novo (the dictatorship; 1937–45), disliking
the imitation of fascist regimes and 'fascist infiltrations', but approving of
what he called the correction of the excesses of the revolution of 1930 and
even of the Republic of 1889.[106]

Regionalism complicated the contrast between Left and Right, as
Freyre noted in the case of the Spanish Civil War.[107] He remembered
Charles Maurras, whose ideas he had encountered in Paris in the 1920s, as
'on the one hand, an intransigent monarchist, but on the other, the theorist of a flexible regionalist federalism'.[108] Freyre, a man whose work shows
his distrust of simple categories, himself resisted categorization.

To conclude this discussion of the public intellectual, it may be illuminating to compare Freyre with figures from other countries. His affinities with the Scotsman Patrick Geddes and the North American Lewis
Mumford are particularly close.

Geddes was a man of vision, an eccentric in the Ruskinian mould
and a scholar gypsy or 'wandering student'. His interests were broad
and he hated over-specialization. Originally a botanist and biologist, he

became a disciple of Herbert Spencer, interested in social evolution, as well as in regional problems (especially those of Edinburgh and its surroundings), in architecture and in museums. Besides Spencer, Carlyle, Ruskin and Morris were major points of reference for Geddes. By 1915 he was already arguing, as Freyre would argue later, for studying the city and the countryside together and for both a historical and an environmental approach to contemporary urban problems.[109] His contrast between the 'Palaeo-technic' age of the nineteenth century, unhappy in its consequences (which included the rise of the 'pseudo-city'), and the possibilities of a future 'Neo-technic' age, were taken up by his followers Mumford and Freyre.

Mumford was another of Freyre's heroes, a fellow admirer of Ruskin and Morris whom he described as 'the master of us all in matters of urban sociology' and as a humanist who was able to combine sociological with aesthetic interests.[110] Mumford never tired of denouncing the 'deterioration of the environment' that followed the Industrial Revolution and especially the rise of what he called the 'non-city', ugly and unhygienic.[111] His nostalgia for the medieval community, like that of Morris, was linked to his utopian vision of the future. Incidentally, when Mumford published a book on *The Story of Utopias*, it was praised by another hero of Freyre's, Alfred Zimmern.[112]

Both Mumford and Freyre were generalists in an age of intellectual specialization. Hence both lived on the edge of the academic world, practising journalism in order to preserve their intellectual independence (from 1931 onwards, Mumford wrote a regular column for the *New Yorker* under the rubric 'The Sky Line'). They both combined a love of tradition with a keen interest in both modernity and modernism, a combination that gave force to their critiques of the world they lived in. Both were interested in ecology and in regionalism (in Mumford's case the Bay Region in California and the area around New York). In his *Culture of Cities*, Mumford wrote about 'the regional framework of civilization', 'the politics of regional development' and the need to adapt cities to their environment, climate included. Both men admired eccentric intellectuals such as Geddes and the sociologist Thorstein Veblen, and they were both a little eccentric themselves. Like Mumford, Freyre took a stand on public issues, but his most lasting achievements are his books. It is time to return to Freyre the historian.

5 Empire and Republic

As we have seen, Gilberto Freyre's life was divided between action and observation, or in the language of the sociologist Norbert Elias, between 'involvement' and 'detachment'.[1] All the same, it would be a mistake to separate the two spheres too sharply. Writing about the agricultural history of his native region, for instance, might be seen as a form of action at a time when the author was concerned to bring the problems of the North-East to the attention of President Getúlio Vargas, who was apparently, his attentive reader, (like 'Professor Salazar', as Freyre liked to call the Portuguese dictator). Freyre's action was necessary because Vargas, like many other Brazilians, was not aware of the problems of the North-East. He came himself from the Deep South of Brazil, where the problems, like the climate, were rather different.

The Ecological Turn

Four years after the publication of *CGS*, Freyre returned to some of its themes in a relatively short essay, *Nordeste* ('North-East'; henceforth *NE*), concentrating this time on the influence of the cultivation of sugar-cane on the environment – land, water and forest – and on the animals and the people of the region. Leaving aside the arid *sertão* or 'backlands' and its pastoral economy, the book focused on the so-called *terras de massapé*, the rich soil that produced the sugar-cane and with it the whole Big House complex.

In his first lines, Freyre warned the reader against expecting a book dealing with the droughts and horrors of the *sertão*, with which the North-East was associated. It is worth emphasizing that at the time that Freyre was writing the first two volumes of his trilogy, together with *NE*, the view of the backlands as the seat of violence in nature and men alike was widespread. Lampião, the most famous leader of a gang of *cangaceiros* (bandits), who was at the height of his activity in the 1920s and 1930s, was attracting the attention of the country to the dark side of the region, as other *cangaceiros* and mystics had been doing for decades. Freyre's aim was to tell the rest of the country about another North-East. Instead of reading about starving people and animals, so extremely thin that they resemble the elongated figures of El Greco, he told his readers, they were going to learn about the 'older North-East', full of fat trees, fat animals and fat people. As contemporary reviews testify, the book revealed a reality that many Brazilians ignored, as it represented 'a true initiation' of the men from the south into the civilization of the North-East'.[2]

NE differed from its better-known predecessor CGS in two major respects. In the first place, in CGS, the landscape was not yet a 'character in the drama' – to use Freyre's vivid description of the work of Euclides da Cunha.[3] Indeed, a significant absence from Freyre's early work is the historical or human geography of the kind practised in France by Paul Vidal de la Blache, a major influence on the French historians of the so-called 'Annales School' such as Lucien Febvre and Fernand Braudel. We might ask ourselves how different CGS would have been if its author had discovered Vidal before writing it.

By 1935, however, Freyre was sufficiently interested in Vidal to use his *Tableau géographique de la France* in a course on 'regional sociology' that he gave in the Faculty of Law in Recife. At about the same time he discovered the work of the American Carl Sauer, whom he described in NE as 'the most humane of human geographers'.[4]

What attracted Freyre most in Sauer's work – as in that of the Indian sociologist Radhakamal Mukerjee – was the ecological approach. As we have seen, Freyre was already concerned with environmental problems in the 1920s. Where Braudel, like Vidal, was attracted by a relatively static geography, Freyre's enthusiasm was for a more dynamic ecology.[5] As he told his students in Recife in 1935, 'Ecology is not a dirty word' (*Ecologia não é coisa feia*). Human ecology did not imply geographical determinism, but was concerned with the relation between people and their environment.[6] 'Ecology' is a term that echoes through the pages of NE, making the book seem surprisingly up to date and so reminding us that both the discipline of ecology and the ecological movement are older than we might think. It is a pity that NE has never been translated into English, and that as a result it has been ignored by workers in the growing field of environmental history, to which it made an early and distinguished contribution.

In the second place, as a result of its focus on the environment, NE differs from CGS by placing considerable emphasis on the negative aspects of the economy and the society of the North-East, going so far as to speak of the 'social pathology' of the region. Where CGS stressed equilibrium,

NE concentrated on disequilibrium.[7] What the author called 'the drama of monoculture' is emplotted as a tragedy, with the dominance of sugar leading to the destruction of the forest, the erosion of the soil, the pollution of rivers, the poisoning of fish and the 'oppression' (the author's term) of slaves, women and children.[8]

The tone of denunciation rose when Freyre discussed recent developments such as the rise of the *usina*, the industrialized sugar factory that was replacing the traditional sugar-mill in his own time and that he blamed for a deterioration of relations between owner and workers and even for the decline 'in the style of furniture, as in that of houses'. As we have seen, his criticism of the sugar-mills provoked a violent reaction from the authorities, and Freyre was put in jail.[9]

Whether the author's aim was to answer his critics, to compensate for an overemphasis on harmony in the earlier book, or to persuade Vargas to do something to remedy the problems of the region – or indeed all of these things – *NE* reads, in parts, at least, as if it had been written by a different member of Freyre's 'collection of selves' from the author of *CGS*. It reminds us of the Freyre who was working for the government in Recife in the late 1920s, interested in the planting of trees and the provision of playgrounds for children. In this book it was the critic and the reformer rather than the traditionalist who had the upper hand, even though the conclusion of the book is balanced – or ambivalent, noting the positive contributions of this 'pathological' culture to the rest of Brazil. Other regional cultures may have been 'more healthy, more democratic, more balanced in the distribution of riches and goods' but so far as political, aesthetic or intellectual values were concerned, 'none were more creative'.[10]

It is also in relation to this topic that Freyre made explicit the assumptions that lay behind his way of doing history: the recognition of the complexity of human affairs and of the relativity of knowledge. Hence, so he argued, our capacity for knowledge is necessarily prejudiced if we approach anything human or social in absolute terms. A relativist approach, he explained in *NE*, is the wisest one to follow when attempting to understand or speak about human affairs, since things are not black or white, right or wrong, good or bad. 'Neither monoculture, nor the great estate, nor slavery, characteristics that affect the social development of Brazil in such a decisive manner ... deserve to be formally condemned by someone who approaches the subject from a relativist viewpoint. And not from an absolute one, so dangerous in judgments about society, disturbing a historical perspective'.[11]

Appropriately enough for a supporter of *mestiçagem*, Freyre did not view history in black and white, though his cultural relativism earned him criticisms from Marxist-Leninists like Rodolfo Ghioldi (discussed earlier) who knew where they stood. Ghioldi denounced this openness as nothing but a disguise for Freyre's 'reactionary ideas' and accused him of being a poker player who places his bets both ways, playing the 'irresponsible game' of 'yes, but' in order to please everyone.[12]

Equally revealing of Freyre's critical and reforming bent at this time is the fact that, although he chose not to write about the North-East that was 'arid and heroically poor, devastated by banditry, malaria and hunger', he sponsored the publication of a book which dealt precisely with the problems that his own book had left out. Already in the 1920s he had been trying to fight against the neglect of the region, by stressing the need to rehabilitate and defend local values and traditions, and there is evidence that in the mid-1930s he even thought about writing a book about the part of the country that Euclides da Cunha had discussed in his *Backlands*.

In fact, as Freyre remarked more than once, Cunha had had the courage and sensibility to reveal what other great Brazilian intellectuals (such as Machado de Assis and Joaquim Nabuco) had avoided, that is, the pain and heroism of the people from a region where 'the antagonisms of race and culture assumed dramatic forms'.[13] As Freyre noted, in insurrections and episodes such as Canudos and Pedra Bonita (to mention just two of the several outbursts which shocked the whole country in the nineteenth century), Brazilian history showed the dramatic loss of its distinctive equilibrium of antagonisms, when, as he put it, 'the macabre was joined by the sinister'.[14] In line with this concern, in 1937, Freyre showed great enthusiasm for a work by Djacir Menezes, a young sociologist from Ceará, that dealt with a region that 'in spite of being the one most talked about is the least well known'. His own strategy, as he explained to his publisher José Olympio, was to present the two North-Easts in counterpoint, one book complementing the other. For this reason, he wanted the book to come out at 'the same time as my own', with the title of 'The Other North-East'.

In other respects, the historical style of *NE* resembles that of its more famous predecessor *CGS*. It was once again based on a wide range of sources, including family papers, photographs, folksongs and the descriptions of the region by foreign travellers such as the Frenchman Louis-François de Tollenare as well as studies by geographers, botanists, agriculturalists and physicians. It celebrated once more the food of the region, especially the sugar-based sweets such as the *goiabada*. It discussed the clothing and even the accent of the aristocrats, and also the physical development – or underdevelopment – of the workers, noting that battalions of soldiers from the North-East could be recognized by the low stature of the recruits, who had grown up undernourished.[15]

The most remarkable section, however, is surely the fourth chapter, on animals, beginning with the contrast between the aristocratic horse and the plebeian ox. The horse was dominant like his master in a culture that Freyre describes as *acentuadamente cavalheiresca* (in this context more 'horsy' than 'chivalrous'). 'Without his horse, the master of the plantation [*senhor de engenho*] would have remained incomplete ... The planter of the North-East was virtually a centaur: half man, half horse.'[16]

If it was the horse that received the most attention from the master and became something of a status symbol, then it was the ox, together with the slave, that did the real work on the plantation. In a bravura passage, written some thirty years before Lévi-Strauss offered his reflections on the names of birds and dogs, cattle and horses as revealing their metaphorical relation to humans, Freyre analysed the names given to two kinds of animals, contrasting the everyday names for oxen (Midnight, Velvet, Boy) with the more 'respectful' names for horses (Rajah, Prince, Sultan and even Bonaparte).[17]

Empire and Republic

Although it does not mention many dates, *NE* was mainly concerned with the nineteenth century. Despite the fame of *CGS*, it may be, and indeed it has been, argued that Freyre's greatest achievement is his work on the nineteenth century, which he knew more intimately than he did the colonial period.[18] If his view of the Empire and the Republic is less well known and appreciated than his portrait of colonial Brazil, the explanation may be that his interpretation of the history of the Empire and Republic is spread over a number of different books.

Freyre began his career as a historian with a study of the nineteenth century. His master's thesis, 'Social Life in Brazil', was essentially concerned with the period 1848–64. His next historical essay, 'Social Life in the North-East', was concerned with the period 1825–1925. It discussed the decline of the 'feudal' system in the 1840s and the rise of the sugar factory or *usina* in the early twentieth century, an institution that destroyed what the author called 'patriarchal cohesion'. After finishing *CGS*, which itself contains some digressions into the nineteenth century, Freyre returned to this period.[19]

Sobrados e Mucambos (henceforth *S&M*; known in English as 'The Mansions and the Shanties'), was originally planned to be part of *CGS*, but as the author confessed, 'the material overflowed'.[20] The first edition of this book, published in 1936, was a slim volume composed of seven chapters dealing in turn with the social landscape, houses and streets, fathers and sons, men and women, mansions and shanties, Brazilians and Europeans and 'the rise of the graduate and the mulatto'. The idea of the equilibrium of antagonisms underlies *S&M* even more clearly than *CGS*, but the book is more dynamic.

During his career as a deputy, Freyre had less time for writing. All the same, in 1948 he was still able to produce a book – or more exactly, a collection of four essays – about the English in Brazil. Another example of the author's anglophilia, six years after his little book *Ingleses* ('English People'; 1942), his *Ingleses no Brasil* (*IB*) focused on their influence on Brazilian culture in the age when Brazil, the major foreign market for British goods, was virtually part of their informal empire. The author wished to combat the idea that the English influence on Brazilian culture was confined to economic aspects and that intellectually speaking, French influence had been supreme. His study had much of interest to say about different kinds of people, such as engineers and consuls (and even a magician); about language, especially the introduction of English words into Brazilian Portuguese; about practices, from football to five o'clock tea and parliamentary democracy; about material culture; and about values, such as religion, comfort and punctuality (itself something of a religion, as Africans observed about Englishmen whose god was their watch). In the long list of Brazilian debts, even English ghosts with fair hair and complexion are included. In spiritualist literature, for instance, the pale and attractive Katie is perhaps 'one of the ghosts most loved by the Brazilian people', so the author claimed.[21]

Although this work is not one of Freyre's best-known books (even in Brazil), it makes an essential contribution to his project of reconstructing the development of the country in its most intimate aspects. If the impact of Britain on their culture was omitted, Freyre argued, an important link would be missing in the 'intimate history' of the Brazilians, and it would be impossible to understand their ethos.

In 1951, soon after Freyre's return to private life, he produced a second edition of *S&M*, nearly double the size of the first, with new chapters on race and class, Orient and Occident and animals and machines, as well as a new introduction and many more notes. It is this version, 'somewhat abridged', as the translator, Harriet de Onís, pointed out, that appeared in English in 1963.[22]

Finally, in 1959, came the long-announced and long-awaited third volume of the planned trilogy on the social history of Brazil, *Ordem e Progresso* ('Order and Progress'). Like the titles of the earlier volumes in the trilogy, *CGS* and *S&M*, *O&P* is surely intended to express not the simple conjunction of order and progress dreamed of by the positivists who chose this phrase for the national flag, but on the contrary, a tension between the two.

O&P is concerned with the period 1870–1920 and especially with the Republic that was proclaimed in 1889. The book itself was not the work of the 1950s alone. On the contrary, it had been planned long before. In November 1936, immediately after the publication of *S&M*, the author described *O&P* as 'already … under construction'.[23] In 1939, however, asked about his progress, Freyre said that he was still collecting material, especially the responses to a questionnaire he had sent to some survivors from this period of Brazilian history.[24]

The writer Monteiro Lobato, one of those to whom Freyre sent a questionnaire, was extremely pessimistic about the outcome of the very 'pretty' programme. It was definitely 'the most intelligent and complete attempt at social measurement that I have yet seen', he wrote, and if it worked, Freyre would have the 'elements for the solution of an enormous *Nosce te ipsum*'. Nevertheless, he believed that the only people who would reply were 'arrogant liars, those petty individuals who try to impress at every moment and do not miss the slightest opportunity to show off'.[25] In any case, the difficulty of persuading people to respond to the questionnaire (discussed below), as well as the diversion of Freyre's energies into politics, delayed the volume until 1959.

A fourth volume, on tombs and cemeteries, was announced as forthcoming in the preface to *O&P*. The project had been in the author's mind as early as 1925, but it was never completed (a sketch of what the book might have been like if it had been written will be offered later in this chapter).

CGS offered a relatively static or synchronic picture of colonial Brazil, bracketing if not ignoring the important changes that occurred during this long period. As we have seen, it has been criticized on these grounds, just like the synchronic pictures offered by the cultural historians Burckhardt and Huizinga. On the other hand, Freyre's later histories, especially *S&M*, are more dynamic or diachronic. It is for this reason among others that Freyre himself, as well as some later critics, described *S&M* as his masterpiece.[26] Together, the later volumes tell a clear story, that of the social consequences of the achievement of independence in 1822, the abolition of slavery in 1888 – the real social revolution, according to the author – and the proclamation of the Republic in 1889.

Interested as ever in the question of regions and regionalism, Freyre discussed the gradual unification of Brazil in the nineteenth century. In

CGS, he had offered a picture of Brazil as divided not only into regions but also into virtually autonomous plantations. The later volumes, by contrast, discuss national institutions such as the emperor, the army and the National Assembly as well as the protection of national industry and what the author sometimes calls 'the mystique of unity'. Unification is examined from a cultural point of view: by 1889, so he suggests, North and South shared 'beliefs, customs, sentiments, games and toys', while one kind of popular song, the *modinha*, is described as 'an important musical agent of Brazilian social unity'.[27]

As for the transition from Empire to Republic, Freyre's main thesis is one of continuity. He described the men who proclaimed the Republic as 'conservative revolutionaries', a phrase that he would later apply to himself as well. As for the regime they established, 'Its anti-monarchism was merely superficial; in great part it was essentially a continuing agent of the former regime.' A chapter of *O&P* is devoted to the cultural consequences of the transition to a republican regime, among them the replacement of England and France by the United States as the dominant cultural model.[28]

The sociocultural changes that Freyre most emphasizes in this series of books about nineteenth-century Brazil are: the decline of patriarchy; the rise of the city; changes in material culture; and the process of what he called 're-europeanization'. The following pages will focus on these four central themes.

The Decline of Patriarchy

Patriarchy is the central theme of Freyre's trilogy on the social history or historical sociology of Brazil. Like *CGS*, *S&M* is described on the title-page as an introduction to 'the history of patriarchal society in Brazil'. The town house or mansion that lends its name to the second volume of the trilogy is sometimes described as the 'patriarchal *sobrado*'. *S&M* also bears the subtitle, 'Decadence of the rural patriarch'. The book itself discussed the decline in the prestige of grandfathers and fathers, no longer formally addressed by their children as *senhor pai* ('Sir'), but as *pai* ('Father') or even *papai*, a linguistic change that revealed the emancipation of the young, whether they were sons, grandsons or students.[29]

In *O&P*, Freyre described the new regime that followed the abolition of slavery and the installation of the Republic as a system in which the patriarch of patriarchs – the emperor – was displaced, the new cult of childhood ran counter to the traditional patriarchal 'mystique' and new forms of forced labour came into existence in the newly explored Amazon region, described, in a somewhat understated manner, as 'in no way patriarchal and not always benign'. The conversion of some traditional *sobrados* into hotels was presented as a symbol of the new age.[30]

Freyre continued to be concerned with women's history, as he had been in *CGS*. The decline of patriarchy, so he suggested, offered new opportunities for women, who were at last able to leave the house on certain occasions, to go to Mass, for instance, or by the later nineteenth century to attend 'elegant colleges for ladies under the direction of French or Belgian nuns'. Some ladies of the period organized intellectual salons. In Pernambuco, the Legislative Assembly once debated the intelligence of women, a discussion provoked by a request for financial support for a girl to study medicine in the United States.[31]

However, in deliberate counterpoint to his narrative of the decline of patriarchy, Freyre also drew the attention of his readers to survivals from the past. For example, women remained legally subordinate to men. The double standard of sexual morality was still in place. 'A lady who went into the street to shop ran the risk of being taken for a prostitute.' As the author confesses, 'We Brazilians liberated ourselves more quickly from racial prejudices than from those of sex'. Hence he described the Empire as a 'liberal-patriarchal symbiosis'.[32]

Even under the Republic, in the later nineteenth century, patriarchal families were still numerous in the Botafogo area of Rio, for instance, families in which 'there was always a birthday or a christening to celebrate' in the traditional grand manner. The *sobrados* turned hotels retained something of the patriarchal tradition of hospitality. As it declined, Freyre saw patriarchy in an increasingly favourable light. It was no longer associated with 'tyranny', as it had been in *CGS*, but rather with hospitality and tables loaded with cakes and sweets.[33]

In this way, as in others, what has been described as the 'tone of satisfaction' in which *S&M* discusses the decline of patriarchy and the rise of social mobility, coexists with another tone, that of nostalgia, increasing the complexity of the author's interpretation of history.[34]

The Rise of the City

The subtitle of *S&M* refers not only to the decline of the rural patriarchs but also to the rise of their urban equivalents. In personal terms, in this book the author shifted from the rural world of his grandparents, to whom *CGS* had been dedicated, to the urban world of his parents, 'in whose still half patriarchal house, now demolished, in the Estrada dos Aflitos in Recife, a great part of this work was written', he told his readers. The theme of the book was summed up in a sentence: 'The square defeated the plantation, but gradually.'[35] *S&M* focused on this gradual process of urbanization. The house remained an important theme but it was now presented as part of a larger entity, the street. House and street (*a casa e a rua*) were complementary opposites like the Big House and the slave quarters. Once again, the author drew attention to social antagonisms. 'Sharper antagonisms arose between the rulers and the ruled, between white children brought up in the house and coloured children brought up in the street … The *muleque* – that vivid expression of the Brazilian street – was showing a growing lack of respect for the mansion as he defaced walls and fences with scrawls that were often obscene. Pissing and defecating on the doorstep of illustrious portals.' [36]

Yet the city was also presented as moderating or softening the antagonisms that it encouraged. The street, the square, the market all helped 'attenuate the antagonisms of classes and races' and create something in between, a typically Brazilian compromise that created moments or zones of 'fraternization'. Again, so the author suggested, the introduction of the tram at the end of the nineteenth century produced a kind of equality, since different social groups were now transported at the same speed and in the same vehicle, without segregation either by colour or by class.[37]

A major challenge that the old planter elite had to face was the rise of the middle class, discussed in *S&M* in one of its most famous chapters, on 'the rise of the graduate and the mulatto'. The city was the site of upward social mobility. Academic degrees were a new means to that mobility and one that according to Freyre favoured mulattos in particular, giving them access to careers in law, medicine or engineering. Degrees were new identity cards, offering their holders what he described as 'patents of sociological "whiteness"'.[38] In the later years of the Empire, several 'people of colour' were ennobled, among them the Baron of Cotegipe and the Viscount of Jequitinhonha, 'who was refused a hotel room in the United States'.[39]

Another means to social mobility was the army, a point that Freyre made by means of an anecdote told by an English visitor to Brazil in the early nineteenth century, Henry Coster. 'When Coster, in Pernambuco, asked whether the captain-major was a mulatto – a fact which, moreover, leaped to the eye – instead of being answered, he was asked "if it was possible that a captain-major should be a mulatto"'. The moral of the story was that 'The title of captain-major aryanized the darkest mulatto'.[40] The Paraguayan War (1864–70, in which the Triple Alliance of Argentina, Brazil and Uruguay invaded Paraguay) offered Afro-Brazilians what the author called 'excellent new opportunities for social advancement', rising through the ranks of the army.

Other social changes followed the mechanization of agriculture, industry and transport, encouraging the formation of a new group, the technicians, and once again offering opportunities for mulattos in particular. In this way 'The machine contributed to making a middle class of the middle race'.[41]

The process of 'democratization', as Freyre called it, was extended after the Republic was proclaimed in 1889. The army and its technical schools now became another important means of social mobility. 'With the Armed Forces playing a more active political part in the affairs of the nation, a military career offered a greater opportunity than ever for the social and political ascension of *mestiços* and humble whites'.[42]

The Empire of Things

One of the most striking and original features of Freyre's work as a social historian was his concern with what, following the archaeologists and anthropologists, we have come to call 'material culture', especially food, clothes and housing. This interest was already visible in some articles that he wrote for *DP* in the early 1920s, when he was living in Europe. Following Ruskin, he suggested, as we have seen, that travellers should read the buildings of a foreign city as clues to its culture. 'There are houses whose facades reveal a whole way of life in its most intimate details'.[43] In this way, by treating details as signs of larger changes, he escaped the dangers of antiquarianism.

IB is the book in which the author devoted most attention to what the novelist Henry James famously called 'the empire of things'. Freyre's eye for the social significance of material objects was sharpened by reading the intimate histories written by the Goncourt brothers (discussed above), and the fiction of their contemporary Marcel Proust, who was extremely sensitive to signs in general – as Gilles Deleuze noted in a brilliant study – and in particular to the social symbolism of everyday things.[44] At a time when the history of consumption was studied, if at all, only from an economic point of view, Freyre adopted a cultural approach. He was already noting the appeal of certain English goods such as tea services as signs of civilization and a means to fashion identity. It would of course be interesting to ask, as social historians do today, about the place of the female consumer in this development, but the sources available to Freyre, notably his famous advertisements, did not offer an answer to this question.

This may be the best place to present what we might call the quasi-manifesto for historical anthropology that Freyre put forward in *IB*. With characteristic lightness and informality, and alongside the immense, varied and colourful inventory of the material traces left by the English in Brazil, Freyre discussed in this book, perhaps more than in any other, some important general questions about cultural encounters and about the methods by which they might be studied. A history of the influences of one culture on another, made up of nuances and unpredictable results – and not of rigid polarities – which allows for the paradoxes, contradictions and complexities of human reality, so Freyre argued, requires the study of what he called 'meaningful details' and of historical personalities who are more or less obscure.

In fact, the way in which the so-called 'minor figures' are presented as important 'agents of British culture in Brazil', like the bakers and cooks who had spread French culture, recalls the famous phrase with which the historian E. P. Thompson announced his work on the English working class of 1963. What he intended, Thompson said, was to 'rescue from the enormous condescension of posterity' the humble artisans, weavers and agricultural labourers who lived amid the anxieties and tensions of the emerging Industrial Revolution. With similar emphasis, Freyre tells us that the most famous personalities and the most grandiose events tell only part of the story. What he wanted, he claimed, was to rescue the memory of those figures who are important despite being obscure, and who 'would not be able to emerge from the tomb of the archives by themselves'. His intention, as he put it vividly, was to salvage from historical forgetfulness 'the Cinderellas of history, considered in its less grandiose aspects; studied through people who despite being forgotten in the obscure and dusty corners of factories, workshops, locomotives, steamers and machines, also contributed a great deal to the encounter and interpenetration of different cultures'. As he insisted, humble machine operators, stokers, mechanics, engineers, actors, magicians and auctioneers can reveal the deepest aspects of cultural influence, expressed in domestic trivia, in the everyday life of workshops, trams, mines and so on.[45]

These trivial details, when meticulously investigated, are exactly the ones that can lead us to an understanding of a reality which is elusive. So we see that, in the 1940s, Freyre was already arguing along the same lines as Carlo Ginzburg in the 1970s, when the latter developed his ideas about the importance of meaningful details in his famous article on clues. According to Ginzburg, in the same way that the art historian Giovanni Morelli showed that trivial variations in the shapes of ears or fingernails could reveal who painted a given picture, and distinguish original paintings from fakes, 'small signs' can lead us to larger phenomena.[46]

Coincidentally, it was an art historian who seems to have reinforced the lesson about the 'infinite significance of trifles' that Freyre had first

learned from the British essayists.[47] Now, studying the encounter between the British and Brazilian cultures, he noted once again that from a
wider historical perspective, 'the trifling details of the relations between
peoples' reveal themselves as having 'more human significance than grand
events'.[48]

The two French Bastides, the geographer Paul Arbousse-Bastide and
the sociologist Roger Bastide, had already recognized Freyre's gift for get-
ting at the global by starting from the individual, his ability for evoking
the 'lost atmosphere ... of the old Brazil' by paying attention to the tiny
details that acquire great significance in his art of 'a painter or a novelist'.[49]
Quoting the French critics and enthusiastically taking over this analogy, Freyre defended in *IB* the idea that history would gain a great deal
if historians would appropriate the 'technique' or the method of portrait
painters whose art consists in paying special attention to the particular, the
individual and the detail in order to attain the universal. Freyre's interest
in this idea became even clearer when he referred to the work that the art
historian Lionello Venturi had just published in 1947, *Painting and Painters*.[50] Basing his arguments on Venturi's view of the portraits by Titian, El
Greco, Rembrandt and Raphael, Freyre suggested that his own ambition
was to be the Titian or the El Greco of Brazilian history. In other words,
his wish was to paint the psycho-sociological portrait of the Brazilian people, starting not from an ideal or abstraction to be imposed on reality, as
Raphael had done, but instead, like Titian and El Greco, from the record
of a 'particular moment' in the life of the sitter.

Inspirations

Venturi had shown that the value of the portraits by Titian, El Greco
and Rembrandt did not consist only in their beauty, but in their ability
to evoke the life and atmosphere that surrounded their sitters, recording
specific moments and 'elusive impressions'. It was this ability that Freyre
wished to imitate. If he were successful, he argued, his picture of Brazilian
society would combine the social with the personal, the universal with
the individual. It is interesting to note in this regard that Titian's paintings
were praised as well as criticized in his own time for their spontaneous,
fluid, and even rough style, which gave them an air of incompleteness as
if, although they had been 'created with a good deal of effort, they seemed
not to have required any at all!'[51] It seems appropriate that centuries later,
Freyre's work should have attracted both praises and criticism for more or
less the same reasons.

Taking even further Arbousse-Bastide's analogy between Freyre's art and that of a novelist, he drew once more on Proust – who from *CGS* onwards had been presented as his model for the project of writing a true novel (*roman vrai*) – and praised him for being a portrait painter in the Titian style. Again, in *IB*, he praised the gift for portrait painting of the British novelists and writers of memoirs such as James Boswell, Rebecca West and others. They are also masters to be imitated, he suggests, because they are exemplary in their 'technique of fixing on the significant detail', in which the social and the psychological appear to be penetrating each other. [52]

Two sources that Freyre considered to be particularly valuable for the recovery of 'the trifling details of the relations between peoples', as he put it, were newspaper advertisements and the correspondence of British consuls, since both of them revealed aspects of the past about which official documents are generally silent. In these sources, which had been 'marginalized by political history', he found a substitute for the field work of the anthropologist.[53]

Freyre was not alone in his interest in the history of Brazilian material culture. The architect Lúcio Costa, for instance, who later became a friend, was already studying colonial art and architecture in the 1920s. Some local historians had interested themselves in the history of vernacular architecture or furniture, at least occasionally.[54] It is also worth noting that on his return to Recife after studying abroad, Freyre had collaborated with his brother Ulisses Freyre in a study of the material culture of the Afro-Brazilians of the city, enlisting the help of a photographer and an artist in order to record forms of slipper, pipe, knife, window and so on.[55]

It is likely that Franz Boas also played a role, sooner or later, in inspiring Freyre's interest in material culture. In his diary-memoir, *TM* (discussed above), describing the time that he spent in museums on the occasion of his first visit to Germany, in 1922, Freyre wrote that he 'asked the advice of the great Boas about these contacts of mine with living museums' (in other words, museums of ethnography).[56] Whether this comment dates from 1922 or later, it recognizes the importance of Boas in this field.

As we have seen, Boas led the anthropological debate on the relative importance of race and culture. His contribution to the study of material culture was also of great importance.[57] Boas began his career working in museums. Before coming to the United States he worked in the Museum für Völkerkunde in Berlin, and it was in the course of cataloguing exhibits there that he became interested in the artefacts of the North West Coast of America. After his arrival in the United States, he was active in the Field Museum at Chicago (1895) and the American Museum of Natural History in New York (1896–9).

It was in the course of his museum work that Boas came to formulate some of his leading ideas. For example, he caused a sensation in the American museum world by criticizing the organization of exhibits in the Smithsonian Institution in Washington. The Smithsonian exhibits were arranged in the way customary at that time, according to the assumption of what Boas called 'a uniform systematic history of the evolution of culture'. What he preferred was what he described as the 'tribal arrangement of collections' in 'culture areas' (a term derived from the German word *Kulturkreis*, used by Boas's own master, Adolf Bastian).

The North West Coast Hall which Boas arranged in the Museum of Natural History in New York illustrates his approach and his view of objects as so many witnesses to the nature of the culture in which they were produced. Exhibits, he argued, could 'show how far each and every civilization is the outcome of its geography and historical surroundings'.[58] Indeed, an object, according to Boas, could not be understood 'outside its surroundings' – or as we often say today, outside its context.

To illustrate this point, Boas took the example of a pipe. 'A pipe of the North American Indians', so he argued, 'is not only a curious implement out of which the Indian smokes, but it has a great number of uses and meanings, which can be understood only when viewed from the standpoint of the social and religious life of the people'. Hence Boas liked to show 'life groups' in the museum, with waxworks of people in the act of using the objects, in order 'to transport the visitor into foreign surroundings', to allow an appreciation of an alien culture as a whole.[59]

Between 1886 and 1900, Boas paid regular visits to the North West Coast and worked among the Kwakiutl (as he called the people now known as the Kwakwakawakw), collecting, sketching and taking photographs of objects (baskets, jars, aprons and so on), as well as observing the local way of life. He was particularly interested in the custom of the 'potlatch', a festival which illustrated 'the method of acquiring rank' by 'the distribution of property'. He quoted the Kwakiutl phrase describing themselves as 'fighting with property', and emphasized the destruction of blankets, canoes and sheets of copper by rival chiefs. One chief would initiate the destruction, 'indicating his disregard of the amount of property destroyed' and so compelling his rival to follow suit until one of them had nothing left.[60]

The work of the original and eccentric American sociologist Thorstein Veblen also inspired Freyre's social approach to material culture. Veblen's famous *Theory of the Leisure Class* (published in 1899) was essentially concerned with differences within a given society, but it resembled the work of Boas in the close attention it gave to material culture. Veblen used the work of Boas on the potlatch, transforming the detailed ethnography into the generalization that 'the motive that lies at the root of ownership is emulation'. He devoted a whole chapter of his *Leisure Class* to the theme of 'dress as an expression of the pecuniary culture', viewing his own culture with anthropological eyes and arguing that top hats and walking sticks for men, like high heels and corsets in the case of women, were 'insignia of leisure' because they were conspicuous hindrances to what he called 'useful exertion', in other words physical labour. [61]

It is likely that Freyre first read the *Leisure Class* around 1939, when he discussed, in a seminar paper given in the United States, the way in which Brazilian plantation owners displayed their wealth via the fine clothes and jewels of their wives and even their slaves, 'a good example, as it has been suggested to me', Freyre commented, 'of what Thorstein Veblen, the economist, called "conspicuous waste"'. A newspaper article in which he discussed the value of Veblen's ideas for cultural history followed in 1943.[62] As we shall see, his reading of Veblen encouraged Freyre to discuss the social symbolism of everyday objects in the second, enlarged edition of *S&M* as well as in *IB* and in *O&P*.

Freyre was also well aware of the contributions to the history of material culture made by two of the most famous architectural critics of the twentieth century, older members of the same generation as himself: Lewis Mumford (discussed above) and Sigfried Giedion. Giedion was a Swiss, another generalist, but as much a supporter of Modernism (and his friend Le Corbusier) as Mumford was an opponent of both. He is perhaps most famous for a social history of technology, *Mechanisation takes Command* (1948), in which he argued that 'for the historian there are no banal things', since 'tools and objects are outgrowths of fundamental attitudes to the world'. Freyre described this study as 'one of the most notable books of our time'.[63] Characteristically ignoring the gulf between their attitudes, he cited the work of both Mumford and Giedion impartially. He saw them as kindred spirits who reinforced his ideas rather than nudging him in a new direction.

This interest in material culture in general and houses in particular is visible not only in Freyre's trilogy on Brazilian history but also in a number of shorter studies, among them a lecture on the mansions of Rio Grande do Sul (1940), a study of a French engineer who worked in Brazil in the nineteenth century (1940) and a much later study, *The Brazilian House* (1971).[64]

Like Brazilian material culture itself, Freyre's history of it diversified when he reached the nineteenth century. He was able to insert many more material objects into his intimate history, thanks to new sources such as advertisements in the newspapers, announcing auctions or attempting to persuade the reader to buy named brands, often foreign, ranging from Colt revolvers to Scott's Emulsion.[65] He referred to the history of gas lamps, lifts, postcards, the *palmatória* (used to beat slaves and children) and various means of transport such as steamships, carriages, trains, trams and bicycles.[66] He had most to say, though, about food and clothes, houses and their furnishings.

Food and Clothes

Freyre's account of Brazilian food and clothes became more complex when it reached the nineteenth century.

CGS had devoted considerable attention to the regional cuisine, especially the famous sweets of Pernambuco. A year later, at the conference on Afro-Brazilian culture that he organized in Recife in 1934, Freyre made a point, as we have seen, of inviting some women to cook samples of these sweets in the atrium of the theatre in which the conference was held. Five years after that, he published an essay entitled *Açúcar; em torno da etnografia, da história, e da sociología do doce no Nordeste canavieiro do Brasil* ('Sugar: concerning the ethnography, history and sociology of the sweet in the sugar-cane region of the North-East, 1939) a text that also included recipes.

On the other hand, when he came to the nineteenth century, Freyre's history of Brazilian food and drink included a long list of innovations introduced from abroad, mainly from England and France, among them biscuits, bread, roast beef, cheese, ale and porter, tea, ice cream, wine, champagne, cocktails, gin fizz and whisky.[67] A fascinating but tantalizingly brief passage introduced readers to the social history of snuff.[68]

Clothes, especially male clothes, also had an important place in Freyre's evocation of nineteenth-century Brazil. Hats, for instance: top hats, bowler hats, derby hats, straw hats and so on, replacing the traditional three-cornered hat. Dinner jackets, cashmere jackets (replacing the traditional calico), overcoats, ties, gloves and especially shoes. The formal dress of upper-class boys, which made them look like miniature adults, is used as evidence that they were deprived of their childhood, while the history of underwear is used to argue for the rise of informality, or as Freyre calls it, 'democratization', at the end of the nineteenth century, when 'Ladies substituted drawers and knickers for their many underskirts'. [69]

True to his long-standing interest in the history of the body, Freyre discussed hair and beards. The beard, the 'patriarchal beard' as he sometimes called it, was discussed in *O&P*, which includes a drawing by the author himself illustrating twelve of the styles of beard most common in the nineteenth century. In the case of women too, 'the mystique of hairdressing developed into a virtual cult', leading the author to describe the 'obsession with hair at the end of the Second Empire' as 'a pyschosis worth the attention of a social psychiatrist'. [70] Women's clothes may seem to be neglected by comparison, despite occasional references to turbans, shawls, lingerie and jewels, but the importance of foreign models for the lifestyle of the upper classes in the late nineteenth century is exemplified by women who lived on sugar plantations but ordered their dresses, hats and shoes from Paris.[71]

Following Veblen, Freyre described objects such as parasols, gloves, boots, whips and umbrellas as so many signs of identity or as part of the 'insignia' of the upper class.[72] One of his most striking examples is that of the walking stick (*bengala*), made from 'noble materials' and furnished with 'symbols of authority' such as the head of a lion or an eagle. He added an anecdote about a plantation owner on a tour of Europe who abandoned his visit to the National Gallery of London because he could not bear to leave his stick behind in the cloakroom.[73]

Houses and Furniture

As might have been expected from the author of *CGS*, Freyre continued to have much to say about housing. Indeed, he suggested that – even when it was diminished in its functions and in competition with other buildings in the city – 'the house of the nineteenth century continued to exert more influence than any other factor on the social formation of the urban Brazilian. The mansion, more European, produced one social type; the shanty, more African or Indian, produced another.'[74]

The urban equivalents of the Big House were the mansions or *sobrados* of Recife, Rio de Janeiro and Rio Grande do Sul. In Recife, so Freyre suggested, 'urbanization proceeded vertically'. Nineteenth-century *sobrados* sometimes had five or six floors. 'The warehouse and slave quarters were on the first floor; the business offices on the second; on the third and fourth, the drawing room and the bedrooms; on the fifth, the dining rooms; on the sixth, the kitchen.'[75]

The dwellings of the urban poor, the *mucambos* or 'shanties' also received attention. As we have seen, Freyre's interest in shanties was not purely historical, but linked to the concern with urban problems that he had shown when working for Estácio Coimbra in the 1920s. His defence of these *mucambos* as a form of housing well adapted to the ecology of the North-East appeared in 1937, a year after the first edition of *S&M*, a book that also made the point that 'the person who lived in a shanty built on a dry, well-drained spot, with a double roof to protect him from the rain, was and is more hygienically housed in the tropics than the rich man and especially the rich woman of the old-fashioned mansion', distanced as they were from the air and the sun.[76] On the other hand, the author admitted that shanties built in the mud were a health hazard, like new forms of slum that Freyre also mentions, such as the tenement (*cortiço*) where conditions were almost 'subhuman', and, more briefly, the now notorious *favelas* on the hillsides of Rio de Janeiro.[77]

Freyre was not the only writer to take an interest in *sobrados* and *mucambos*, but his only serious rivals in this respect were two novelists. His friend José Lins do Rego included in his 'sugar-cane cycle', mentioned earlier, the story of *O Moleque Ricardo* ('The Boy Ricardo'; 1940), in which the protagonist left the plantation for Recife and lived in a *mocambo* in a swamp in which on rainy days the mud came into the house, unpleasant smells were strong and vultures strutted about outside – altogether a less rosy picture than Freyre's, even allowing for the community spirit of the street's inhabitants.[78]

As for the *sobrado*, it played a central role in another Brazilian classic, Erico Veríssimo's *O Tempo e o Vento* ('Time and the Wind'; 1949–62), a historical novel of epic proportions set in the Deep South of Brazil in a small town in Rio Grande do Sul ('Santa Fé', not too far from the author's native Cruz Alta).[79] More exactly, a particular *sobrado*, belonging to the Cambará family, may be described as a leading figure in the novel; as one of the characters remarks, 'for me the *Sobrado* is like a person.' The house – its bedrooms, study, dining-room, kitchen and parlour (*sala de visitas*) – forms the location for a protracted siege during one of the region's civil wars, as well as the scene of regular visits from family and friends and of animated conversations on Positivism, Marxism, Modernism and regional politics. Set at the turn of the nineteenth and twentieth centuries, the novel describes the process of modernization via the story of the entry into the house of gas, electricity, the telephone and the gramophone.

Although Freyre did not visit Rio Grande do Sul until he was nearly forty, he quickly developed an interest in the history and the architecture of the region, viewing the local *sobrados* and giving a lecture in which he compared and contrasted them with those of Recife. He made the acquaintance of Veríssimo, collaborated with him in editing a journal and published a review of the first part of *O Tempo e o Vento*. Despite making a number of criticisms, he recognized the novel's 'moments of grandeur', compared it with the 'intimate history' that he appreciated and practised and concluded that it was a 'great book' in the manner of Balzac.[80]

One characteristic of Freyre's thought was that it developed by taking ideas that he had discussed in one context and re-employing them, suitably adapted, in other situations. In his studies of the nineteenth century, for instance, Freyre extended his social history of the Big House and the slave quarters not only to the *sobrado* and the *mucambo* but also to a wide range of new urban and suburban forms of building.

One of these was the *chácara*, a small house in the country or the suburbs, which the elite of São Paulo preferred to the *sobrado*.[81] Another was the 'cottage' or the 'bungalow'. In their design as in their name these houses followed English – or in the case of the bungalow, Anglo-Indian – models. Somewhat later there arrived the fashion for the chalet in Rio and Recife, 'imported from Switzerland and inappropriately situated even in commercial streets'.[82] Freyre's concern with the interior spaces of houses, described and analysed in *CGS*, reappears in his discussion of the nineteenth century, from the social history of the hall – introduced by the English at the beginning of the nineteenth century – to the rise of the private swimming pool around the year 1900.[83]

Public buildings such as the railway station and the hotel also received some attention. *O&P* described nineteenth-century hotels as 'cathedrals of a new cult' (though less so or at any rate later in Brazil than elsewhere), linking their rise to the decline of patriarchal hospitality. The author lingered lovingly over the splendour of their 'rococo' decorations, huge mirrors, for instance – decorations that were imitated in private houses – and pointed out how hotel restaurants, saloons and terraces became new centres of sociability, whether for business or for pleasure.[84] Freyre's interest in traditional furniture remained apparent in the later studies. References to the 'patriarchal table' were particularly frequent, its size a symbol both of large families and of traditions of hospitality.[85] Chairs, sofas and beds made from local woods such as *jacarandá* and *vinhático* were once again lovingly described.

However, change, both for the better and for the worse, is the central theme in this account of nineteenth-century material culture. *IB* noted, for instance, the replacement of traditional wooden shutters by glass windows in shops and houses alike in the early nineteenth century, as a result of the sweeping government decree of 1808 which ordered the operation to be completed in six months. On the grounds that this replacement was going to liberate Brazil from these so-called 'Gothic' or 'Turkish' symbols of 'barbarism', and give it a symbol of modern European civilization in return, many urban houses lost a characteristic feature of the colonial period.[86] The decline of traditional furniture under the Republic, replaced by iron beds and upholstered armchairs imported from abroad, was also described by the author in a tone of regret.[87] Even Freyre's novel or 'semi-novel' *Dona Sinhá e o Filho Padre* ('Mother and Son'; 1971) included comments on furniture, notably the passage in which one of the main characters, returning to Brazil from France late in the nineteenth century, noted with distaste some recent changes such as the iron bed and 'the invasion of Brazil by the so-called Austrian furniture that was coming to replace *jacarandá* and *vinhático*'.[88]

Other changes noted by Freyre include the rise of the fork, the mirror and the mosquito net and the increasing use of English furniture, tea tables, tea sets and cutlery. Water closets arrived in Brazilian cities, together with showers and 'sumptuous porcelain urinals', first in the houses of English merchants and then in those of the Brazilian bourgeoisie,.[89] The 'vogue of the piano during the Second Empire' was analysed from a sociological point of view. 'The huge grand piano became a status symbol, a manifestation of taste and social prestige, whether in the aristocratic villas of the suburbs, the middle-class city homes or the mansions of the more cultivated planters'.[90]

It seems that no object was too small to escape the sharp eye of the social historian who once remarked on the need to include even pencils in a history of Brazil.[91] *O&P* includes discussions of palm-leaf fans, dolls, lace napkins, iron frying pans, heavy wooden pestles to grind coffee and earthenware water coolers that gave the water a distinctive taste, according to one of the most sensuous and 'proustian' memories of his informants.[92] It was in this context that Freyre praised the British traveller Maria Graham for her remarkable powers of observation, 'eyes that remind us of those of the best English novelists, such is her capacity for noticing significant details'.[93] The eye for domestic details may well be a predominantly feminine one, illustrated by Jane Austen and George Eliot as well as by Graham. All the same, the phrase, 'capacity for noticing significant details', is one that applies equally well to the author himself.

Unlike the few earlier studies in the field, such as Clado Ribeiro de Lessa's study of Brazilian furniture, Freyre's work was not antiquarian.[94] As a sociocultural historian he was concerned to read domestic objects as expressions of the attitudes and values of the period in which they were made and used. For example, Freyre treated the hammock and the rocking-chair as symbols, or more exactly as materializations, of the voluptuous idleness which Brazilians in general, so he suggested, had inherited from the planters of Pernambuco. Dining-room tables for twenty persons symbolized patriarchy, large families and generous hospitality. Again, *S&M* noted the hierarchy of materials for furniture; only noble woods such as *jacarandá* could be employed to furnish noble houses. Yet again, the author described *O&P* as 'an attempt to reconstruct the essential social order existing between 1870 and 1920 through its value system, reflected in material things.'[95]

The integration of a multitude of concrete details into a general picture was assisted by the author's interest in the analysis of the process of cultural change. *IB*, for instance, introduced two important ideas in this respect. The first of these is the idea of a semi-oriental old regime in houses and furnishings. The second key idea is that of a revolution, a 'gentle, velvet revolution' (*revolução branca, macia*), inspired by the British.[96] As Freyre insisted, the majority of changes that the English promoted did not imply 'the total abolition' of what existed before. In contrast with the French, who are described as 'radical or absolute revolutionaries', the English are great experts in quiet revolutions.

In this way, as Arbousse-Bastide once commented, Freyre presented material objects as expressions or translations of 'immaterial realities, of mentalities'. His book on the activities of the French engineer Louis Vauthier in Recife during the 1840s – which dealt with the intriguing and unexplored question of the way in which an essentially material activity like building bridges could leave immaterial marks on a culture – was greeted by Bastide with the greatest enthusiasm. The author, so he argued, had the great merit of 'revealing all the sociological interest of technical contacts, even the most humble in appearance', and of showing that 'the most modest French artisan always brought a certain view of life along with his tools.' On the other hand, as Bastide also pointed out, Freyre sometimes reversed the equation and presented 'ways of thinking' as the result of 'ways of living.'[97] His attitude to the relation between material and immaterial culture offers a typical example of the author's frequently criticized conceptual 'fluidity', his habit of looking at the same phenomena from a variety of points of view that he never tried to reconcile in a definitive synthesis. In this context, it is worth noting that the English historian Asa Briggs (a great admirer of Freyre, as we have seen), once commented that the alternative to conceptual fluidity is 'conceptual rigidity', which also suffers from disadvantages, such as restraining the 'historical imagination.'[98]

Re-europeanization and Reaction

Where *CGS* had stressed the interaction between three cultures, the Amerindian, the European and the African, Freyre's studies of the nineteenth century emphasize what he describes as the 're-europeanization' of Brazil, a concept he used to discuss both immigration and the following of cultural models.

During the nineteenth century, there was a new wave of Portuguese immigrants to Brazil. New kinds of European immigrant also entered the country, first the Germans, especially in Rio Grande do Sul, and then the Italians, both there and in São Paulo. They were welcomed by the government not only as workers, on the coffee plantations, for instance, but because they contributed, according to the prevalent ideology of the period, to what was described as the 'aryanization' or 'whitening' of Brazil.[99] The new immigrants made some impact on Brazilian culture, 'Italianizing' it in some respects, for instance, but they came to be assimilated in the long run. Hence the major theme of Freyre's discussion of re-europeanization was the influence of English and French culture on upper- and middle-class Brazilians.

The old cultural regime still in force around the year 1800 bore many traces not only of Africa but also of what the Freyre liked to call the 'Orient', including both the 'Moorish' or *mourisco* tradition of Portugal and some imports from the Far East. The Moorish tradition, so he suggested, still affected social life. In North-Eastern Brazil in 1800, people lived their lives in a rhythm that was 'more oriental than European', in city streets that were narrow 'like the streets of the Moors' (*mouriscamente estreitas*), while upper-class women were confined to the house, sitting with their 'legs crossed in the Moorish fashion', observing street life through the shutters, as in the world of Islam.[100]

S&M devoted an entire chapter to the contrast between 'Orient and Occident', beginning with a long list of Asian influences on Brazil that were absent from the rest of the Americas: 'the palanquin ... latticed windows, women's shawls and turbans, the whitewashed or brightly painted house in the form of a pagoda ... tiles, Indian mangoes and palm trees, the elephantiasis of the Arabs, couscous ... the cinnamon of Ceylon, the pepper of Cochin China, the tea of China, the camphor of Borneo, the nutmeg of Banda, the fabrics and porcelain of China and India, the perfumes of the Orient'.[101]

After 1800, however, European influences competed with these traditions. Take the case of Freyre's 'velvet revolution', which he also described as the 'anglicization' of Brazil. This anglicization is presented as a consequence of an encounter between unequals. On many occasions this encounter is described by the author in the strong language of 'imperialism', 'domination', 'shock', 'invasion', 'flood', 'penetration' or 'conquest'. At times, as in the case of the introduction of glass windows into Brazilian houses, Freyre argued that cultural change came about as a result of economic imperialism and that the British were in a position to impose their supplies without waiting for local demand.[102]

The irony of this violent imposition – as Freyre liked to emphasize because it revealed history as disconcertingly complex and challenging the beliefs in absolute progress or absolute failure – is that what was aimed at keeping the Brazilian economy 'passively colonial' ended up being beneficial to its intellectual culture. As Freyre had argued in *NE*, an absolutist, all-or-nothing or black-and-white approach is 'an obstacle to historical perspective' as well as 'a danger for assessments of society'.[103] The case of the official decree imposing windows was similar to the case of the railways, which revealed both the good and the bad sides of foreign capital. On one side, it is true that they served 'slavocrat' monoculture and British capitalism; but on the other side, they simultaneously opened the way for democratic polyculture and for laws in defence of workers.[104]

In the case of the imposition of windows, the fact is that alongside glass for windows and doors, large shipments of lenses for spectacles and telescopes also arrived in the busy ports of Recife, Salvador and Rio de Janeiro. These novelties represented something positive for the country. For example, 'The import of reading-glasses', Freyre pointed out, 'coincided, in fact, with an increase in the production and the imports of books, journals, magazines and newspapers.' That is why he wrote of the decree of 1808 as provoking a revolution that was not only 'aesthetic' but also 'psychological'.[105]

However, the poorer and more backward culture sometimes resisted the richer and more powerful one, so Freyre liked to argue. If it is true that in most cases the irresistibly seduced Brazilians fell for English products and habits – spending summer in the mountains, playing and listening to the piano, attending public lectures on art, politics, chemistry etc. – it is also true that the penetration of Brazil by England sometimes encountered passive resistance. One example that he mentioned was the relative lack of impact of the British suffragettes, who found very few followers on Brazilian soil.[106]

In similar fashion, in *O&P*, the author told a double story. Many cultural and social changes of the period were presented as the result of the Brazilians' desire to imitate foreign models. In architecture, for example, Freyre described and denounced the tendency – in the name of progress – to abandon the tradition of decorating houses with coloured tiles. He had particularly harsh words for the Church, for adopting the Gothic style of architecture. These words, from a former follower of Ruskin and Morris, may sound like treason, but they are actually in the spirit of Morris, since the author's point is that a local tradition that was well adapted to the environment was now abandoned in order to follow a foreign model.[107] Other examples of the inappropriate imitation of foreign models include the vogue of English ghosts, of 'blonde, blue-eyed dolls' (whose owners were usually brown-eyed brunettes), and in the case of men the fashion for dark woollen suits made in London or Paris but worn in the tropical sun as status symbols – a typical example of the hindrances to 'useful exertion' described by Veblen.[108]

Freyre continued to take pleasure in shocking some of his readers as well as pointing to the active role played by women in the process of social and cultural change. Where *CGS* had reflected on the civilizing mission of the Indian and African women who had introduced the Portuguese to bathing, as we have seen, *O&P* noted the educational function of the French *cocottes*, 'instructors in civility, courtesy and refinement', who taught their young clients about literature, dancing and wine as well as the art of sex. At the end of the book, the author mischievously and mysteriously included the messianic anti-republican leader António Conselheiro in a list of Brazilians who had contributed to national progress.[109]

However, the story told in *O&P*, as in *IB*, is not a simple account of one-way 'influence'. On the contrary, the author noted the existence of cultural traffic in both directions, 'transculturation', as he sometimes called it (using a term coined by his Cuban contemporary Fernando Ortiz), or employing a favourite expression of his, the 'interpenetration of cultures'.[110] A few items of Brazilian culture were taken up in Europe. Monkeys and parrots were definitely not the only Brazilian items that the Europeans took home in their luggage. *Guaraná* was a success in France, for instance.[111] It is true that 'unambiguous expressions of Brazilian influence on the British are rare', he admitted, but examples of the 'invader' being penetrated by the 'conquered' culture could be found. The Brazilian taste for eating sweets with cheese, for instance, was taken back home, while some Englishmen could be found drinking Brazilian rum (*cachaça*) and eating dried meat (*carne seca*). They came to have a particular love for furniture made from *jacarandá*, some of them were converted to Catholicism and others were even seduced by the 'sweet taste of the sin' of owning slaves and by the comfort of being carried by them in 'palanquins'.[112]

O&P also found a place for nationalist reactions against foreign influence, notably in the brief chapter devoted to 'the tropical challenge to Brazilian civilization', especially concerned with what the author called 'sanitary or medical nationalism'.[113] He noted medical criticisms of unhygienic garments and the gradual shift towards wearing clothes more appropriate to a tropical climate, a favourite topic of his own in later years, for Freyre himself belonged to this critical tradition.[114] More generally, he criticized the imitation of foreign models as producing an artificial culture in which people paid too much attention to self-presentation, to playing an elegant role in the theatre of everyday life, whether in the domain of clothes or in that or public speaking. He made about Brazil a point that would be central to Yury Lotman's interpretation of eighteenth-century Russia, in which the preoccupation with styles of behaviour among the nobility was explained as a consequence of the rapid Westernization of elite culture in the age of Peter and Catherine the Great.[115]

In short, as in the case of *CGS*, Freyre's studies of Brazil in the nineteenth century expressed not the simple nostalgia often attributed to the author but a certain ambivalence, related to his perspectivism. The social and cultural changes that he discussed were viewed in some ways and on some occasions as progressive, a liberation from patriarchy and a fixed social hierarchy. However, they were also viewed in a negative light as the abandonment of valuable local traditions in order to follow inappropriate foreign models that invaded the country in the age of informal or economic imperialism.[116] In a sense, we might describe Freyre as both a Westernizer and the equivalent of a slavophile, the antagonism between the two elements in his make-up co-existing in a somewhat precarious equilibrium.

Taking some steps towards a possible resolution of this conflict, Freyre presented the reception of many foreign products, whether objects, institutions or ideas, not as purely passive but as active and transformative. In the case of clothes, Freyre commented on what we might call, following Japanese precedent, the 'double life' of middle-class Brazilians at this time, wearing English clothes in the street but traditional clothes at home.[117] The invading French, English and also North American products were often domesticated, brazilianized or tropicalized. Pianos, for instance, originally imported, came to be made in Brazil from local wood.[118] As for the music itself, the opera by Carlos Gomes on an Amerindian theme, *O Guarani* (1870) was discussed as an example of the tropicalization of Italian models.[119]

Again, according to Freyre, the design of English furniture was modified by local craftsmen, often slaves, as if responding to differences in cultural tradition. Drawing one of his favourite contrasts, between hard and soft, straight and curved, Freyre called attention to the disappearance of 'those English straight lines' (*essas linhas anglicanamente secas*), 'the English style of furniture becoming more round (*arredondando-se*) in the Brazilian climate' (just as the hard sounds of Portuguese became softer in African mouths). It was 'England being modified in Brazil'.[120]

It is worth noting that this fascinating passage about furniture echoes but also inverts a passage from a book by the brothers Goncourt about French society in the age of the Revolution. In this study, they described

as a 'revolution' within the French Revolution the introduction of the ancient Greek and Roman style of furniture, a reaction against the rounded
forms (*rondissements*) of the rococo style that was associated with the old
regime. The new style, with its straight lines (*lignes raides, droites, mal hos-
pitalières, inexorables*), was linked to 'revolutionary taste'. In other words,
even furniture had a place in the history of ideas.[121]

Although hybridization contributed to the resolution of the conflict
between Brazilian traditions and European culture in its nineteenth-century forms, it is worth noting that the author did not see this resolution or
synthesis as complete. On occasion, he associated hybridization itself with
Brazilian traditions and suggested that these traditions were threatened by
Euro-American cultural imperialism.[122]

Sources

Like *CGS*, the author's later work stands out for its use of an unusually
wide range of sources, including gravestones, lithographs, photographs,
literature (the novels of Machado de Assis, for instance) and even popular
songs (*modinhas*).[123] The testimony of travellers such as the Englishmen
John Luccock and Henry Coster and the Frenchmen Auguste de St-Hilaire,
Pierre Denis and Georges Clemenceau was used to good effect in the same
way that their predecessors had been used in *CGS*.[124] The later books also
drew on new kinds of source, including some that were virtually untapped,
notably advertisements, autobiographies and questionnaires.

Freyre made skilful use of the evidence of advertisements, employing
them in order to show that the furniture of the *sobrados* in the deep South
of the country increasingly resembled those of the North. Tea services, for
instance, came into use, even in the area where drinking *chimarrão* (the
local word for *maté*) from a gourd (*cuia*) through a metal straw (*bombilla*)
was, as it remains, a popular activity.[125]

O escravo nos anúncios ('The Slave in the Advertisements'; 1963) is
Freyre's fullest study of this kind of source, based on 10,000 advertisements
describing runaway slaves in the hope that someone would recognize and
recapture them.[126] It emphasizes the value of advertisements in giving
access to 'the most intimate habits and sentiments of our ancestors' and
studying them from 'an anthropological point of view', but also notes the
need for source criticism.[127] This essay was a pioneering attempt at a history of the slave body, using the descriptions of the runaways to compare
and contrast different ethnic types and to note the deformations of the
body by physical labour and punishment.[128] It is as remarkable a *tour de
force* as the study of the physical condition of recruits to the French army

in the nineteenth century, made by Emmanuel Le Roy Ladurie and his colleagues in 1972.[129]

However, the greatest variety of uses of this source occurs in *S&M* – advertisements for carriages, for machinery, for French cooks and so on – while the closest analysis is that made in *IB*, where the growing vogue for English products such as crockery, cutlery and furniture among the Brazilian middle classes is charted in detail on the basis of advertisements for auctions.

Freyre's own practice of journalism made it especially appropriate for him to exploit this source, but he was not the first person to see its potential. Santo Thyrso, a Portuguese diplomat and writer whom he read in his youth, had described advertisements in newspapers such as the 'agony column' in *The Times* as sources for 'the history of humanity'. One of Freyre's favourite novelists, George Meredith, was also aware of the interest of advertisements, while North American historians and anthropologists had begun to use them in their work.[130] What can reasonably be claimed, though, is that Freyre exploited the potential of this source for social and cultural history more fully than anyone had done before him.

A similar point may be made about Freyre's use of autobiographies or more generally of personal documents, what are coming to be known as 'ego-documents'. An enthusiastic reader of autobiographies and memoirs, as we have already noted, he was already in the 1920s seeking out people who had lived in the imperial age, including the widow of Joaquim Nabuco, in order to listen to their reminiscences.[131]

As we have seen, Freyre regretted the relative absence of Brazilian autobiographies and journals, though he did his best to compensate for this absence in his own case. By the nineteenth century, however, some notable exceptions to the rule can be found. A foreigner who lived in Brazil from 1840 to 1846, the French engineer Louis Vauthier, kept a diary which Freyre edited and published, as he published the memoirs of Félix Cavalcanti, a relative of his and the head of a patriarchal family.[132]

However, Freyre's most extensive use of this kind of source was in *O&P*. In order to make this study of the recent past, Freyre invited around a thousand Brazilians who had been born between 1850 and 1900 (the date of his own birth) to write their autobiographies. These texts were supposed to be structured around the answers to a questionnaire about their social attitudes and memories of everyday life. The result was 'a kind of sociological spying into the souls of Brazilians' that occasionally produced 'something like the secrets of the confessional'. Besides the customary sociological enquiries into place of birth, education, occupation, religion and so on, respondents were asked some typically Freyrean questions about toys, dances, fashions, and 'the heroes of your childhood', especially the aviator Santos Dumont. They were also asked about their reading, whether they read Nietzsche, for instance, or Herbert Spencer.[133]

In April 1939 Freyre was thinking in terms of a hundred or more responses. By December of that year, he had 170 responses but was hoping for 200 to 300. In 1943 he still needed more testimonies from Minas and São Paulo and was complaining about the difficulty of obtaining them (his request was turned down by President Vargas, for instance). The book that was eventually published in 1959 refers to 'nearly 300 usable replies', though it lists only 183 respondents.[134]

As in the case of advertisements, Freyre was not the first scholar to make use of this kind of source in order to write social history, but he exploited it with unusual effectiveness. He knew the work of the Polish sociologist Florian Znaniecki, who made use of 500 'directed' autobiographies of peasants and workers preserved in the Polish Sociological Institute in Poznań, as well as the study of personal documents by the American psychologist Gordon Allport, whom he had met at the famous UNESCO conference discussed earlier.[135]

How Freyre chose his sample of Brazilians he does not tell us. The group is presented as 'typical' of the wider society, and includes people from different regions and social classes, but the presence of family and friends suggests that the sociologist relied on his personal network in order to elicit responses. So does the prominence of his native region. Of the female respondents (twenty-one out of the 183) seventeen came from the North-East and thirteen from Pernambuco alone.

Sociologists of a quantitative bent will doubtless be horrified by the informal and unsystematic way in which Freyre collected his 'sample', but it should be noted that the results were never supposed to be a basis for statistical analysis. They were individual testimonies, no more and no less. What Freyre was doing in the middle of the twentieth century, generating his own sources, resembles what oral historians began to do a generation later.

Take the case of one of the best-known British oral historians, Paul Thompson. As he explains in *The Voice of the Past* (1978) he found oral evidence to be particularly precious for the history of the family, in his case the family in Edwardian Britain, since other sources for this history of intimacy were generally lacking. Like Freyre, though more systematically, he chose informants on the basis of a statistical sample, so that 'the men and women recorded broadly represent the regions, city and country, and occupational social classes of early twentieth-century Britain as a whole.'[136] If Thompson's work is superior to Freyre's in this respect, it

might also be said that Thompson and other oral historians might have
learned something from Freyre's questionnaire, its emphasis on the sense-
impressions of childhood, for instance. In some cases, incidentally, Freyre did collect oral testimonies. Three
of his female respondents are described as 'illiterates', among them the
professional medium Maria Joaquina da Conceição, who came from the
interior of Pernambuco, while as early as 1932, he had interviewed an ex-
slave in order to discover how the old regime looked from below.[137]

Social Science or Literature?

Like CGS, Freyre's studies of the nineteenth century are both works of
literature and contributions to the social sciences, to anthropology, sociol-
ogy and psychology as well as to history. The approach followed in these studies remained personal and essayistic. Even O&P, despite its size – 961 pages of text in the fifth edition
– is described by Freyre as an 'essay'. The tone remained colloquial and
conversational but became more confident, with fewer references to the
secondary literature than was the case in CGS, when the author was making his academic début. Freyre's love of lists continued to be apparent, and
the lists themselves became longer and longer – one of them continues
for three pages without a full stop.[138] The organization, clear and tight in
S&M, loosened and became more obscure in O&P, in which the mass of
examples taken from the personal testimonies escaped control and threat-
ens to overwhelm the reader. In one chapter of the latter book (the seventh
in the English translation), the author seems to rely on free association as
the principle of organization, moving from business to businessmen, to
hotels, to drinks, to the historian Capistrano's 'almost Germanic devotion
to draft beer' and so on. Of course, as we noted in the case of CGS, the
way in which to organize a study of social history has always presented
a problem, but in this case the author faced it with conspicuous lack of
success.

Freyre's concern for 'sensuous history', one of the most spectacular
features of his early work, as we have seen, remained very much in evidence in the later books. NE presented the image of the plantation owner
'on horseback, in black boots with silver spurs, his whip in his hand', with
his people 'receiving his blessing as if he were a king', or still more vivid,
the image of a Wanderley naked from the waist up but wearing his riding-
boots and spurs in the Big House. [139]

The sounds of the past continued to reverberate through these studies. S&M noted the sound of traffic on stony roads, church bells, people

shouting in order to be heard at the end of the huge dining-table, Wanderley's spurs clinking and the arrival of a stranger in the house 'immediately followed by the rustle [*ruga-ruga*] of departing skirts' and the sound of slippers on the stairs.[140] In *O&P*, we hear the sound of whistling, of pianos, of 'the carriages which, on party-giving days, clattered noisily through the iron gate opened only on special occasions; the street calls of the fruit, fish and poultry vendors; the beggar's rattles; the cries of the mendicant nuns or the ordinary beggars asking for alms "for the love of God"; the band playing marches on the way to a ball or to the bandstand in the cathedral square; the guitar serenades' and so on.[141]

The smells of the past were also evoked. 'The whiff of cinnamon coming from a house meant either a wedding or a baptism, or that a son had just returned from Europe or the capital. The smell of lavender meant a new baby. The smell of incense, mass in the chapel or a death in the family.' The smell of bedrooms in the *sobrado* was described as 'a mixture of semen, urine, unwashed feet and armpits, cockroaches and damp'.[142] *O&P* noted the bad smell of churches 'heavy with the accumulated odours of centuries of worship by persons of all colours and from all walks of life', as well as the special taste of water drunk from earthenware jars.[143]

Vivid as it is, Freyre's work on the nineteenth century also drew on social theory. Compared to *CGS*, it made less use of anthropology and more use of psychology. *S&M* discussed fetishism, pathology, perversion, the 'psychoanalytic function' of confession, Carnival as psychological liberation and Lusophobia as a kind of 'sublimation' of or 'compensation' for parricidal fury.[144] Freyre referred to Freud and still more often, to his old favourite Havelock Ellis, Freud's popularizer in England. However, the author now seemed to be more aware than before of the problems of drawing on psychoanalysis. His remarks on the value of confession as a kind of 'mental therapy', for instance, referred to 'some of the less controversial generalizations of psychoanalysis'.[145]

O&P was less psychological in approach, despite references to the 'psychosis' of self-hatred and to the ideas of the psychoanalyst Erik Erikson, whose controversial study of the young Martin Luther had been published two years earlier.[146] Although Freyre suggested that the display of hair during the Empire deserved the attention of a psychoanalyst, he also implied a certain scepticism by adding that the analyst would need to be 'convinced of the possibility of extending his science to the psychosocial intimacies of a still recent past'. Elsewhere, Freyre seems to have deliberately avoided the phrase 'inferiority complex', preferring to speak more sociologically of status insecurity.[147]

Freyre continued to make considerable use of sociology. Indeed, *O&P*, with its social survey or public opinion poll of the past, may be regarded as his most sociological essay on history. He also continued to make references to sociologists, not only to Thorstein Veblen, as we have seen, but also to Georg Simmel, William I. Thomas and Max Weber.

Critiques

Freyre's studies of nineteenth-century Brazil received a good deal of acclaim. *NE* was translated into Spanish (1943), French (1956) and Italian (1970), while *S&M* appeared in English in 1963, Italian in 1972 and German in 1982. *S&M* has been described by some readers, among them Fernand Braudel and the Brazilian historian Evaldo Cabral de Mello, as 'the best of his books' (towards the end of his life, the author also expressed the view that it was better than *CGS* in some ways).[148] *IB*, despite its unjustifiable neglect since, was the best-seller of the week in 1948.

CGS might be described as having appeared at the right moment, when miscegenation was a topical issue. *O&P*, by contrast, was published in the 1950s, the age of Kubitschek, when economic development, about which the book had little to say, was the main national concern. All the same, thanks doubtless to the fame of its author, *O&P* sold 10,000 copies in about six weeks on its publication in 1959. An abridged English version was published in 1970. The planned Italian and German translations do not seem to have materialized, owing doubtless to the book's formidable length.[149]

However, both *S&M* and *O&P* became the object of serious academic criticisms, more or less from the moment that they were published. Sérgio Buarque de Holanda, for instance, criticized *S&M* for its treatment of patriarchy as a realistic description of a particular society rather than as an abstract model or ideal type to which reality never corresponds exactly. Like some critics of *CGS*, he faulted Freyre for extending a model that might be valid for the North-East, or part of the North-East, to the whole of Brazil. Sérgio also made the point that patriarchy, which Freyre seemed to assume was distinctively Portuguese, was actually an example of 'European and baroque models'.[150]

As for *O&P*, it has often been criticized. One reviewer drew attention to the book's lack of a clear organization, comparing it to 'An Asian bazaar after it has been looted'. The American Brazilianist Thomas Skidmore published a review essay that, despite a respectful tone and a characterization of the work as a 'tour de force', focused on its defects, describing it as 'ill-proportioned', 'chaotic' and lacking in 'sustained analysis', as well as paying insufficient attention to chronology and to institutions. The author's method was described as insufficiently rigorous and the volume was compared at one point to a 'historical scrap-book'.[151]

Among the most common criticisms of Freyre's later work, as in the case of *CGS*, were his impressionism, his unmethodical or anti-methodical approach, his lack of discipline, his emphasis on the picturesque, his distaste for statistics and his tendency to present hypotheses or even speculations as if they were documented facts.

As in the case of *CGS*, a recurrent criticism of the later work concerned Freyre's emphasis on the North-East or even its Pernambuco-centrism, a criticism that was sometimes made in a crude manner and sometimes, as in Sérgio's case, for instance, in a subtle and nuanced way. Freyre's response to the criticism of his provincialism was ingenious even if it was not completely convincing. He argued, for instance, that the North-East was the most truly Brazilian part of Brazil, as well as drawing on Georg Simmel's distinction between the form and the content of a society, claiming that he had been speaking about fundamental forms, while his critics had only noticed the more superficial differences of content. Sérgio rejected Freyre's use in his defence of Simmel's distinction between social form and social content, claiming that form and content were not properly distinguished in *S&M*.

In any case, the emphasis on the North-East became less and less justifiable in the volumes concerned with the nineteenth century, as Rio de Janeiro and later São Paulo increased in economic and political importance at the expense of Recife and Salvador. In a preface to a new edition of *CGS* in 1949, defending himself against the charge of provincialism, the author had claimed that *O&P* would be 'dedicated to the study of the South and the Centre rather than the North of Brazil', but he did not fulfil his promise. By the early twentieth century the city of São Paulo had a quarter of a million inhabitants and the influx of Italians in particular led to many cultural changes. *O&P* mentions these changes, but only briefly. As we have seen, the author relied heavily on North-Eastern respondents to his questionnaire.[152]

Again, as Skidmore and others have pointed out, the author's focus on patriarchy, even taking its 'disintegration' into account, became progressively less useful as a key to Brazilian society as he approached the present. Planned in the 1930s as a history of the family, the trilogy was gradually turning into a sociocultural history of Brazil, but the original programme was never sufficiently adapted to the change of aim. An accurate title for what Freyre actually wrote might be 'Aspects of Brazilian Cultural and Social History with special reference to the upper and middle classes in the North-East'. Such a title for a wide-ranging essay intended for general readers would have been insufferably pedantic, but the actual titles, especially that of *O&P*, invite misunderstanding.

Another serious criticism concerns Freyre's interpretation of the social changes of the nineteenth century. Like the author's description of the old slaveholding regime, this interpretation has been criticized as too rosy, as placing too much emphasis on the opportunities for social mobility, which were in fact limited, and for underestimating the importance of the obstacles, including race prejudice, especially in the cities of the South – a point that will be discussed more fully below in the context of the idea of 'racial democracy'.[153]

Despite these criticisms, Freyre's studies of the nineteenth century include some of his best work. One reason for this was that the richer sources fitted his intimate approach better than the sources for the colonial period did. Another reason was that his location in the declining North-East detached him from a conventional Grand Narrative. For a historian from the South, in contrast, there might have been a temptation to write a more triumphalist account of order and progress that failed to note the tension between these ideals.

If the merits of *S&M* are widely appreciated, it remains true that *NE*, *IB* and *O&P* are not read or appreciated as much as they should be. It is especially unfortunate that the fascinating study of the British in Brazil has never appeared in English. As for *O&P*, its length, lack of clear organization and a style that sometimes verges on self-parody discourage even Brazilian readers. It might be characterized, as Henry James famously described the classic Russian novel, as a 'loose baggy monster'. All the same, *O&P* is an extremely suggestive essay, full of new ideas about the culture and society of the late Empire and the early Republic. Nearly half a century later, some of its suggestions are still to be taken up and developed. In a paradox that Freyre would not have enjoyed, his approach was developed most systematically in a four-volume *History of Private Life* in Brazil, apparently inspired not by his work, which is rarely mentioned in the text, but by the *Histoire de la vie privée* planned by the French historians Philippe Ariès and Georges Duby.[154] Had Freyre's work been taken more seriously by his compatriots, a Brazilian history of private life might have appeared earlier than the French one.

Tombs and Shallow Graves

The fourth volume in the sequence, long announced, was to have been a study of the history of death, burial and cemeteries. The title, *Jazigos e covas rasas* ('Tombs and Shallow Graves'), followed the model of *CGS* and

S&M, using material objects as symbols of social classes and juxtaposing aristocrats and plebeians. Freyre was already interested in this topic in the 1920s, as an early essay reveals.[155] Although the book was described in 1959 as 'about to be published', it never appeared; the manuscript, or the notes for it, appear to have been lost. All the same, as in the case of the planned but unwritten history of Brazilian childhood, it is possible to reconstruct at least some elements of the project.

CGS, for instance, illustrates a general point about the cohesion of the patriarchal family with the example of burials in the Big House, 'the dead remaining under the same roof as the living', indeed 'controlling and keeping watch on the living', remaining part of the family. The author speaks of a 'domestic cult of the dead' that is reminiscent of ancient Greece and Rome.[156] Later books continued the story. *IB*, for instance, described the English cemetery in Recife. The introduction to the second edition of *S&M* discussed the future book, describing the monumental tomb as the extension of the *sobrado* and the shallow grave as the extension of the *mucambo*. The tomb, decorated with 'dragons, lions, angels, owls, palm fronds, saints, the Virgin and Christ' as if they were defending it, was viewed as an 'expression or ostentation of the power, prestige and wealth of the survivors, the descendants'; 'a dead man is in a certain sense a member of society'.[157] The parallel between the author's descriptions of the decoration of aristocratic tombs and walking-sticks as insignia of power is worth noting.

O&P introduced the themes of religion and hygiene. It discussed the practices of burying members of religious fraternities in shallow graves under the church floor or in a vaulted gallery (practices that were prohibited in 1850 as a danger to health), as well as the secularization of cemeteries, a measure proposed by Joaquim Nabuco in 1879.[158]

Occasional references elsewhere in Freyre's writings offer further indications of the shape of the planned book. An old interest in African rites of burial in Brazil was stimulated by Freyre's opportunity to observe tombs in Africa itself in the course of his visit to Ultramar and led to a short essay on Afro-Christian tombs.[159] Notes in his books show that Freyre was aware of the journalist Jessica Mitford's *The American Way of Death* (1963) as well as the study of *Death, Grief and Mourning* (1965) by the British anthropologist Geoffrey Gorer.[160] The burials and the graves of the poor would doubtless have been described in more detail had the book been completed.

Instead, Freyre turned in the 1970s towards social theory, the subject of the following chapter.

6   The Social Theorist

If Gilberto Freyre had written nothing but his trilogy on the history of Brazil, his reputation as a sociocultural historian or a historical anthropologist would still be secure. His most solid and enduring intellectual achievement was his work as a historian; his contribution to social theory did not have the same importance. All the same, he did make a serious attempt to use his knowledge of the past both to understand and to influence the present and the future. The student at Columbia University who had once attended the lectures of Franklin Giddings on sociology and Franz Boas on anthropology made a distinctive contribution to both disciplines as well as working for their establishment in Brazil.

It is true that Freyre was not a great inventor of new concepts – with the rather unhappy exception of Luso-Tropicalism, to be discussed below. His originality showed itself in other ways, partly in his view of sociology, in which he was swimming against the mainstream tendencies of his day, and partly in his gift for what Michel de Certeau used to call 're-employment'. He had the gift of taking up concepts and extending and adapting them to fit new situations. Whether we speak of him as contributing to sociology, social theory or social thought, it remains true that some of his leading ideas remain provocative, good to think with – and sometimes against.

Despite his determination to preserve his independence and live from his writing, Freyre was – briefly – a professor of sociology on three occasions in his career: at the Escola Normal of Pernambuco in 1929; in the Law Faculty of Recife, where he gave a course on regional sociology in 1935; and at the new University of the Federal District in Rio de Janeiro, from 1935 to 1937, where he was also professor of anthropology.[1] Out of the courses that he gave in these institutions developed his *Problemas brasileiros de antropologia* ('Brazilian Problems of Anthropology'; 1942), a collection of essays and his *Sociología* ('Sociology'; 1945). Although this last work was written as an introductory textbook, it departed from the usual objective tone of such introductions and offered a personal and at times a polemical statement in favour of a particular approach to the subject. It went through five editions, and the author was working on a sixth edition as late as the 1980s, revising his ideas on the subject almost until the end of his life.[2]

The variety of Freyre's contributions to cultural and social theory is suggested by their titles: *O mundo que o Português criou* ('The World that the Portuguese Made'; 1940); *Região e Tradição* ('Region and Tradition'; 1941); *New World in the Tropics* (first published in English, 1959); *Arte, Ciência e Trópico* ('Art, Science and the Tropics'; 1962); *The Racial Factor in Contemporary Politics* (published in English, 1966); *Sociología da medicina* ('Sociology of Medicine'; 1967); *Contribuição para uma sociología da biografia* ('Contribution to a Sociology of Biography'; 1968); *Além de Apenas Moderno* ('Beyond the Hardly Modern'; 1973); *Rurbanização: que é?* ('What is Rurbanization?'; 1982) and *Insurgências e Resurgências* ('Revolts and Revivals', 1983).

In this shelf of studies, most of them published after *O&P* and illustrating the final phase of the author's intellectual career, discussing the present and emphasizing the actual and potential contribution of Brazil to human civilization, Freyre made contributions to the sociology of food, clothes, housing, cities, the countryside, medicine, religion, language, biography, literature, leisure, time, modernity and postmodernity. He also gave a course in Recife on the sociology of art at the end of the 1950s, at a time when the topic had not attracted much attention. Space does not allow the discussion of these contributions topic by topic, so what follows will focus on the whole at the expense of the parts and on the structure of his ideas rather than their development, emphasizing his views on sociological method, place, time, mixture, racial democracy, Luso-Tropicalism and the tropicalization of medicine, architecture and of social theory itself.

Social Thought, Social Theory, Sociology

It is more exact to speak of Freyre's 'social theory' or 'social thought' rather than his 'sociology', since, as he emphasized in a characteristically brilliant and egocentric essay, the author both was and was not a sociologist. He considered himself at least as much an anthropologist as a sociologist, and sometimes more, and in any case he identified himself as a writer rather than a scholar.[3] His admiration for Lafcadio Hearn, whom he praised for being able to see much more 'as a simple writer, than many sociologists', testifies to Freyre's pride in being a writer and also, perhaps, to his doubts about the knowledge that sociology could convey.[4] His disagreement of the 1950s and 1960s with the sociologists of the University of São Paulo, was among other things, as we shall see later, a conflict between two conceptions of sociology, one more open and humanistic and the second more professional and scientific.

For this reason it might be appropriate to speak of Freyre's contribution to 'social theory', or indeed to 'cultural theory' – were it not for the fact that he was as suspicious of formal theory as he was of formal method.[5] He both employed and discussed general concepts such as race, culture, patriarchy, regionalism or democracy, but in an intuitive, unsystematic way. Hence the charge of 'theoretical nihilism' brought against him, as we have seen, by Rodolfo Ghioldi.

It has already been pointed out that Freyre liked to think comparatively. His studies of Brazil were never inward-looking. On the contrary, the author made comparisons and contrasts with North America, the Caribbean, Britain and even on occasion with China and with Russia – another huge country, with serfs in the place of slaves. He also saw an analogy between the debates over 'Westernization' in Brazil and in Russia. Indeed, in his first preface to *CGS*, he compared himself to the Russian Romantics, in other words to the so-called 'slavophiles' who believed that Western ideas and practices needed to be adapted to local Russian circumstances. Once again, these comparisons were not pursued in a systematic or a sustained manner. In some cases, such as the reference to China, they are little more than metaphors (it should be remembered that Freyre was, among other things, a poet). In this respect, as in many others, he was deliberately impressionistic. The vaguer term 'social thought' might therefore be more appropriate than 'sociology' or 'theory' when describing his work, despite his early contribution to the establishment of sociology in Brazil.[6]

Freyre's interest in social thought went back a long way in his career. As an adolescent he seems to have read some of the writings of Comte, Spencer and Marx. Spencer, in particular, who was regarded, together with Comte, as the 'Aristotle of the modern world' and enjoyed more fame and influence in his time than Karl Marx, had a deep impact on Freyre, as he had on a whole generation, some of whom participated in a kind of cult that extended from Russia to the United States.[7] As the social theorist and economist John A. Hobson put it in 1904, one year after Spencer's death, 'we are all Spencerians today, whether we like it or not.'[8] As a young man Freyre read Spencer a great deal – 'at home and even in the trams' – using books that he could find in his father's library.[9]

Following what was probably his first contact with the discipline, he discovered that his appreciation for Spencer was shared by writers he admired such as Flaubert, Maupassant and Lafcadio Hearn, who confessed he revered him as a 'Godfather'. Besides inspiring Freyre with his idea of the equilibrium of antagonisms and its essential role in the doctrine of evolution, as we have noted, Spencer's acknowledgement of the complexity of reality and 'the relativity of all knowledge' (the title of one of the chapters in his *First Principles*), left deep marks on the young man. As we mentioned in the last chapter, he clearly stated both in *NE* and in *IB* that only relativism (*o critério do relativo*) was appropriate to deal with complex social issues; while an absolutist, all-or-nothing or black-and-white approach was an obstacle to 'historical perspective' as well as a 'danger for social analyses'.

According to Spencer, when we consider the limits of human intelligence in grasping the complexity of reality, 'the more defensible position' for dealing with the antagonisms (whether religious and others) by which people are divided 'is that none are completely right and none are completely wrong'.[10] Or, as he put it in the draft of the prospectus of his *First Principles*, 'truth generally lies in the co-ordination of antagonistic opinions'. To the ones who criticized what they saw as the 'fundamental incoherence' and inconsistencies of his thought in his attempt to make impossible compromises – between realism and idealism, for instance or between empiricism and transcendentalism – Spencer replied that the 'spirit of no-compromise' (when both sides in a dispute 'claim the whole truth') was the great obstacle to any mode of reconciliation or combination. As he put it, those who espouse one of two antagonistic views of reality get into the habit of taking these as the only alternatives, and are 'puzzled by a hypothesis which is at once both and neither'. However, since there is almost always 'an element of truth' in conflicting doctrines, Spencer concludes, 'the controversy ends by combination of their respective half-truths'.[11]

Freyre took courses in sociology at Baylor, and at Columbia University he took two more courses by Franklin Giddings (a follower of Spencer and one of the first professional sociologists in the United States), as well as two by the anthropologist Franz Boas. His copy of the *Outlines of Sociology* (1917) by F. W. Blackman and J. L. Gillin is heavily underlined, as if he read it relatively early in his career. Both Giddings and Boas he later described as his 'masters', together with four others; Robert Park, the founder of the Chicago school of urban sociology; William Thomas, best known for his concept of 'the definition of the situation' and his study, with Florian Znaniecki, of the Polish peasant in Europe and America; the Indian Radhakamal Mukerjee; and Lewis Mumford, Freyre's model as a cultural critic as well as 'master of us all on matters of urban sociology'.[12]

Besides Boas and Roquette-Pinto, the anthropologists whom Freyre admired included Boas's students Melville Herskovits and Ruth Benedict, together with Bronisław Malinowski (described as 'a man of science with touches of almost Conrad-like romanticism'), George Pitt-Rivers (whose ideas about the clash of cultures are regularly cited in *CGS*), Alfred Radcliffe-Brown (praised for the balance he achieved between fieldwork and theory) and, later, Edward Evans-Pritchard, whom he once visited in Oxford.[13]

Sociologists whom Freyre studied relatively early include the 'classics', Emile Durkheim, Max Weber and Vilfredo Pareto, once viewed as a kind of 'Holy Trinity' of sociology. He seems to have had a particular sympathy for Thorstein Veblen, whose love of shocking his readers he shared and whom he appreciated as a social scientist 'with a scientific and even a poetic imagination'.[14] There were also the Germans Hans Freyer, Karl Mannheim, whose perspectivism he appreciated, and Georg Simmel, whose distinction between social form and social content he discussed more than once and with whose essayistic and impressionistic approach he naturally felt an affinity (even if much of Simmel's work was virtually inaccessible to him because he read German only with difficulty).[15]

Freyre kept up his wide reading until late in his life. For example, he was familiar with the work of gurus of the 1960s such as Elias Canetti, Erik Erikson, Liam Hudson, R. D. Laing, Marshall McLuhan and George Steiner. In the case of anthropology, he was aware of studies by Clifford Geertz, Georges Balandier, Dell Hymes and Marshall Sahlins. In sociology, he cited (among others) C. Wright Mills, Daniel Bell, Peter Berger, David Riesman and the Frenchmen Gabriel Le Bras, Georges Gurvitch, Jean Duvignaud and Alain Touraine.

All the same, it is probably fair to say – thinking of the annotations that he made in his books – that in later life, like most of us at that age, Freyre read either in order to acquire information or to confirm positions that he already held, rather than to learn about radically new ideas, which had interested him so much when he was younger. In the 1960s, for instance, he discovered the work of Marshall Sahlins on Fiji, but what he underlined was the remark about the new fashion for houses of European style, 'unsuited to the native climate and mode of life', a point he had already been making about Brazil in the 1930s.[16]

To have attended a few courses of lectures is not exactly a professional training, even if these lectures were later supplemented by wide reading.[17] Freyre seems to have learned most of his sociology in the course of teaching it. His sense that he was unprepared for teaching is revealed by his writing to Melville Herskovits in 1935 to ask for information about courses in anthropology and sociology in the United States and about important books on the subject. Herskovits sent him the information about anthropology that he had requested, including his own course outlines and a textbook by Alfred Kroeber, and put him in touch with Arthur J. Todd (the Chair of the Sociology Department at Northwestern University), who sent similar information about sociology.[18]

Although he became extremely well informed about trends and controversies, he may therefore be described as an autodidact in the social sciences.[19] His work shows both the strengths and the weaknesses of this form of learning: unusual breadth and originality on one side and a certain lack of rigour on the other. It was only when he was in his forties, with CGS and S&M behind him, that he published general discussions of sociological theory and method.

Freyre's Discourse on Method

Sociología was and remains a rather unusual textbook. A massive work in two volumes of 772 pages, it was, as the author warned his readers, 'not always orthodox'.[20] He later described the book as 'irregular, disorganized and unacademic'.[21] The fundamental concepts of sociology are not explained one by one, as one might expect in a text written to introduce students to a new subject. The work begins with a discussion of the limits and limitations of sociology. In this respect it is probably unique among sociological textbooks. Ironically enough, the book was dedicated not to sociologists but to two anthropologists, Heloisa Alberto Torres and Edgar Roquette-Pinto.

As Freyre confesses, his book was really an 'essay', quite an appropriate genre for a discipline that was so far from having the 'conceptual precision' of a science and the 'mathematical rigour' that ends divergences.[22] In any case, the book is not even an 'attempt at systematic sociology with didactic pretensions'. On the contrary, it aims, as he firmly announced, at being a 'companion of the anxieties and preoccupations' of teachers and students alike – and without 'keeping them away from the basic problems of the material' – to suggest the great complexity of the discipline and to widen their perspectives, awakening their interest in the 'neighbouring fields', even in literature.[23]

The great educationalist Anisio Teixeira, who had invited Freyre to teach sociology in 1935 at the University of the Federal District that he had just founded, introduced the book with the greatest enthusiasm, praising it for being 'wisely unsystematic' in the 'still obscure but extremely promising world of the science of social reality'. In a private letter, he also praised its conversational tone, capable of seducing and instructing the readers: 'with books like this, Gilberto, one might do without schools. For to communicate knowledge it is essential for it to become personal, human, warm and imaginative in this way'.[24]

More exactly, *Sociología* is a sequence of separate essays. Some of these essays examine different aspects of the discipline (regional or 'ecological' sociology, historical sociology, the sociology of art and literature and so on). Others are concerned with the relation of sociology to neighbouring disciplines, notably biology, psychology and history, as well as to literature. Long sections are devoted to some of the author's favourite themes, notably biological and cultural hybridity, so important in *CGS*, and material culture, especially status symbols, already discussed in *S&M*. Once again, the author emphasized the importance of significant details, noting that 'things that are dumb or generally despised by cultural sociologists' offer eloquent testimony about a given culture if they are studied with care.[25]

Freyre developed his ideas about sociology in dialogue with alternative views, notably those of the Marxists on one side and contemporary North American sociology on the other. His attitude to Marx was complex and even ambivalent. He admitted that the scientific development of sociology owed much to the work of Marx and Engels as well as that of Comte. He also praised the author of *Capital* as an 'artist', a 'poet' and an apocalyptic visionary who offered a synthesis of the sociocultural experience of the Industrial Revolution. On the other hand, given Marx's view that sociology is simply part of political economy, as well as his general stress on economic factors, an autonomous sociology needs to be in a certain sense 'anti-Marxist', more social and more cultural.[26]

Much more extensive is Freyre's polemic against the dominant style of sociology at the time that the book was published, the North American style represented by Pitirim Sorokin, Talcott Parsons and Paul Lazarsfeld (though he praised the last for being less exclusively devoted to quantitative methods than some of his colleagues).[27] Freyre, who claimed to have more affinity with anthropologists, geographers and historians, sometimes criticized American sociology as simplistic and once described William Thomas as 'so penetrating that he does not seem to be a North American sociologist'.[28] The American paradigm, as we might call it, is criticized on three main counts: it is too scientific, too pure and not historical enough.

In the first place, Freyre criticizes the claim of sociologists to impersonality and scientific objectivity, ideals that he regarded as both impossible and undesirable. He mocked Sorokin for his ambition to be the Thomas Aquinas of sociology, in other words to produce a summation of orthodoxy. Faithful to his early perspectivism, what Freyre emphasized was precisely the variety of human points of view.[29] Associated with his critique of pretensions to objectivity is Freyre's polemic against abstraction and against quantitative methods, to which he prefers impressionistic descriptions packed with concrete and sensuous details. He used to recommend students of sociology to begin by observing everyday life in the street in which they lived, the number of houses and their inhabitants, the lighting, the paving, the hygiene, the security and so on.

As for the critique of sociological 'purity', Freyre began by emphasizing what he called the 'insufficiency of sociological methods'. Sociology, he wrote, should be 'polytheist' rather than 'monotheist'. 'It has to be mixed or amphibious in order to concern itself with both nature and culture.' Sociology depends on its neighbours: anthropology, ecology, social history, folklore, psychoanalysis, biology and other disciplines. The triple approach to society through sociology, psychology and history was particularly illuminating.

For these reasons, individuals on the margin of the profession, 'semi-sociologists' as he called them (thinking of himself) had a special contribution to make. Indeed, to understand society, creative writers were more useful than most sociologists. In the manner of his early praise of Lafcadio Hearn, he regarded José Lins do Rego (whom we have already discussed) as a leading sociologist of the North-East, and claimed that 'a novelist such as Proust ... painted a better psychological-sociological portrait of the French aristocracy at the end of the nineteenth century and the beginning of the twentieth than all the disciples of Durkheim together.'[30] In similar fashion, in his preface to *CGS*, he referred to Henry James as a social historian.

North American sociology was also criticized for lacking a historical dimension (Freyre would later recognize the contributions of George Homans and Barrington Moore). A historical perspective was necessary, he argued, not only for the analysis of social change but also in order to base general theories on the totality of human experience rather than that of one generation. Freyre viewed his own work, especially *CGS* and *S&M*, as examples of applied or historical sociology or anthropology just as much as contributions to social or cultural history.

We should note that Freyre did not condemn the American style of sociology *in toto* but made exceptions. His old teacher at Columbia University, Giddings, was an illustrious and memorable example. Indeed, his humanist sociology was extremely inspiring for Freyre's development. As we already mentioned, he recognized with regret later in life that he had left his old mentor 'in the shade' in contrast with Franz Boas, whom, since *CGS*, he had never failed to acknowledge as a great inspiration of his work. It was through Giddings – who had given himself the role of the systematizer and the popularizer of the ideas of his master Spencer – that Freyre learned, as we pointed out, about the centrality of the equilibrium of antagonisms in the doctrine of evolution, an idea that he would tropicalize and make essential for his interpretation of Brazil.

However, Giddings' importance for Freyre's development was more than that of a mediator, since his whole style was extremely appealing to the young student. It was a great 'intellectual pleasure' to hear this 'world-famous' sociological theorist who had something of a writer in him and managed to combine science with art, as the mature Freyre recalled when looking back to his Columbia days. He had the gift of being exact and precise but, at the same time, 'as expressive as if he were … an oral essayist' (*um ensaísta oral*), he remembered. The fact that Giddings had a career in journalism alongside his academic life might explain the vivid style that captivated readers and listeners alike. His lectures, according to the testimonies of his students, were both 'logical' and full of passion, and being 'unsystematic' they offered space for heated debate and passionate criticisms concerning current issues. The enforcement of peace and the improvement of basic education were among the problems to which the Columbia professor was devoted. He was also impressive in his breath of knowledge and interests, and his capacity for making social science relevant to current debates. 'No one who heard him lecture could ever be narrow in his outlook … Professor Giddings is a splendid illustration of the usefulness of the sociological theorist in practical life', as a critic put it.[31]

The role of history and literature in his sociological work was also remarkable and Freyre could not be indifferent to the way in which his teacher brought a discipline that was normally dry and cold close to what was his eternal passion, literature. The great facts of social evolution, wrote Giddings in one of his books, could also be found in historical sources, newspapers and literature. For this reason, alongside authors such as Spencer and Adam Smith, his pupils were encouraged to widen their reading to include the essayists William Hazlitt, Daniel Defoe, Joseph Addison and Richard Steele, as well as Plutarch, Homer, Herodotus, Gibbon, Spinoza and even passages from the Bible.[32]

No wonder, then, that in his *Sociología*, Freyre referred to Giddings as one of the important exceptions in the general ahistoricity of American sociology, a fact that – regrettably – was not, as he said, generally acknowledged by scholars.[33] Perhaps it is not too far-fetched to imagine that Freyre had his teacher's work and lectures in mind when he wrote his own sociological textbook and brought such figures as Proust, Shakespeare, Samuel Johnson and Ernest Renan to the attention of students of this subject.

North American sociology was faulted not only for a lack of a sense of time but also a lack of a sense of place. Freyre's views on the region, which we are about to discuss, were an important element in his social thought.

The Importance of Place

As we have seen, Freyre was devoted to his region – the Brazilian North-East in general and his native Pernambuco in particular. While he was living outside Brazil he developed an enthusiasm for regional writers such as Thomas Hardy on 'Wessex', Maurice Barrès on Lorraine and Hermann Sudermann on East Prussia. He also discovered the regionalist politics of Charles Maurras. Other thinkers whom Freyre admired were interested in regions and their ecology. Boas, a former geographer, remained interested in what he called 'ecotypes', while Roquette-Pinto once called Euclides da Cunha 'an admirable ecologist' for his vivid description of the 'backlands' (*sertões*), in other words the deserts of North-Eastern Brazil.[34] These readings sensitized Freyre to the ecological element in the work of thinkers he encountered later, such as Patrick Geddes, Lewis Mumford, Radhakamal Mukerjee and Carl Sauer. After his return to Brazil, Freyre's regionalism was apparent, as we have seen, in the foundation of the *Centro Regional do Nordeste* (1924), in the volume he edited on the culture of the North-East (1925) and in the organization of a Regionalist Congress (1926), as well as in his most famous book, *CGS*.

The fullest exposition and defence of Freyre's regionalism is to be found in *Region and Tradition*, a collection of essays explaining the position of the group of North-Easterners in which he played a central role. In this collection, the regionalism of the North-East was defined against the Modernism of São Paulo and the group of artists and writers surrounding Mário de Andrade, discussed above. The culture of the North-East was both described and celebrated: the popular culture (cuisine, folklore, vernacular architecture) and the works of art and literature inspired by that popular culture, from the paintings of Cícero Dias to the novels of José Lins do Rego (who wrote a preface for the book). The purpose of the collection is to defend this regional culture, under threat in an age of europeanization, 'the mechanization of life' and what Freyre sometimes described as 'yankeezization' (*ianquização*).

One threat to regional culture that preoccupied Freyre was urbanization. As we have seen, he was already interested in urban problems in the 1920s, with Lewis Mumford as his guide. He was worried about the rapid growth of Recife, and interested in policies that would foster an equilibrium between the city and the countryside, with mixed areas in which rural values might survive. These areas are reminiscent of the 'conurbations' recommended by Patrick Geddes or the 'rurbanization' described by some North American sociologists (curiously enough, Freyre did not cite Geddes in his *What is Rurbanization?*). Thinking as usual in terms of hybridity, he analysed as well as recommended a mixture or compromise between urban and rural, as he did between regional and national, traditional and modern.[35]

Time

The discussion of tradition brings us to Freyre's life-long preoccupation with time. When he was at Columbia University, one of the ideas of Franklin Giddings that impressed him most, as we have seen, was the idea that the struggle between old and new is never won. One of his most vivid memories of his visit to Oxford was that of students wearing gowns but riding bicycles, an image that symbolized for him a happy marriage between tradition and modernity. In his master's dissertation, Freyre already noted the co-existence of different times in mid-nineteenth-century Brazil. 'In their material environment and, to a certain extent, in their social life, the majority of Brazilians of the Fifties were in the Middle Ages: the elite only was living in the eighteenth century'.[36] In *S&M*, Freyre discussed the process of industrialization of Brazil in terms of the 'europeanization of work' and the imposition of a 'new rhythm of life' that required mechanical clocks and watches instead of natural timekeeping by the movement of the sun.[37] *IB* included among the effects of English influence a changing sense of punctuality.[38]

By the 1950s, Freyre had become familiar with the work of the sociologist Georges Gurvitch (whom he had met at the conference on tensions that cause wars) concerning the multiplicity of social times.[39] It was in this decade, in *O&P*, that he first wrote on the history of time at any length, contrasting 'social, cultural and psychological times in Brazil' with those dominant in Europe and the United States.[40] A recurrent theme in the book is what Freyre, employing some of his favourite concepts in a new context, calls the 'accommodation' or 'interpenetration' of past, present and future, vividly illustrated in this case by his example of an electric light-bulb mounted on an old candlestick.[41] Although a Brazilian newspaper article of 1888 had described time in modern fashion as money that could be wasted, traditional attitudes long continued to be dominant.[42]

A little later, Freyre developed and generalized his ideas about 'triple time' (*o tempo tríbio*), in other words the interaction of past, present and future, especially the survival of the past in the life of the present and the penetration of the present by a sense of the future. Drawing on Patrick Geddes and Lewis Mumford on the contrast between the 'palaeo-technic' age of the Industrial Revolution, and the coming 'neo-technic' or post-industrial age, he turned his attention to futurology – on which he gave a course of lectures at the University of Brasília in 1959 – and especially the problem of leisure in a post-industrial society.

By now Freyre was contrasting two attitudes to time, the modern or northern (relatively mechanical and rigid) and what he called the 'Iberian' sense of time, more relaxed, more flexible and more natural.[43] In a series of essays and lectures, some of them reprinted in *Além do apenas moderno* ('Beyond the Hardly Modern'; 1973), he went on to suggest that if northern or modern time had been well suited to the age of industry and capitalism, Iberian time was more appropriate for the post-capitalist or postmodern age. Like some European and North American sociologists of the 1950s, Freyre argued that automation was solving the problem of work, but also creating a new problem, that of how to spend the lengthening hours of leisure. The increase in the expectation of life made this problem still more acute, since retired people could now look forward to decades of leisure. The solution to the problem, so he suggested, was a return to the more traditional, Iberian or tropical sense of time. In other words, progress depended on going back – a point not infrequently made in different contexts by this self-styled 'conservative revolutionary' or 'Morris from the periphery'.[44]

The reference to postmodernity in the previous paragraph is not anachronistic. Like Arnold Toynbee, whose work he admired, Freyre regularly employed the term 'postmodern' (in the sense of 'post-industrial') from the 1950s onwards, lecturing, for instance, on 'postmodern challenges to the Brazilian'. In his work, though, the term had traditionalist overtones, referring among other things to a repudiation of the modern and nostalgia for the pre-modern.[45]

Freyre's ideas on time have tended to be either ignored or inflated. So far as work, leisure and automation are concerned, his diagnosis of the world's problems followed that of earlier North American or European sociological studies (Elton Mayo and Georges Friedmann on work, for instance, and Jacques Ellul, Josef Pieper and David Riesman on leisure), studies that he was instrumental in introducing to a Brazilian public. The idea of the 'contemporaneity of the non-contemporary' (*Gleichzeitigkeit des Ungleichzeitigen*), was memorably formulated by the German philosopher Ernst Bloch – though it is worth noting that Bloch's discussion dates from 1935, while Freyre's first reference to the topic is in his master's thesis of 1922.

In short, what was most distinctive in Freyre's approach was the suggestion, part of his 'tropicalism', that the tropics may offer some solutions to the social problems generated by Northern industry and capitalism.

Polarities and Mediations

Freyre loved binary oppositions. The titles of his books make this point obvious enough, contrasting as they do masters and slaves, mansions and shanties, order and progress, adventure and routine. The titles of individual chapters, especially in *S&M*, often follow the same model, contrasting 'the house and the street', 'fathers and sons', 'men and women', 'Brazilians and Europeans', 'frontiers and plantations'.

Contrasts between hard and soft, rough and smooth, fixed and fluid, angular and curved recur in Freyre's work, like that between the angular, thin Don Quixote and the round, plump Sancho Panza or between the angular English and the curvaceous, baroque Brazilians. So does the contrast between Dr Jekyll and Mr Hyde, or that between Catholic cultures and Protestant cultures. The polarity of male and female recurs as a metaphor for the relations between Europeans and Africans, masters and slaves, and even for economies, the 'masculine' economy of the United States, for example, being contrasted with the dependent, feminine economy of Brazil.[46]

A favourite polarity is that between the Apollonian and the Dionysian, noted by Nietzsche, although Freyre admitted to discovering it in the pages of Ruth Benedict's *Patterns of Culture* (1935). The idea of the Dionysian might have been devised for a discussion of Brazil in general and the North-East in particular, so appropriate was it to this part of the world. Freyre introduced the contrast into later editions of *CGS* and exploited it in a variety of contexts: types of fashion, types of intellectual and – notably and most memorably, as we have seen – types of football, contrasting the Apollonian English style with the Dionysian play of Brazilian mulattos. He wrote about the opposition between Apollonian friendship and Dionysian cordiality, and noted the irony of the Apollonian ascetic Euclides da Cunha writing a masterpiece about Dionysian, sensual Bahia.[47]

Another favourite contrast of Freyre's was that between the East and the West. There are many examples in his pages of the orientalism famously described and condemned by Edward Said: of stereotypes of the east such as oriental luxury, languor, fatalism, feminine submission, the riches of 'nabobs' and the despotism of 'sultans' and 'pashas'.[48] However, the uses of this orientalist language were very different from the ones described by Said. Freyre employed these terms and phrases not to describe the Ori-

ent but to describe Brazil. Whether his point was to make comparisons
or to establish connections (noting the influence of Islamic culture on the
Portuguese, for instance), he was deliberately undermining the binary opposition between East and West.

A similar point might be made in response to the possible criticism that tropicology essentializes the tropics in the same way that orientalism essentializes the Orient.[49] Freyre regularly used terms such as
'semi-tropical'. Undermining apparently rigid binary oppositions was in
fact a recurrent strategy of his. It was linked to his search for mediations
between opposites and revealed in his rich vocabulary for describing
such mediations, including 'accommodation', 'acculturation', 'adaptation',
'adjustment', 'assimilation', 'compromise' (*contemporização*), 'concilia-
tion', 'fraternization', 'interpenetration', 'mixture', 'transculturation' and of
course 'hybridization', as well as more concrete and specific terms such as
'brazilianize', 'anglicize', 'africanize', 'europeanize', 'tropicalize' and so on.
He viewed such mediations as characteristically Brazilian. 'Almost everything in Brazil tends to be softened into middle terms', he wrote, 'poison-
ous plants, illnesses, theories, ideas, passions, vices and virtues'.[50]

This concern with mediations is linked to Freyre's interest in what
he calls 'flexibility' or 'plasticity', in other words the capacity or propensity for compromises of the kinds that he associates with the British and
Portuguese – at least at one point in their history, as we have seen already
and will discuss again later. On occasion, he also associates plasticity with
Islam, allowing that religion to succeed in Africa in places where Christianity failed.[51] He is fascinated by the effects of cultural encounters, not
only between Portugal and Brazil, Europe and America, or Orient and
Occident but also between past and present, republic and empire, order
and progress, town and country, male and female, the authoritarian and
the democratic systems. He emphasizes the importance not only of the
mestizo or mulatto as an agent of mediation but also that of the nanny, the
cocotte, the emperor, the army or the street.

His concern with mediation and hybridity explains Freyre's love of
qualifying terms such as *meio, semi-, quase-* and *para-* , softening harsh
contrasts. The author of two 'semi-novels', as he called them, and a book
called *Quasi-Politics*, Freyre's work is full of references to 'semi-feudal',
'semi-military' or 'semi-patriarchal' conditions, for instance, or to 'para-
democratic', 'para-fascist', 'para-political', 'para-national', 'para-scientific'
or 'para-socialist' ideas. He once described Getúlio Vargas as a 'quasi-boss',
and even himself as a 'para-political figure' (*para-homem público*). A good
example from *O&P* is that of the military schools under the Republic, described as 'semi-military' and 'semi-political' and as producing 'semi-grad-

uates', 'semi-doctors' and 'semi-polytechnicians'.[52] It is in this spirit that we describe Freyre as a quasi-theorist in the sense of an anti-theoretical theorist, critical of abstractions and umcomfortable inside systems.

It is worth emphasizing the reflexivity of these central concepts at both the national and the individual level. Freyre argued that mediation was a distinctively Brazilian process, an argument followed by later sociologists or anthropologists such as Roberto DaMatta. His own writings are attempts to mediate between art and science, sociology and literature in which the author tried to combine a view from inside and a view from outside, involvement and detachment, intuition and analysis. Not the least of the lessons that he has for us today – in an age of even more intense cultural mixing than his own – is that of his 'mestizo logic'.[53]

Racial Democracy

The most famous kind of mixing discussed in Freyre's work is the ethnic and cultural mixing presented in *CGS*, as we have seen, as central to the Brazilian identity. As a kind of shorthand for the positive social consequences of miscegenation, the author used the expression 'social democratization' in his first preface to that book. Later, especially when writing for North American readers, he came to prefer the expressions 'ethnic democracy' or 'racial democracy', though he did not use them very much.[54] The phrase 'racial democracy' seems to have been first used by the Brazilian psychologist Arthur Ramos in 1941, and then, in 1944, by Roger Bastide when describing a conversation with Freyre. It has since passed into common usage in Brazil, according to sociological and anthropological studies made in the 1950s and the 1990s.[55]

The point of these phrases was to suggest that in the past and the present alike, Brazil was unusually democratic, though not in the sense of having a political system in which everyone voted and still less in the sense of having an economic system in which everyone was more or less equal. In 1937 Freyre had already contrasted Brazil with what he called 'the merely political democracy of the English'. Questioned about his idea of democracy in a newspaper interview in 1945, when he entered active politics, Freyre suggested that what was distinctive about Brazil was 'the democratization of personal relations' in the sense of a 'fraternal tendency'.[56] Phrases like these suggest that his social theory, or, we might say, his 'quasi-theory', owed something to his 'intimate history'.

In short, what distinguished Brazilian society, according to Freyre, was not so much liberty or equality as fraternity. From *CGS* onwards, he liked to speak of tendencies to fraternization or zones of fraternization between colonizers and colonized, masters and slaves, rich and poor. He explained these tendencies in terms of miscegenation. On the plantation, the master's children and the slave children (some of whom were also the master's children) played together, developing personal ties that lasted into adult life. In the city, the mulatto descendants of the unions between masters and slave women had the opportunity of rising socially. Under the Empire, there developed 'a social and not simply a political democracy' in the sense of increasing opportunities for plebeians and mulattos to rise socially. On these grounds he once described Brazilian history (in the preface to the first English-language edition of *CGS*) as 'a march toward social democracy'.

Freyre's theory of social, ethnic or racial democracy was originally welcomed and followed by some sociologists and anthropologists, including North Americans such as Donald Pierson and Charles Wagley as well as Brazilians. Pierson, for instance, noted the comparative absence of race prejudice in Brazil, and more especially in Bahia, thanks to miscegenation: 'Such prejudice as does exist is *class* rather than *caste* prejudice.' In similar fashion Wagley began his introduction to a collective study of race and class in rural Brazil with the words, 'Brazil is renowned in the world for its racial democracy'.[57]

All the same, the theory is vulnerable to a number of criticisms.[58] 'Democracy' may not have been the best choice of term to describe either fraternization or social mobility. The praise of mixture comes perilously near at times to an assertion of superiority, a position that Rodolfo Ghioldi criticized as 'a new racism: mulatto racism'. A more moderate version of this criticism suggests that Freyre's praise of mixture 'was as lacking in a scientific basis as the condemnation of it before the publication of *CGS*'.[59]

Again, Freyre was widely understood and criticized as saying that Brazil had already achieved the happy state of racial democracy, though he denied this explicitly: 'No one should understand me as implying that Brazil is a perfect ethnic democracy. It is not.' He claimed only that Brazil was 'inclined toward' it, that it was 'becoming more and more a racial democracy', or that it was closer than other countries to this goal.[60] In similar fashion, Pierson and Wagley admitted the existence of racial prejudice, racial discrimination and racial conflict in Brazil, arguing only that the conflicts were unusually mild in that country. One might say that a certain image of a racially harmonious Brazil existed in the North American social imagination. A telling example of this image or expectation can be found in a letter from a journalist who had lived in Brazil that was published in the *New York Times* in May 1922 under the title 'Black and White in Brazil'.

If there exists an antagonism between white and black in this country, the letter says, it is insignificant and certainly much less marked than, for example, that between the Piedmontese and the Sicilians in Italy.[61]

Rüdiger Bilden had also insisted that although the abolition of slavery did not free the 'Negroid element' from 'its dismal and insidious heritage' and that some degree of racial discrimination and tensions among the different ethnic groups still existed, the Brazilian racial situation was unique: 'Today, Brazil has progressed far on the road toward a harmonious blending of diverse and supposedly incompatible ethnic elements into a new tropical race.' And again: 'It is the only land of European origin and background where three fundamental divisions of mankind meet on terms of comparative equality, live in peace side by side, and intermingle to form a new human compound, suited to the tropical milieu and endowed with distinctive gifts.' No wonder then that he, instead of echoing those who viewed Brazil as a 'country of mongrels', described it as a 'laboratory of civilization.'[62]

This positive view of Brazil was naturally welcomed by the Vargas regime. It is expressed very clearly in a book that was encouraged if not commissioned by the regime and intended especially for foreign readers, *Brazil: Land of the Future* (1942) by the Austrian writer Stefan Zweig. Without referring to Freyre, Zweig paraphrases and indeed exaggerates his views – and those of Bilden – in references to 'the experiment of Brazil, with its complete and conscious negation of all colour and racial distinctions'. 'All these different races – visibly distinct by their colour alone – live in fullest harmony with one another.' Zweig concluded that Brazil had solved the race problem in a manner that 'demands not only the attention but the admiration of the whole world'.[63] In 1953, when Vargas was President once more, the official representative of Brazil at the coronation of Queen Elizabeth, Freyre's friend Chateaubriand, presented his country to the British in Freyrean terms as 'a Brazil of authentic *mestiços*', revealing 'the vast experience of crossings that we undertook in the tropics'.[64]

This interpretation of Brazil in both the past and the present has been strongly criticized. In the case of the colonial period, a leading specialist, Charles Boxer, argued in the 1960s that 'The social ascent of the Negro which Freyre claims was fostered in Brazil, was, on the contrary, deliberately retarded in that colony by the maintenance of a rigid colour-bar on full-blooded Negroes during the whole of the colonial period, in so far as municipal office-holding was concerned' (the qualification at the end of this sentence should be noted).[65]

So far as Brazil in the present is concerned, the story of the reception of Freyre's views is a somewhat ironic one in which unintended consequences played an important role. In 1951 and 1952 UNESCO gave its support to research on race relations in Brazil.[66] The original idea came from Arthur Ramos, who was then head of UNESCO's department of social science, but after his sudden death it was taken up by the anthropologist Alfred Métraux, head of the section on race relations. The paradox is that Métraux was thinking in Freyrean terms as a possible model for other parts of the world (he had written to Freyre in 1940, calling *CGS* a 'masterpiece').

The first scholars he asked to direct research on the situation in São Paulo, the Frenchman Roger Bastide (a sociologist best known for his studies of Afro-Brazilian religion) and the American Donald Pierson (who was unable to accept), were both admirers of Freyre's work on race relations. Freyre himself was interested in the project and wished to involve the new Instituto Joaquim Nabuco. When the research was carried out, however, its main conclusions turned out to be diametrically opposed to the suggestion of Ramos and Freyre that Brazil was something like a racial democracy.

The sociologists and anthropologists who carried out this research came in the most part from the University of São Paulo (henceforth USP). There was also a group led by Charles Wagley (a former student of Boas and a professor at Columbia University) and the Brazilian Thales de Azevedo, that studied Bahia and was also supported by UNESCO. Among the scholars from USP whom Bastide recruited for the project were Florestan Fernandes, Octávio Ianni and Fernando Henrique Cardoso, who had not yet embarked on his political career.[67]

The conclusions reached by the Wagley group, like those of Pierson, supported Freyre's ideas, with the exception of the young Marvin Harris, who emphasized race prejudice in his study of a small town in Bahia, Minas Velhas.[68] However, what Bastide and his group discovered undermined Freyre. The case studies of race relations made at USP were all located in the South of Brazil, concentrating on the cities of São Paulo, Curitiba, Florianópolis and Porto Alegre. Three of these studies of the South were historical, comparing and contrasting the situation before and after slavery.[69] Where Freyre had told an optimistic story, emphasizing the rise of the mulatto and the opportunities for education and social mobility in the nineteenth century, Florestan and his colleagues presented a pessimistic account, stressing the negative consequences for Afro-Brazilians of urbanization and the rise of capitalism and class society. Where he saw fraternization, they saw discrimination. With the exception of Bastide, who always expressed his respect for *CGS*, they made relatively few references to Freyre.[70]

The other publications by the USP group focused on the present, combining personal observation with interviews and questionnaires.[71]

The authors were careful not to essentialize race, defining it simply as what provides 'the attributes that are socially selected and imputed to particular people in particular conditions of social existence'.[72] What they found was a good deal of evidence of discrimination by skin colour.

As a result, they all rejected what they called 'the myth of racial democracy', described by Florestan as 'one of the great myths of our time'.[73] As Fernando Henrique remembers, race had been a taboo subject in Brazil in the 1950s because the official line was that the country was a racial democracy – an idea expressed by some of the respondents to interviews and questionnaires.[74] The São Paulo group broke the taboo, arguing, for instance, that miscegenation was not proof of lack of prejudice, since white males saw coloured females as objects of pleasure rather than as possible wives, and also that the social mobility of Afro-Brazilians, when it happened, was perceived by whites as a threat, leading to 'racial solidarity' between Brazilians of European descent.

The evidence for racial discrimination that Florestan and the others discovered in the course of their research cannot be dismissed. Indeed, Freyre was already aware of the problem, witness the speech he made as a deputy in 1950 when the Hotel Esplanada in São Paulo rejected the North American Black dancer Katherine Durham.[75] All the same, a comparison between the studies of Bahia and the studies made by the USP group suggests the existence of differences in attitudes to African-Americans between the North and the South of Brazil, along similar lines to the United States, with unofficial and everyday prejudice being stronger, ironically enough, in the regions that lack the historical experience of plantations and slavery. If such a difference existed, then we may say that both Freyre and his critics fell into the trap of extending conclusions about particular regions to the whole of Brazil.

If Freyre's thesis is formulated with all the necessary nuances, an important point remains, which Florestan shows that he accepted when he warned readers against 'the risk of considering as *perfect* a racial democracy that is still in the process of formation'.[76] Relative to other former slave societies, Brazil stood out and indeed still stands out as a society in which, despite extreme inequality in the distribution of both wealth and power, relations between blacks and whites are unusually warm and personal. A similar point might be made about relations between employers and employees. This 'fraternization', as Freyre liked to call it, still impresses many visitors to Brazil, and suggests that for better or worse – or both – the family, especially the patriarchal family, hierarchical but warm, remains the model for other forms of social organization.

Luso-Tropicalism

Miscegenation, together with other forms of mixing, is the link between the idea of racial democracy and that of Luso-Tropicalism. *CGS* already described the Portuguese regime in Brazil as softer, less violent and more flexible than that of the colonial regimes of the British, Dutch, French or Spaniards, explaining the difference in terms of the greater propensity of the Portuguese to interbreed with native women, their capacity 'to fraternize with the so-called inferior races' or more broadly still, of their 'social plasticity'.

According to Freyre, it was easier for the Portuguese than for the British or Dutch to survive in the tropics because so far as climate is concerned, Portugal 'is more Africa than Europe'. This 'acclimatability' (*aclimatabilidade*), as he called it, was accompanied by an adaptability to local customs. The Portuguese in the tropics ate the local food, wore the local clothes, slept in hammocks and had sex with the local women, while the northerners (according to him) generally did not. The English, for example, 'thought that this adoption of tropical dress habits compromised European dignity'. Freyre also claimed that there was less colour prejudice and that slaves were better treated in 'the world that the Portuguese made' than elsewhere.[77] We should note that such a view was not uncommon. The issue was discussed by Alfred Zimmern, for instance, the British classicist who became a specialist in contemporary international relations and a great supporter of the League of Nations. In a lecture in New York published in 1926, Zimmern referred to the great difficulty that the 'Anglo-Saxons', in contrast to the Latin nations, had in dealing with non-white peoples in the colonies.[78]

It is therefore easy to see why the Portuguese government should have invited Freyre to visit Ultramar. It was in the course of this tour of the Portuguese colonies, discussed in an earlier chapter, that he coined the term 'Luso-Tropical' to describe what he considered to be the particular aptness of the Portuguese for the task of colonization. This claim was appropriated by the Salazar regime and pressed into service to legitimate the Portuguese empire at a time, the 1950s, when it was increasingly challenged by the colonized.

An irony that should be pointed out is that the Portuguese authorities chose to ignore or seem not to have been aware of Freyre's dismissal of modern Portugal in *CGS*, the very book in which he pointed to the virtues of the Portuguese colonizers. Their plasticity, adaptability and other virtues were, according to him, long gone. Since the end of the sixteenth century, he argues, the modern Portuguese, 'so spotted with decay', have lived arrogantly and 'parasitically' on a past whose splendour they exaggerate, trying to look much better and civilized than they actually are.

Freyre's words to describe the behaviour of the Portuguese are direct and merciless, and deserve to be quoted at length, since, strangely enough, they have not been noted by later scholars. In fact they raise rather awkward questions about the changes in Freyre's attitude and also about Freyre scholarship. Full of 'pretensions to greatness' and 'far from resigning itself to the honest poverty of a nation fallen into decay ... Portugal, after Alcazakebir went on imagining itself to be the opulent land of Dom Sebastian's lifetime. It went on feeding upon the fame acquired by its overseas conquests.' Instead of behaving like modest Holland, who 'devoted herself to the making of cheese and butter', when she ceased 'being the mistress of a vast empire', Portugal 'went on deluding itself with an imperial mysticism that no longer had any base. Went on poisoning itself with delusions of grandeur.'

The picture of the modern Portuguese that Freyre painted comes close to the pathetic at times, especially when they are portrayed as desperately trying to appear to the world what they definitely are not. Struggling to counterbalance the feeling of being either neglected or dismissed as inferior by foreigners, 'he turned himself into a Portuguese-for-English eyes, although the English have been the most perspicacious of all in portraying him from the life, restoring to him his precise contour and colouring.' In short, without mercy, Freyre described a people who for four centuries 'have more and more tended to simulate those European and imperial qualities which they possessed or incarnated for so brief a period. The Portuguese people live by making themselves believe that they are powerful and important. That they are civilized in the European manner. That they are a great colonial power.'

The future does not promise any improvement, according to Freyre. 'Switzerland might go on condensing its milk and Holland making its cheeses, but Portugal continues to stand on tiptoe in an effort to appear to be one of the great European powers.'[79]

All these rather denigrating if not downright offensive remarks were apparently ignored by those who invited Freyre to visit Portuguese Ultramar in 1951 – and, for that matter, even by the guest himself. Very different was his tone in the rare critical remarks that he made about the Portuguese in the Africa he saw, as if 'apologizing for having made them'. His visit to Ultramar, as he reported it in his book *Aventura e Rotina* (1953; henceforth *A&R*), was, with very few exceptions, 'a prolonged experience of happiness', as the diplomat-historian Alberto da Costa e Silva has put it.[80] The Freyre of 1953 seems to be a different person from the Freyre who lived in Portugal in 1930 and described the Portuguese in 1933. Had he really changed his mind? Or had he decided to play a particular role? It is impossible to answer this question, adding to the complexity of this intellectual. As for modern scholarship, it is to say the least rather intriguing that these passages seem to have been passed over, with the result – once again – of simplifying Freyre's rather complex attitudes.

To return to the idea of Luso-Tropicalism – perhaps the closest thing to a theory that Freyre ever enunciated – it was first put forward, so he tells us, in a lecture in Goa in 1951. It was also discussed in *A&R*, an account of his tour in the form of a diary. The book is a travelogue, full of vivid description and personal observations, but although it was written by a critical student of travelogues, it betrays excessive confidence in the penetration of the traveller's gaze. Freyre told his readers that he immediately felt at home in Luanda and also in Goa (seeing its capital, Pangim, as something like the city of São Luis in Maranhão, in the north of Brazil). He went on to argue that the creation of the Portuguese empire was 'a process in which women, old people, children, adolescents and *mestiços* ... participated from the start ... and not simply adult white males'.[81]

Like the speeches its author made during his tour, *A&R* has been interpreted, as we have seen, as a defence of Portuguese colonialism. Partly for this reason, the idea of Luso-Tropicalism that it expounds has been generally rejected, not only by active opponents of colonialism such as Amílcar Cabral but by scholars as well. Melville Herskovits, for instance, so close to Freyre in other respects, dismissed it as a romantic idea. As for Marvin Harris, his characteristically blunt comment was that it is 'hard to imagine' how 'Freyre could have been hoodwinked into finding resemblances between race relations in Angola and Mozambique and Brazil'.[82]

As in the case of 'racial democracy', it is not always clear quite how far the author wanted to take the idea: whether he was claiming, for instance, that the Portuguese lacked race prejudice, or only that they were less prejudiced than other European colonists; whether he was aware of all the differences between Brazil and the Portuguese colonies in Africa; or whether he distinguished between different periods of colonial history, whether British or Portuguese. As we have just seen, Freyre claimed in 1933 that the Portuguese had lost their plasticity forever. They now kept themselves apart from the 'natives' and their treatment of Africans has been described by a specialist on Angola as 'not appreciably better or worse than their counterparts from the other European colonizing nations'.[83]

Change also occurred in the case of the British in India, an example against which, despite his usual anglophilia, Freyre defined the plasticity of the Portuguese and their empire. In 1945 he had suggested that the British Empire 'seems to us to be superior to its current competitors (although it perhaps yields in creativity to the Portuguese and the Spanish)'.[84] By 1953, however, he had changed his mind and at least at that moment, he described the British as inflexible, criticizing what he called in one of his vivid phrases 'the British-style monocle-wearing (or 'one-eyed') arrogance of the sub-Kiplings' (*a arrogância britanicamente monocular dos subkiplings*). He had apparently forgotten, or come to reject his earlier remarks about the modern Portuguese as full of arrogance and pretence.[85]

Freyre does not seem to have known that the British in India, until about 1830, often wore Indian dress, ate the local food, smoked hookahs, took Indian mistresses (known as *bibis*) or married Indian women. Famous examples of these 'white Mughals' were Sir David Ochterlony, an officer in the East India Company, and Lieutenant-Colonel James Kirkpatrick, the British Resident at Hyderabad and the husband of Begum Khair-un-Nissa.[86] Apparently unaware of such examples, Freyre regarded the British colonizers as unwilling to mix and believing that 'East is East and West is West', while the Portuguese, in contrast, had shown that the twain could meet. Unusually for him, the historical dimension was lacking in his references to colonial India.

In short, Freyre criticized the British in India as if they had always behaved as they did in the age of Kipling (who grew up in India in the 1860s and lived there again in the 1880s).[87] However, if we reformulate his contrast between the two colonizing nations to refer to the Portuguese in Brazil in the sixteenth and seventeenth centuries and the British in India from around 1830 to 1947, he might be said to have made an important point. The equivalent in India of the Brazilian mestiços and mulattos were the Eurasians, usually the children of British fathers and Indian mothers. They were a relatively small group, and they found it difficult to fit into society in India, where social and cultural frontiers were sharper than in Brazil. The situation of this group at the time of Indian independence was dramatized in *Bhowani Junction* (1954), a novel by John Masters, a former army officer who lived much of his life in India. The heroine of the novel, Victoria Jones, is presented as trying and failing to become both English and Indian, before accepting her separate destiny as a Eurasian.[88]

In spite of all the problems raised by Freyre's quasi-theory, we should avoid throwing the baby out with the bathwater. If the 'Luso' part of Luso-Tropicalism is obviously open to criticism, as a sociological hypothesis as well as an instrument employed by the Salazar regime in defence of colonialism, the 'Tropicalism' part is still worth taking seriously. It describes a project intended to combat what Freyre called the persistent notion that 'everything tropical is the negation of refinement and civilization.'[89] The project included reflections on tropical medicine, the idea of an interdisciplinary tropicology and the argument for the tropicalization of social theory.

Tropicalism, Tropicology, Tropicalization

Freyre published a book on the sociology of medicine in 1967, relatively early in the development of a field that had emerged only in the 1950s. He was particularly interested in tropical medicine, not only in the treatment of tropical diseases but also in alternative medicines, such as Ayurvedic medicine, that had been developed in the tropics and made use of tropical herbs. On his visit to Goa, he visited the medical school and commented soon afterwards that 'traditional Indian medicine' included 'valuable anticipations of more modern medicine'.[90]

This interest in medicine had developed out of Freyre's collaboration with his cousin the psychiatrist Ulisses Pernambucano, and it was reflected in his concern with the history of the body from CGS onwards. He cited professional journals such as Brasil Medico, the Boletim Sanitario, the Annães da Faculdade de Medicina do Rio de Janeiro, distinguished different physical types of slave in colonial Brazil, noted the deforming effects of physical labour and punishment on the bodies of the slaves and discussed female illnesses, syphilis and so on. He also argued that inhabitants of the tropics follow a healthy diet, eating more fruit and vegetables than inhabitants of the temperate zones.

Another aspect of his interest in medicine was Freyre's concern with hygiene in the past and the present alike. Already in 1921 he was reading and writing about sanitation in nineteenth-century Brazil. In the 1970s he was arguing that tropical traditions of clothing, such as pyjamas and sandals, are superior to European traditions because they are better adapted to hot weather. The young man who had sported an English tweed jacket during the hottest season in Recife turned into the old man who liked to wear his shirts outside his trousers, 'a custom', he remarked, 'that the Portuguese inherited from the orientals'.[91]

Hygiene was also central to Freyre's defence of the *mucambos* of Recife, stressing the fact that they were built from natural, local materials such as palm fronds. Architecture fitted into Freyre's tropicology because he thought that the built environment should always be related to the natural environment, moderating the harsh light of the tropics as well as providing air and shade.

He also believed, as we have seen, that the modern architecture developed in Europe by Le Corbusier and others should be adapted rather than imitated in other places in order to take account of local traditions, such as the colonial style in Brazil. However, like his master Mumford, Freyre did not support the slavish imitation of traditional buildings. His regionalism was a critical one. The point was not simple conservation or conservatism but the exploitation of the strong points of traditional architecture, including the design of parks and gardens, so well adjusted to the Brazilian way of life.[92]

At a more general level, Freyre suggested that Brazil might become a leader in the process of making 'civilized man in cold regions' aware of the aesthetic values of the tropics. He predicted a movement that might be described as cultural imperialism in reverse, with the tropics leading and Europe following, not least because Brazil had been a pioneer in the racial and cultural mixing that was becoming characteristic of the world in the late twentieth century.[93] He offered a critique of European reason and modernity from a tropical point of view. His main point, frequently reiterated, was that the tropical way of life was better adapted than the 'Western' way to the demands of a post-industrial or postmodern society.

Freyre's prime example of the adaptation of the tropics to the future was that of attitudes to time. As we have seen, he liked to contrast English time (precise, mechanical and 'chronometric') with what he called 'Iberian' time, less precise and more rooted in the earth (*tellúrico*, a favourite word of his). In the tropics, the idea of time as money had not penetrated so deeply. It should therefore be relatively easy for their inhabitants to adapt to the coming culture of leisure.[94] To sum up the argument in a single phrase, the tropics are already postmodern because they had never been really modern. The future is theirs.

Underlying Freyre's wide range of publications on sociology and anthropology was a single ambitious project, nothing less than tropicalizing social theory (a project that was of course too vast for any individual to accomplish singlehanded). Freyre's essential criticism of the social theory of his day was that it had all been produced in the West and bore the marks of its origins there. Its generalizations were based too exclusively on the social experiences of the temperate zone, making too little room for other parts of the world, including Brazil (some European anthropologists and sociologists such as Georges Balandier and Jean Duvignaud made the same point).[95] 'If there are transplants which fail because the organism rejects them', Freyre wrote in his vivid metaphorical way, 'they are transplants of concepts, methods and solutions of a social and economic type.'[96] It was therefore necessary to modify or tropicalize social theory in order to make it more widely applicable and thus to contribute to what Freyre called a 'pan-human civilization'.[97] He was treating European social theory in the way that Heitor Villa-Lobos treated European classical music, using it but brazilianizing it.

Sociología had already suggested that there was a 'Brazilian style of sociology', evident in the work of Sérgio Buarque and Caio Prado Jr.[98] In an interview of 1959, Freyre spoke about the 'Brazilianization of sociology'. Again, in an interview of 1971, he stressed the need for Brazilian intellectuals to develop their own concepts and methods in social sciences to fit their own ecology and avoid what he called 'European "isms"' such as Marxism, Freudianism or Weberism.[99] In other words, he explored the positive side of the criticism once levelled at the author of *CGS*, that of practising '*xique-xique* sociology' (*xique-xique* is the popular name for a kind of cactus that grows in the North-East of Brazil). He viewed tropical societies as the new models for humanity. In short, he was already participating in the collective enterprise recently described as 'provincializing Europe'.[100]

By the early 1960s, Freyre was calling for a 'tropical anthropology' and attempting to found an institute for the study of the subject within the Faculty of Medicine of the University of Recife.[101] This tropical anthropology or sociology came to be known as 'tropicology'.[102] Freyre had already used this term in a book title of 1953.[103] By 1975 he was calling it a 'new science' that drew on ecology, anthropology, sociology, history and other disciplines, employing a comparative approach to discover common features in tropical societies and cultures, their illnesses, dwellings, food, clothes, mentalities and so on. In other words, tropicologists would pursue collectively and systematically the comparative, interdisciplinary approach that he himself had long pursued in an individual and less systematic manner.

Freyre's proposal at the 1948 UNESCO Conference about the 'tensions that cause wars' had stressed that the possible liberating influence of the social sciences depended on their avoiding being used in the service of ethnocentrism and 'aggressive nationalisms', and even of being closely connected to a particular nation. 'It is time to try to contain the excessive development of the so-called "Chilean sociology", "Peruvian sociology", "Bolivian sociology", Brazilian sociology", "French sociology", "German sociology"', he declared, since these sociologies are easily perverted by national interests and aspirations and so harm not only science but international understanding as well. Transnational and regional studies – in which a political or national criterion is replaced by an ecological or cultural criterion – help solve the problem of bringing peoples together and opening up ways of common understanding and communication between them. As an example of what he had in mind, Freyre suggested the implementation of a transnational scientific study of great regional or 'Pan-Latin American' problems carried out by the combined efforts of individuals from different disciplines and different nations.[104]

In short, Freyre both wanted and did not want a Brazilian sociology. He opposed a narrow nationalist Brazilian sociology just as he opposed a narrow nationalist German sociology. On the other hand, he supported a Brazilian sociology in the broad sense of a tropical sociology that would reveal the insufficiencies of a study of society based on Western European and North American experiences alone, thus contributing to what we might call an ecumenical sociology.

The new science of tropicology found a home in the institute that Freyre helped to found, the Instituto Nabuco in Recife.[105] From 1966 onwards, regular interdisciplinary seminars (modelled on the seminars at Columbia organized by the Latin Americanist Frank Tannenbaum) were held at the Instituto Nabuco on the comparative study of tropical societies, and many of the papers presented there were published in the journals *Ciência & Trópico* and *Anais do Seminário de Tropicologia*.[106] The first Brazilian Congress of Tropicology (1986) marked the twentieth birthday of the seminar.

What counted as the tropics was not altogether clear. As always, Freyre was hostile to precise definitions and impassable frontiers. He used the term 'tropic' on different occasions to refer to a region, the North-East; to Brazil as whole (although it is not a completely tropical country); and to parts of Asia, Africa and the Americas. He sometimes extended his idea of plasticity to include the Spaniards, writing about the *hispano-tropical*.[107] Occasionally he included the French as well, or drew an analogy between the tropics and the Mediterranean world. As we have seen, he loved to think with binary oppositions such as tropical and temperate, but also to undermine them. 'Paratropical', for instance, was an intellectual umbrella that he used to cover European artists and writers such as Gauguin or Rimbaud who went to live in other continents and whose conceptions of space were, he claimed, essentially tropical.[108] 'Eurotropical' was another term he used to describe cultural mixing.[109] In short, Freyre's tropicalism reveals what Luiz Costa Lima has called his 'conceptual fluidity'.[110]

This fluidity, which admirers might describe as openness and detractors as a lack of intellectual rigour is also revealed, as we have seen, in Freyre's broad conception of sociology. Contrasting paradigms of sociology were among the points at issue in the disputes between Freyre and some younger Brazilian sociologists, most of them associated with USP.

Recife and São Paulo

The long story of the relationship between Freyre and the sociologists of São Paulo, especially USP, went through several phases of which it may be useful to distinguish three. The first phase was the rejection of Freyre's hypotheses about race relations in Brazil, described earlier in this chapter. There was no debate, though there might and perhaps should have been one. Repeated attempts by the USP group to involve Freyre in dialogue came to nothing. He was asked to participate as one of the examiners of the doctoral theses of Ianni and Cardoso in 1961, but he refused the invitations.[111]

In the second phase, the original disagreement gradually widened to include sociological method. Florestan Fernandes, Octávio Ianni and Fernando Henrique Cardoso all considered that Freyre had overemphasized harmony and consensus in his approach to Brazilian society, offering a myth or an ideology rather than a serious analysis, still less what Florestan called a 'critical sociology' that would assist the transformation of society. In fact, a major reason for Florestan's rejection of Freyre's style of sociology was what he viewed as its failure to measure up to this serious role of changing the world, transforming rather than simply analysing society.

In the third phase, after the military coup of 1964, the disagreement was politicized. All three of the USP sociologists were on the Left, and their intellectual distance from Freyre became still greater at this time. On one side, as we have seen, Freyre supported the new regime. On the other, all three sociologists had to leave USP. Cardoso went into exile in Chile, Fernandes was forced into early retirement and Ianni migrated to PUC (the Pontifical University, which offered employment to some left-wing scholars who had lost their former posts). In the hot intellectual climate of this 'McCarthian moment' (as we called it earlier), Freyre denounced what he called 'archaic-Marxist sociologists', 'sectarians' or 'fanatics' (although he still did not reject Marx himself), while Florestan described Freyre's criticisms as 'praise for our work.'[112] Historians and literary critics who taught at USP were also critical of Freyre at this time, among them Antonio Candido, Alfredo Bosi, and Carlos Guilherme Mota, who described Freyre's interpretation of Brazil as an 'ideology' and his intellectual role as the sociologist of the Big House.[113] Freyre was 'banished' from academic circles in the sense that students were often discouraged from reading his books. In 1979, he claimed to be the victim of a 'conspiracy of silence.'[114]

In what follows, we concentrate attention on the second phase, the disagreement about the nature of sociology and Freyre's place in the sociological tradition. When the second edition of Freyre's *Sociología* was published, it was reviewed by Octávio Ianni, dismissing it on the grounds that it lacked what was required by 'the present state of the preoccupations of Brazilian specialists' and confused the methods of scientists (including sociologists) with those of artists. Ianni also rejected some of the author's claims to be a pioneer in the social sciences by citing predecessors for some of his approaches, including *Middletown* (1929), the sociological portrait of a community in the American Mid-West by Robert and Helen Lynd. Freyre published two indignant replies defending his priority on the grounds that his distinctive approach went back not to *CGS* but to his historical essays of the 1920s, which were published before the Lynd's work.[115]

The disagreement about the nature of sociology has been described, with perhaps a slight exaggeration, as a 'struggle for hegemony' between the Northeast and the South.[116] Paulo Duarte, 'the most combative of Brazilian liberals', as Freyre called him, an archaeologist and also a leading figure in USP, claimed that 'scientifically oriented' sociology in Brazil effectively began in São Paulo.[117] Returning to Michel de Certeau's famous question to scholars, 'Where do you speak from?', it is worth noting that Freyre not only came from the North-East but treated it as a model for the rest of Brazil, while Florestan and the others not only came from the South but carried out their research in that part of the country.

This dispute was also one between two generations.[118] Freyre was born in 1900, but Florestan in 1920, and Octávio Ianni in 1926; Fernando Henrique was still younger, having been born in 1931. The two generations entered the intellectual field at two different stages in its development, since sociology was becoming professionalized and institutionalized in Brazil in the middle of the twentieth century. In the 1920s and 1930s, when Freyre held academic posts in sociology in Recife and Rio, few such posts existed in Brazil. By the 1950s and 1960s, the situation had changed. Roger Bastide was Professor of Sociology at the University of São Paulo from 1938 to 1957. Fernando de Azevedo became head of the Department of Sociology and Anthropology in 1947, while Florestan Fernandes, who was to become the leading Brazilian sociologist of his time, succeeded to Bastide's chair.[119] In 2006, eleven years after Florestan's death, the President of Brazil would sign a decree naming him the 'patron of Brazilian sociology', a kind of canonization.

The contrasts and conflicts between Freyre and the social scientists of São Paulo should not be exaggerated. After all, in 1935 Azevedo, who was then director of social sciences at USP, had considered bringing Freyre to the university.[120] Again, Bastide was not only an admirer of Freyre but a scholar who, like him, combined ideas from sociology with anthropology and psychology. Florestan himself began his career with a work of historical anthropology, a study of the Tupinambá. Like Freyre, he drew on French and German traditions of sociology, from Marx's dialectic to the functionalism of Durkheim and the interpretive method of Weber, as well as on the North Americans. In 1958 he described Freyre as a scholar 'considered by many to be the first Brazilian specialist with a scientific training'.[121] On the other side, before he came to reject Florestan as a 'fanatic', after 1964, Freyre had described him as a sociologist 'whom I particularly admire', possibly because of the historical dimension present in his work.[122] His anti-professionalism should not be exaggerated either. After all, his textbook of sociology noted the need to fight the dilettantism characteristic of the nineteenth century. He presented himself as a 'semi-sociologist', on the margins of the university, but claimed that from this position he could make a valuable contribution to the discipline.[123]

All the same, the contrast and the incompatibility between Freyre's paradigm of sociology and that of Florestan will be obvious enough. The positivist Florestan admired the current North American sociology against which Freyre, as we have seen, defined his position. Florestan thought of sociology as a science concerned with objective facts that should be described and analysed in a language that was impersonal, precise and sometimes technical. Freyre, on the other hand, saw sociology as an art and deliberately wrote about society in a language that was personal, vivid, colloquial and imprecise. He was aware of quantitative sociology, but dismissed it.

Ironically enough – though we should not expect methodologies to depend on politics – it was the right-wing Freyre rather than the left-wing Florestan who agreed with the radical American sociologist C. Wright Mills's famous critique of the 'grand theory' of Parsons and the hyper-empiricism of Lazarsfeld, as well as with his emphasis on 'the sociological imagination' and on the effects of social change on the lives of individuals.[124]

There were other contrasts between the two scholars. Freyre's forte was the microscopic approach. Tristão de Athaíde once described him as 'the man who introduced micro-sociology into Brazil', while Roger Bastide noted his 'almost infinitesimal micro-analyses'.[125] Florestan, on the other hand, was concerned above all with broad social trends and criticized Freyre for 'the reduction of the social macrocosm inherent in the regime of orders and castes to the social microcosm inherent in the plantation or estate'.[126] He took economic factors more seriously, while Freyre placed a greater stress on culture.

Although Florestan carried out some important historical research, believing that the present situation (racial discrimination, for instance), could not be explained without reference to the colonial past, he believed that sociology was a science with its own methods and that 'sociological explanations have a scientific character' ('scientific' was one of his favourite adjectives). He criticized the use of historical explanations in sociology and linked this reliance on history to the 'essayists' whom he viewed as 'precursors' rather than as true members of the guild. Fernando Henrique also criticized studies of Brazil 'in the form of essays … lacking the habitual rigour of scientific analysis'.[127]

Neither scholar had much sympathy for Freyre's deliberately anti-methodical, informal and multi-disciplinary approach, once described by a Marxist sociologist from Recife, Gláucio Veiga, as 'sociology in its underwear' (a criticism reminiscent of the 'shirt-sleeve style' of *CGS*). Like Ghioldi, Veiga also criticized Freyre for being insufficiently dialectical, and later, for criticizing Marxism, and pointed to the 'absence of a scientific basis' to his work.[128] Even when the two men were reconciled and Veiga proposed the foundation of a chair in Freyre studies at the Federal University of Pernambuco, he insisted on the need for an objective critique of Freyre's work, a critique that was all too rare (Veiga thought) among those who wrote about him.[129]

In short, Florestan and Freyre held incompatible views of sociology and more generally, of intellectual activity. One valued intellectual rigour more highly, the other imagination. The two men might even be said to have represented what the sociologist Karl Mannheim used to call different styles of thought. With his concern for generalization, Florestan was closer to the universalist style of the French Enlightenment, while Freyre, more concerned with uniqueness, was closer to the German conservative-historicist style.[130] Each of them embodied something that the other rejected. For Freyre, Florestan was a purist, and he did not care for purists. For Florestan, Freyre was, or came to seem, an amateur, and he had little time for amateurs in his discipline.

Freyre in comparative context

A few comparisons with other social thinkers, such as Max Weber and Norbert Elias, may help us place Freyre's work in perspective.

Freyre frequently cited Max Weber – on understanding, on ideal types, on patrimonialism, on prophets, and so on – and once described him as the most important modern sociologist.[131] As a Catholic who was educated by the Baptists and briefly turned Protestant, Freyre found

Weber's reflections on the contrast between Catholics and Protestants particularly fascinating. In some respects he extended Weber's ideas, notably to the kitchen. A note on the flyleaf of a history of England in Freyre's library refers to 'culinary puritanism'. In similar fashion, the essay on cuisine in R&T suggests that Dutch cooking was harmed by 'the grey wave of Calvinism' that spread over that country in the seventeenth century.[132] In other respects, though, Freyre turned Weber on his head, accepting the contrast between Protestant and Catholic cultures but claiming in his studies of time and other topics that the future lay not with the precise and rational Protestant North but rather with the more fluid, sensuous and emotional Catholic tropics.

On the other hand, Freyre does not appear to have known the work of the most creative of Weber's followers, Norbert Elias, whose famous study of *The Civilizing Process*, published in 1939, was generally neglected in Europe, the United States and elsewhere until the 1970s. This failed encounter is a pity, for Freyre would surely have appreciated many features of the work of Elias: his historical approach, his use of literary sources, his interest in Freud, his concern with the civilizing process at an everyday level, the anthropological eye that he turned on his own culture and his discussion of forks, time and football. He would doubtless have criticized Elias as Eurocentric (given his own discussion of the contribution of the Indians and Africans to Brazilian civilization) and perhaps as too Apollonian as well.[133] In similar fashion, Freyre appears to have missed a possible encounter with the work of Mikhail Bakhtin, another thinker who failed to attract much attention (outside Russia) until the end of the 1960s. He would surely have appreciated Bakhtin's concepts of carnivalization, dialogic and heteroglossia, so much in tune with his own ideas.

Freyre's humanist anthropology, informed by literature and philosophy, has more than a little in common with the approach of a later generation, most notably Clifford Geertz, some of whose work he discovered in the 1960s.[134] His concern with analysis at the micro-level has come to be widely shared not only in anthropology but in sociology and history as well. The anecdotes he loved, once dismissed as unscientific, have been rehabilitated.[135]

There is even a broad sense in which Freyre's work may be viewed as postmodern. As we have seen, Freyre was one of the first intellectuals to use the term 'postmodern', in the 1950s, alongside the critic Irving Howe, the historian Arnold Toynbee and the sociologist C. Wright Mills. In some respects, Freyre might even be described not only as a postmodern but also as a post-colonial thinker, an awkward ancestor who is omitted from the official genealogies.[136]

There are of course obvious reasons for this omission. Post-colonial theory is usually understood as anti-colonial theory and this obviously excludes the inventor of Luso-Tropicalism. Post-colonial theorists are generally on the Left, while Freyre moved towards the Right as he grew older. If Edward Said had opened Freyre's books, he would have been quick to note the author's orientalism, as we have noted. All the same, we believe that it makes sense to speak of a post-colonial Freyre, and not simply because he was writing after Brazilian independence.

Some of Freyre's central interests and preoccupations resemble those of post-colonial thinkers such as Edward Said, Ranajit Guha, Paul Gilroy, Homi Bhabha and Gayatri Spivak.[137] They draw on Gramsci, but he made use of Marx – enough for *CGS* to have been read in some quarters, as we have seen, as the work of a Marxist or at least of a materialist. They draw on Lacan, but he made use of Freud. They employ ideas from Foucault and Derrida, but he made use of one of the masters of Foucault and Derrida, Nietzsche – notably the idea of perspectivism that we have mentioned earlier.[138]

Four analogies or affinities between the ideas of Freyre and those of post-colonial theorists are particularly worth noting, even if we allow for differences in both emphasis and application. In the first place there is his life-long concern with the subaltern as well as the dominant, with 'the Cinderellas of history', with slaves as well as masters and with women and children as well as adult males. In the second place is his interest in cultural identity, at its clearest in *CGS*. In the third place comes his preoccupation with hybridity, cultural as well as biological, and especially with the two-way process that Fernando Ortiz, who is sometimes cited as an ancestor of post-colonial theory, famously called 'transculturation'. Particularly striking are the similarities between the ideas of Freyre and those of the Argentinian-Mexican anthropologist Néstor Canclini, whose analysis of hybrid cultures includes, like Freyre's, the hybridization of tradition and modernity.[139] In the fourth place is his critique of Eurocentrism, most apparent in his programme for provincializing Europe by tropicalizing social theory.[140] Like this group of theorists, Freyre was trying to think beyond colonialism. It may be worth adding that a leading post-colonial writer, Kemau Brathwaite, cited Freyre with approval in his history of Creole society in Jamaica.[141]

Today, the post-colonial theorists have the great advantage of representing the periphery but living in the centre, in London or New York, using the Western loudspeaker (publishing houses, journals, television networks and so on), to broadcast their ideas. Freyre, on the other hand, spent most of his life in provincial Recife and usually wrote his books and articles in Portuguese, a language that many Western scholars do not read. All the same, a global history of social thought ought to find a place for his name as well as theirs.

Freyre's Place in Social Thought

There are two basic questions to ask about Freyre as a social thinker or quasi-theorist. In the first place, a relatively precise question: how original were his ideas? Secondly, and more generally: what is his place in the history of social theory?

In later life, Freyre liked to describe himself as having anticipated many theories and approaches in the social sciences, from ecology to 'rurbanization', and later scholars have sometimes taken his word in this respect. If 'anticipations' are defined as ideas which had not previously occurred to anyone, the claim is exaggerated. As he himself admitted, Freyre learned about ecology from Radhakemal Mukerjee and others; he found the term 'rurbanization' in the work of Charles Galpin; his discussions of work and leisure drew on Josef Pieper and Jacques Ellul; his futurology drew on Bertrand de Jouvenel and so on. In this way he mediated between cultures, bringing certain European or North American problems and ideas to the attention of Brazilian readers.

If, on the other hand, the term 'anticipation' refers to the gift for taking up ideas with a great future at a time when their potential has not been fully recognized, then Freyre was a great anticipator. His *NE,* for example, was a pioneering study of what is now known as environmental history. Again, his perceptive discussion of the reciprocal influence of the languages of the masters – and mistresses – and the slaves in *CGS* was published some twenty years before the emergence of the discipline of sociolinguistics, although some linguists had already studied language from a sociological point of view. When sociolinguistics did emerge, Freyre was quick to refer to it.[142]

In fact, Freyre had, to an unusual degree, the capacity to see the importance of a new idea, to take it up and to employ it in a new context, often qualifying or developing it in the process. One might say that he imitated in order to create, quite consciously so. Very early in his intellectual career, Freyre noted, as we have seen, the role of imitation even in the development of a genius such as Shakespeare, whom the young Freyre once described as being at the same time a genius and a plagiarist, a telling example of the fact that 'in the world of culture, nothing is an absolutely new creation'.[143] He read widely, he soaked up ideas and information like a sponge and he cannibalized earlier thinkers, but he gave to what he absorbed and digested a distinctive colouring, very often a tropical colour-ing.

Let us turn to the second question, about Freyre's place in the his-tory of social thought in general and sociology in particular. At first sight, his concern with social harmony and equilibrium makes him look like a follower of Emile Durkheim and the functionalist anthropologists and sociologists. However, this reading of his ideas is too simple, ignoring his concern with social conflict. An 'equilibrium of antagonisms' is far from a simple consensus. The idea of an equilibrium of antagonisms he took, as we have seen, from Spencer and Giddings. His originality lies in the way in which he developed and employed this concept to interpret Brazilian history, culture and society.

At its most generous, the answer that the São Paulo school would have given to our question would have been to describe Freyre as the last of the amateurs, a major figure in the transition from essays in the inter-pretation of Brazilian society to scientific sociology. As Asa Briggs put it, he 'was sociologically aware even when he was not sociologically sophis-ticated'.[144] He appeared to be unsophisticated and old-fashioned because he practised in the middle of the twentieth century the kind of sociology that had been dominant a generation earlier, in the age of Simmel, Park and Thomas and the now obscure Giddings.

All the same, this judgement requires certain nuances. In the first place, Freyre was not so much pre-scientific as anti-scientific. He was aware of the claims made for scientific sociology, but he rejected them. In any case, the age of scientific sociology was followed by a reaction against it. In the history of ideas, as in other kinds of history, one can never be sure who will have the last laugh.

What we can say, then, is that Freyre was not original in the strong sense of launching new and fruitful concepts. On the other hand, he not only appropriated but also elaborated on ideas from different sources. His kind of sociology, which took individuals seriously, considered change over the long term and placed imagination higher than quantification, may have been dismissed as old-fashioned in his own day but it is closer than that of his rivals to the humanistic, historical or cultural sociology practised in our own time (by scholars as different as Peter Berger, for instance, Michael Mann or Jeffrey Alexander). We might add that Freyre's work illustrates a recurrent paradox in intellectual history. Defending the approach of Simmel and Park and adapting it to meet the new challenges of the age of Parsons and Lazarsfeld, Freyre was an innovator thanks to his very traditionalism.

7   Gilberto Our Contemporary

Gilberto Freyre's place in history is secure, thanks in particular to his interpretation of Brazilian culture – the most famous of the three classic interpretations, alongside those of Caio Prado Jr and Sérgio Buarque de Holanda. His wide interests and his global vision justify the obituary in which the Spanish philosopher Julián Marías described him as 'a universal Brazilian'. However, in the seventy-five years since *CGS* was published, the world, including Brazil, has changed almost beyond recognition. So why should one read Freyre today? Three points are worth making in answer to this question.

In the first place (and it was certainly the first place for him), Freyre was one of the finest writers of Portuguese prose in the twentieth century, dancing with the language, inventing new words and fusing a colloquial with a literary style. An 'extraordinary writer', as one of the great Brazilian novelists, João Guimarães Rosa, once called him.[1] We have said relatively little about this achievement in a book intended primarily for a public that does not read Portuguese, but the point deserves to be remembered. Among the most memorable tributes paid to Freyre were the ones from two leading Brazilian poets, Manuel Bandeira and Carlos Drummond de Andrade, both of them emphasizing the poetic qualities of his prose.[2]

In the second place, Freyre was one of the most brilliant and original sociocultural historians of the twentieth century to be found anywhere in the world, and one from whom we can still learn. In the third place, his central ideas about hybridity and tropicalization make a distinctive and still valuable contribution to social thought. In order to define Freyre's achievement more precisely, we will offer a few more brief comparisons and contrasts, more general this time, between his work and that of other historians and sociologists.

Freyre as a Historian

In some ways, Freyre's work recalls G. M. Trevelyan's *English Social History*, a book that he admired and annotated in some detail. Both historians emphasized social harmony more than many of their colleagues, both had powerful historical imaginations, both expressed a certain nostalgia for the past and both were unusually sensitive to the 'poetry of history'.[3] On the other hand, Freyre's concern for the 'Cinderellas of history', as we have already noted, recalls a very different approach to social history from Trevelyan's, that of Edward Thompson.

As a historical essayist, concerned to paint the portrait of an age, Freyre has already been compared with Jacob Burckhardt and Johan Huizinga.[4] The affinities between Freyre and Huizinga are particularly close, despite the difference in generation and also the contrast in personality between the introverted, Apollonian Dutchman and the extrovert, Dionysian Brazilian. Their paths to history, via the aesthetics of decadence, ran parallel. Both men wrote literary masterpieces in a style that owed a good deal to *fin-de-siècle* literature. As we have seen, Freyre admired Walter Pater and Oscar Wilde, and to some extent imitated their style. As for Huizinga, when he was a student at the University of Groningen in the 1890s, he joined a group of aesthetes who read the poems of the Symbolist Paul Verlaine and the novels of Joris-Karl Huysmans.

Huizinga, like Freyre, was a man of wide interests, so wide that he found it difficult to settle down and specialize in history, let alone a particular period. Both were active as journalists, artists and cultural critics (and as critics both concerned themselves with the mechanization of modern life). Huizinga was interested in Buddhism, learned Sanskrit and wrote a thesis on the role of the clown in the ancient Indian drama. When he later turned to the history of his own country he could to some extent see it, like Freyre, with foreign or anthropological eyes. He did in fact read a good deal of anthropology as well as some psychology (he disliked Freud but like Freyre he was attracted to the ideas of William James).

Both scholars produced a cultural history that was unusually sensuous, sensitive to the colours, the sounds and even the smells of the past. Both believed that the history of culture could best be understood in terms of polarities and oppositions: Huizinga contrasted Erasmus with Luther, for instance, Rembrandt with Rubens, the court with the small town.[5] The two historians also shared an interest in material culture – in the history of clothes, for instance, and in symbolism. Huizinga wrote a famous passage about the religious meaning of apples in the Middle Ages; Freyre one about the symbolism of bananas in Brazil.[6]

Freyre's approach to history was also close to that of the French historians associated with the journal *Annales*, emphasizing past structures rather than events and social and cultural life more than politics.[7] It is unlikely that Freyre had much influence on the practice of French historians, or they on him, but independent moves in the same direction led eventually to the discovery of intellectual kinship, what Goethe called 'elective affinities'. Fernand Braudel and Lucien Febvre both praised the work of Freyre, while he did the same for Febvre and Marc Bloch. The parallels with Freyre are closest in the case of two French historians of his own generation, Fernand Braudel and Philippe Ariès.

Fernand Braudel, who was two years younger than Freyre, shared his wide vision, his interest in varieties of time and also his concern for the minutiae of everyday life and material culture (*civilisation matérielle*, as he called it). In the 1960s Braudel wrote about the social history of chairs and tables; in the 1930s Freyre was already discussing the hammock and the rocking-chair. When he was teaching at the new University of São Paulo in the late 1930s, Braudel discovered Freyre's work and wrote an enthusiastic review essay, published in 1943, discussing *CGS*, *S&M* and *NE*, describing the author as 'a born writer', and praising his work as both innovative and rich in detail.[8]

Freyre's affinities were still closer to the so-called 'new history' (*nouvelle histoire*) preached and practiced in France from the 1960s onwards, emphasizing topics such as the family, sexuality and collective mentalities. He was closest of all to Philippe Ariès. Freyre dreamed of writing a history of childhood, while Philippe Ariès actually wrote one, virtually launching the academic study of the history of children in 1960 with his claim that childhood did not exist in the Middle Ages.[9] Ariès argued that childhood, more exactly 'the sense of childhood' (*le sentiment de l'enfance*), was invented in early modern France. His study of childhood, like his later study of death – another concern he shared with Freyre – exemplifies the interest in the history of mentalities associated with the so-called *Annales* school in France, as well as the history of private life that he would launch in the 1980s. The historical studies written by Ariès also resemble those of Freyre in the attention they pay to iconographical evidence and material culture (notably clothes and toys) as expressions of changes in adult attitudes to children.

Ariès was not a professional scholar but a 'Sunday historian', as he described himself in his autobiography, whose working hours were spent as an archivist in an institute for research on tropical fruit. His position, like Freyre's, was on the margin of professional history.[10] This was not the only similarity between the two men, who were not acquainted and appear

Chapter 7

not to have known each other's work. These two great conversationalists would surely have had much to say to one another had they had a chance to meet. Both scholars defined themselves as essayists. In the 1940s, so he tells us, the ambition of Ariès was to write a 'historical essay', although in France at that time 'the two terms, essay and history, appeared to be contradictory'.[11] Both men were critical of industrial society and looked back to the past with a certain nostalgia. Both were regionalists, with Southwest France playing for Ariès the role that the North-East of Brazil played for Freyre. Both were public intellectuals, active as journalists and cultural critics. They expressed similar views on politics. Where Freyre described himself as a 'conservative revolutionary', Ariès called himself an 'anarchist of the Right', suspicious of the increasing power of the state. Both had admired Charles Maurras and sympathized with *Action Française*, Freyre from a distance and Ariès as an active supporter of the movement.[12] Both became politically marginalized, Ariès as a young man, after 1945, thanks to his participation in the collaborationist Vichy regime, and Freyre as an older man, thanks to his support for the military coup of 1964.

Most important of all for their style of history, the two scholars had a similar upbringing. The family of Philippe Ariès were Creoles who had settled in Martinique in the eighteenth century. Both his mother and father had been raised by black nurses, descendants of slaves, whom they called 'Da'. He was especially close to his mother and saw the social world of Martinique through her nostalgic eyes. When the family moved to Bordeaux, a few years before Philippe's birth, the Ariès household remained a group of nine or more people, a mixture of relatives and family servants, providing what he remembered as a close-knit and emotionally warm milieu (*un monde dense et chaud*). Even in the cemetery the family remained together. In the eyes of Ariès, as in those of Freyre, the family tomb resembled 'a patriarchal house'.[13]

It was on the basis of these personal experiences as well as on documents that the two men reconstructed their past worlds of childhood. The contribution of tropical society to the history of the child is thus more important than is generally realized. For both Freyre and Ariès, their upbringing in an extended family was at once a stimulus to the study of childhood and the family and a help to the understanding of patriarchal societies in the past. It led them to appreciate what Freyre called 'intimate history' and Ariès, 'the history of private life'.

Freyre as a Semi-theorist

Like his history, Freyre's social thought is close to that of our time. Indeed it is closer to our time than it was to the sociology of his own day in its concern with the micro-level, the everyday, and the use of literature and personal testimonies. His independence from academic life allowed Freyre to avoid joining any school and to swim against the current. It was relatively easy for him to work in an interdisciplinary manner because he did not need to limit himself to a single discipline for professional reasons. He had wide interests that discouraged specialization. It was also easier for him than others to be post-modern because he was in a sense pre-modern, a defender of tradition.

Freyre's intellectual career, like that of Franz Fanon, Fernando Ortiz, Radhakamal Mukerjee or M. N. Srinivas, illustrates the growing importance of social theory produced outside Europe and the United States. His project for tropicalizing social thought and so provincializing Europe remains extremely relevant to our time. As the Introduction remarked, a comparative social theory, like a comparative political theory, should find a place for Freyre's ideas.[14]

Among these ideas the most important is surely what Freyre variously called mixture, hybridization or interpenetration, terms that suggest comparisons and contrasts between him and the Cuban sociologist Fernando Ortiz, in other words what Ortiz called a 'counterpoint'.[15] Ortiz and Freyre belonged to the same generation. Both had a remarkable range of interests that centred on sociology, anthropology and social history. Both combined a deep attachment to their own region and a profound knowledge of it with a global perspective, encouraged by their studies abroad, one in the United States and the other in Spain.

Both men were remarkable stylists who liked to describe their work as 'essays' and enjoyed elaborate sexual metaphors. Both combined an almost antiquarian love of historical detail with a strong interest in social theory. Both of them were interested in Marx, without being Marxists, and in Freud, without being Freudians. Both were particularly close to social and cultural anthropology: one attended the lectures of Boas, the other became a friend of Malinowski. Both had a racist phase (Ortiz was attracted by the ideas of the Italian criminologist Cesare Lombroso, who believed that criminals had distinctive physical features), but left it behind. They both came to criticize the idea of race and to spend much of their lives in the study of the interaction between cultures, what Ortiz called 'transculturation' (*transculturación*).

Both men were concerned with the everyday: with the social history of the body, with clothes and with food, especially sugar. Both studied the world of the plantations. Both were interested in language. Ortiz learned several African languages in order to study African elements in Cuban culture, while Freyre was a pioneer in the study of language contacts and reciprocal influences, as we have seen.

There were also contrasts between the two. Both men studied the civilization of sugar, but Don Fernando's real enthusiasm was for the culture of tobacco. He lacked Freyre's enthusiasm for architecture, but he had a more profound and detailed knowledge of music. Ortiz was more concerned with conflict, Freyre more with social harmony. Ortiz was closer to Marx than Freyre was and he discussed imperialism, capitalism and the formation of class consciousness among the proletariat. He accepted Castro's regime in Cuba, while Freyre accepted the military regime in Brazil. They both had a European culture but they focused on different Europes. Where Freyre looked towards France and especially England, Ortiz was more interested in Spain and Italy

Gilberto Freyre and the twenty-first century

Some of Freyre's interests sound surprisingly contemporary. In the 1920s, he was already expressing concern for the devastation of the Brazilian forests. In the 1930s, he promoted Afro-Brazilian studies. He was interested in alternative medicine long before this interest became fashionable. He wrote about the history of the body, the history of sexuality and even the history of smells before these topics became part of the repertoire of sociocultural historians. He even had something to say about attitudes to animals, a topic which European historians would only begin to take seriously in the 1980s.[16]

However, Freyre's importance for our own time is not simply that he was a pioneer, concerning himself with problems that have been taken up later. Unlike many scholars, Freyre studied the past not for its own sake alone but from a concern with the problems of the present: with identity, ecology, slum clearance and so on. On these accounts he still has something to teach us because he approached these problems, which are also our problems, in a manner that is often different from ours and still potentially illuminating. In the past, his ideas tended to be neglected because he was not part of any school.[17] Today, that individualism is one of his great attractions. No wonder then that the Joaquim Nabuco Foundation has established a working group entitled 'Freyre and the Contemporary World'.

When he was a deputy in the Constituent Assembly, Freyre was criticized by a colleague for his historical point of view. Freyre's reply was that 'the past is never over; the past continues' (*O passado nunca foi; o passado continua*).[18] As we have stressed throughout this study, Freyre's historical writings might be described as attempts to understand the present by examining the continuing power of the past. The present he was trying to understand in the 1930s and 1940s is now the past, but his approach might and should inspire other scholars to approach our present, whether in Brazil or in the world at large, in a similar way.

So far as Brazil is concerned, a study of the country from 1900 till today along the lines of his trilogy is very much to be desired. Such a fourth volume might be entitled *The Condominium and the Favela*, since these kinds of building are the contemporary equivalents of the Big House and the slave quarters.[19] The condominium is a block of flats for the middle class, guarded against armed robbery and served by porters and maids who clean and cook for the occupants. Porters and maids, usually darker-skinned than the people they work for, often live in *favelas*, clusters of homes that, even if they are often improved later, usually begin by being built hurriedly and without permission on land that happens to be vacant. They are constructed in the first instance out of scrap and connected unofficially to services such as electricity.

Other topics to be considered in a possible Freyrean history of contemporary Brazil include the motel (thinking of Freyre's pages on sex as well as on the hotel); the shopping mall, mediating between the street and the house and providing a controlled environment in which people can walk or sit; the supermarket, replacing the traditional neighbourhood baker's (often a kind of general store); the spread of Italian and Lebanese restaurants and the rise of North American fast food; new forms of dress (T-shirts, jeans, tennis shoes and new hair styles); transport and its problems (overcrowded buses, traffic jams, and motorcyclists weaving between lines of cars), modern advertising (extending Freyre's pages on newspaper advertisements to hoardings and television screens), sport (even if his observations on Brazilian football remain up to date) and of course new media of communication and new genres of communication such as the Brazilian soap opera (*telenovela*), which has become a major export and is watched in many parts of the world.

Underlying these topics there would be a more general Freyrian theme, relevant to many countries today besides Brazil, that of the relative importance of local traditions and foreign, increasingly global models. Have these models been adopted uncritically, leading to the Americanization or (as Freyre himself sometimes said) the "yankeezization" of the country, or have they been adapted to local circumstances? In short, what is the importance of cultural mixture or hybridization?

Popular music may be a good example to help answer this question in an age in which Brazilian contributions are conquering the world. The famous *bossa nova* of the 1950s owed a good deal to North American models, yet Tom Jobim did not sound like Frank Sinatra. The North American element was blended with Brazilian and more especially with Afro-Brazilian tradition, 'chewing gum with banana' (*chiclete com banana*).[20] More recently, the funk singer Fernanda Abreu has once again described blending Brazil with the United States, 'black with swing' (*black com suinge*).[21]

In short, Freyre's ideas have not lost their relevance to today's world, even if they continue to be contested. In an age in which globalization and immigration is changing the culture of many countries, with Turks established in Germany, Moroccans in Paris and Malmö, and Senegalese arriving in Italy by the boatload, the contemporary relevance of his ideas about cultural mixture increases. As we have seen, Freyre was not in favour of ethnic cultures that were separated from the mainstream, such as German-Brazilian culture in the 1940s. On the contrary, he celebrated interaction and interpenetration, declaring that mixed is beautiful and predicting that this idea would be increasingly recognized in the choice of actresses and fashion models. He was a fan of Sonia Braga, (whom he believed to be mixed), the actress who won an international reputation for her role in *Kiss of the Spider Woman* and he would have appreciated Naomi Campbell, the English model of Jamaican and Chinese descent.

Our age of cultural globalization is also an age of trends and counter-trends in which Freyre's ideas are still regularly invoked, whether to agree or disagree. In other words, they remain good to think with.

For example, Freyre is denounced as responsible for the myth of racial democracy, 'the myth of the friendly master' or 'the Freyrian myth of the affectionate Big House'.[22] His key idea of hybridity is increasingly criticized in Latin America on the grounds that it denies the separate cultural identity of both indigenous peoples and African-Americans.[23] In Brazil, a movement of counter-hybridity is growing, modelled on the Black Consciousness movement in the United States. The Brazilian movement began after the First World War but it became stronger with the foundation of the Marxist *Movimento Negro Unificado* during the military regime (1978). One sign of change is the fact that a few samba schools now exclude white participants, notably *Ilê Aiyê* (the name means 'House of Life' in Yoruba), founded in Salvador in 1975.

In this new context, the idea of racial democracy is widely criticized as hypocrisy or mystification, as a mask for white racism. For some years now there has been pressure in Brazil for 'quotas', in other words for laws to oblige universities, the civil service and other institutions to reserve places for students of African descent (and also for indigenous peoples), and the Lula government has come out in favour of affirmative action.

An awkward problem raised by the quota policy is that the question, who counts as 'black' or 'Afro-Brazilian', is not always easy to answer in a country notoriously mixed, in which the North American 'one-drop rule' was never accepted. When identical twins recently applied for places at the University of Brasília under the quota scheme, one was accepted as black and the other rejected, on the basis of photographs. In this context it may be instructive to return to another anthropologist, Franz Boas, who argued against the prohibition of mixed marriages, partly on the grounds that the more difficult it is to decide whether someone is black or white, the weaker race consciousness will become. On similar grounds, he argued that mixed marriages would eventually eliminate anti-Semitism.[24]

A recent attempt to solve the problem of identification is the so-called 'Molecular Portrait of Brazil' (*Retrato molecular do Brasil*) produced by a team of geneticists from Belo Horizonte, using blood samples to show that many Brazilians who look white are actually mixed (a point that the anthropologist Melville Herskovits, a former student of Boas, had made about whites in general in the 1920s).[25] The results are controversial, not least because they have been interpreted in some quarters as a means of 'bringing new blood to the dying myth of racial democracy'. They have attracted a good deal of public attention in Brazil, with articles on the subject in dailies and weeklies as well as television programmes.[26]

Abroad, the interest in the Brazilian model of race relations associated with Freyre continues to be acute. Ironically enough, at the very time that some Brazilians are attracted by the North American model of Black separatism, South Africa has moved from the ideology of apartheid to that of the 'rainbow nation', and a mixed-race movement has developed in the United States (a response to the 'biracial baby boom' following the repeal in 1967 of the anti-miscegenation laws).[27]

A recent article in the *Guardian* by the historian Timothy Garton Ash and the reaction to it bears witness to British interest in this question. Garton Ash summarized the findings of the 'molecular portrait' and the debate over quotas, to conclude, in Freyrean style, that Brazil reveals 'an anticipation of all our futures, in a world where peoples will be increasingly mixed up together', and to hope that 'Brazil moves closer to making a reality of its old myth of "racial democracy"'. His article provoked scores of blogs. Some of them were supportive: 'I would simply love the world to be one cinnamon spice race', or 'the sooner we're all a golden-pinkish-brown the better.' Others rejected his position: 'I will regret the loss of black people, white people, Asian people'.[28]

In reaction to the rise of black consciousness and especially to the idea of quotas, former critics of Freyre such as Fernando Henrique Cardoso, discussed earlier, or the Anglo-Brazilian anthropologist Peter Fry have moved closer to his position. By the 1980s and 1990s, Fernando Henrique was writing about the importance of CGS. 'Freyre captivated me ... because he had been capable of formulating a founding myth' or 'quasi-myth'.[29] As President, by a decree of 13 July 1999, he officially declared the year 2000 (the centenary of Freyre's birth) to be the 'National Year of Gilberto de Mello Freyre'. He even gave an interview in which he declared that although the idea of racial democracy contains an element of mystification, 'it also contains an element of truth'.

As for Fry, he asserts the relevance of S&M for the understanding of Brazilian society today and criticizes the so-called 'racialization of public policy' in Brazil. He opposes affirmative action and the quota system on the grounds that it makes official and so strengthens the 'myths' of two separate races and of racial conflict, weakening the more beneficent myth of mixture and fraternity. He describes racial democracy as a 'utopia', an ideal at which to aim, and the 'new black and mulatto heroes' of Brazilian popular culture as a counterweight to racial antagonisms. In short, although he was once a severe critic of Freyre's ideas, Fry now sees him as an ally.[30]

The founders of the Tropicalist movement in Brazilian music have proceeded in a similar direction. This movement, which originated in the 1960s and 1970s, may sound Freyrean, but its protagonists were critical of Freyre himself. It was indeed to distinguish his position from Freyre's that the Bahian singer-composer Caetano Veloso preferred the term *tropicália* to *tropicalismo*. In 1968 the Tropicalist group made a production for TV Globo which was intended to include an interview with Freyre as part of a parody of Luso-Tropicalism.[31]

More recently, however, both Caetano and his colleague Gilberto Gil have moved closer to Freyre's view of cultural hybridity and even of racial democracy. In the speech he made on being appointed Minister of Culture in the Lula government in 2003, Gil spoke of 'cultural multiplicity' and 'tropical syncretic culture', affirming that 'we are a mixed people'. For his part, Caetano Veloso declared that 'Freyre has been very important to the building of our best myth as a nation, the myth of racial democracy'.[32] He also signed the manifesto against quotas in 2007. The praise of miscegenation and cultural hybridity remains a theme in Brazilian popular music, witness the song 'Etnia' by the band 'Chico Science & *Nação*

Zumbi', a song that has been described as 'a kind of postmodern musical interpretation' of Freyre. Beginning 'We are all united, a miscegenation ... Indians, whites, blacks and mestiços, nothing wrong in their principles' (*Somos todos juntos, uma miscigenação ... Indios, brancos, negros e mestiços / Nada de errado em seus princípios*), the song turns to hybrid performance, 'psychodelic *Maracatu*' (a North-Eastern performance) or 'electric *birimbau*' (the traditional instrument that accompanies *capoeira*).[33]

The black consciousness movement is growing in Brazil, or at least has become more visible than before, with more and more protests about discrimination. On the other hand, it does not appear to attract a large following, thanks in part to the persistence of the idea of racial democracy, still invoked by some poor dark-skinned people, although they do not all understand the phrase in the same way and generally view it not as a fact but as a dream (a point already made by Freyre himself, as we have seen).[34] Sociologists and anthropologists continue to note that Afro-Brazilians lack a 'unified racial identity'. Like the discrimination against which it reacts, 'black identity crystallizes only episodically'. It is strong in the domain of employment, for instance, where Afro-Brazilians are at a disadvantage, but weak in the domain of sport, where fraternization often takes place.[35]

The history of race relations in Brazil over the last century might be summarized in terms of a struggle for hegemony between three myths or discourses. First came the discourse of aryanism or white superiority, defeated – thanks in part to Freyre – by the discourse of racial democracy. Today, on the other hand, the struggle is between the discourse of racial democracy and the discourse of African identity, symbolized by the semi-playful suggestion that the state of Bahia 'the capital of African culture in the Americas', should leave Brazil in order to join Africa. All three myths or discourses screen out information that does not fit their narratives. The myth of racial democracy minimizes discrimination and prejudice in past and present alike, while the myth of African identity denies hybridization, for instance the adaptation of African cults such as *candomblé* to Brazilian circumstances.

Which discourse will triumph in Brazil – or whether some kind of compromise or equilibrium will be achieved between the idea of mixed identity and that of African roots – it is difficult to say. On the other hand, it is relatively easy to imagine how Freyre would have reacted to the current situation. He would have criticized black purism and separatism as much as the white purism and separatism with which he was more familiar. Indeed, he did criticize the idea of *négritude* on occasion, while his friend Jorge Amado spoke of 'black racism'.[36]

Whether we are for quotas or against them, whether we think that 'mixed-race' should or should not be or become an official category, Freyre's ideas and ideals remain highly relevant to the discussion. He has not lost his power to provoke and he remains a reference point in the debate. In this domain, as elsewhere in his work we should treat his ideas in the way that he treated the ideas of others, quick as he was not only to appropriate but to transform them, adapting them to new contexts and situations. Looking beyond Brazil, in an age of racist revival and racist violence, it is clear that the world still has something to learn from Gilberto Freyre's 'mixophilia' and his encouragement of harmony and fraternity.[37]

We know all too well today that the myth of purity, especially in the form of 'ethnic cleansing', can have tragic consequences. On the other hand, cultural historians, Freyre among them, have argued that history shows that no individual or community is pure. This example only confirms the point about the ethics of history that Freyre made at the UNESCO conference in 1948. He suggested that while political and military history, pursued in a nationalist style, often drives peoples apart, 'the study of social and cultural history' is or might be a way 'to bring peoples together' and open 'ways of understanding and communication between them'.[38]

Chronology

Further details in EC, 661ff.

1900   born Recife
1917   conversion to Protestantism
1918   to Baylor, Waco; began to write for *DP*
1920   BA; met Yeats
1921   to Columbia University
1922   'Social Life in Nineteenth-Century Brazil'; travels: Paris, Oxford, Germany, Portugal
1923   return to Recife
1924   lecture 'Apologia pro generatione sua'; foundation of Centro Regional do Nordeste
1925   'Vida Social no Nordeste'; 'Região, Tradição e Cozinha'
1926   visit to Bahia and poem 'Bahia de todos os santos...'; poem 'O outro Brasil que vem aí'; visit to RJ, met Sérgio Buarque de Holanda and Pixinguinha; visit to SP, met Paulo Prado; visit to American South with Simkins; Bilden visit Freyre in Recife; Regionalist Congress in Recife
1927–30   *oficial de gabinete* to E. Coimbra
1928   professor of sociology and anthropology at Escola Normal, Recife
1930   revolution; visited Senegal; in exile in Portugal
1931   visiting professor, Stanford
1933   *Casa Grande e Senzala*
1934   organized Afro-Brazilian congress in Recife; *O Estudo das ciências sociais nos universidades americanas*; *Guia da Cidade do Recife*
1935   arrest and interrogation for criticism of law of national security; denounced as agitator for attempting research into workers in rural Pernambuco; wrote manifesto against racial prejudice with Roquette and Ramos

1935–7	taught a course in sociology in the University of the Federal District
1936	*Sobrados e Mucambos*
1937	*Nordeste*; visited Paris exhibition together with Paulo Prado
1937	visit to Lisbon to Congress of Portuguese Expansion
c.1937	visit to Spain
1939	visiting professor at Michigan
1939	*Açúcar*; *Olinda*
c.1939	*Mucambos do Nordeste*
1940	*Um engenheiro francês no Brasil*; *O mundo que o Português criou*; lecture *Uma cultura ameaçada*; first visit to Rio Grande do Sul; 'Sobrado no Rio Grande do Sul'; 'Social Development'
1941	married Magdalena
1941	*Região e Tradição*
1941	'Racial Minorities'
1942	briefly imprisoned for having denounced Nazism in Brazil; *Ingleses*; *Problemas brasileiros de Antropologia*
1943	'Paulo Prado'
1944	gave Patten lectures at University of Indiana; 'Perfil de Euclydes'; *Na Bahia*
1945	*Brazil: an Interpretation*
1945	*Sociología*
1946–50	served as deputy in Constituent Assembly
1946	English trans. of *CGS* published
1947	chosen by deputies as Nobel candidate
1948	*Ingleses no Brasil*; *Guerra, Paz e Ciência*; at UNESCO conference in Paris; speech proposing Instituto Joaquim Nabuco; began to write for *O Cruzeiro*
1949	presented project for Instituto Joaquim Nabuco; visit to United States, delegate to fourth UN conference
1950	*Quase Política*
1951	second, enlarged edn of *S&M*
1951–2	in Portugal and colonies
1953	*Um brasileiro em terras portuguêsas*; *Aventura e Rotina*
1955	'História além dos textos'
1959	*Ordem e Progresso*; *A Propósito de Frades*; *Túmulos afro-christianos*; official invitation to Brasília; film, 'Mestre de Apipucos'
1962	*Talvez Poesia*
1963	*New World in the Tropics*; *O Escravo nos anúncios de jornais brasileiros do século xix*
1964	*Dona Sinhá e o filho padre*

1964	Came out in support of military regime
1965	at University of Sussex
1966	'The Racial Factor in Contemporary Politics'
1967	*Sociología da medicina*
1968	*Como e porque sou e não sou sociólogo; Brasis, Brasil e Brasília; Oliveira Lima: Dom Quixote Gordo; Contribuição para uma sociología da biografia*
1971	interview, *Realidade; A Casa Brasileira*
1972	exhibition of Freyre's drawings
1973	heart operation; *Além de Apenas Moderno*
1975	*Tempo Morto*
1977	*O outro amor do Dr Paulo*
1978	*Alhos e bugalhos*
1979	*Heróis e Vilões no Romance brasileiro*
1981	*CGS em quadrinhos*
1983	*Insurgências e Resurgências*
1984	'Uma Paixão Nacional'; *Camões: Vocação de Antropólogo*
1985	*Cultura e Museus*
1986	*Ferro e Civilização*
1987	*Assombrações do Recife Velho; Modos de homem e modas de mulher*; died Recife

Notes

Chapter 1: The Importance of Being Gilberto
1. J. Pedro de Andrade (directed), 'Mestre de Apipucos' (1959).
2. R. L. Euben, *Enemy in the Mirror: Islamic Fundamentalism and the Limits of Modern Rationalism. A Work of Comparative Political Theory* (Princeton: Princeton UP, 1999), 9.
3. The ambiguities are emphasized in R. Benzaquen de Araújo, *Guerra e Paz: Casa-Grande e Senzala e a obra de Gilberto Freyre nos Anos 30* (RJ: Editora 34, 1994), as well as in *VT, passim*.
4. Meneses.
5. *C&P; TM*.
6. *VT*, 43.
7. N. Shakespeare, *Bruce Chatwin* (London: Cape, 1999), 339.
8. R. Bendix, *Max Weber: an intellectual portrait* (New York: Doubleday, 1960).
9. S. Collini, *Absent Minds: intellectuals in Britain* (Oxford: OUP, 2006).
10. Earlier English translation as *The Waning of the Middle Ages*; if Freyre knew the book he might have read it in this translation or in French or Spanish.

Chapter 2: Portrait of the Artist as a Young Man
1. Freyre knew and admired Joyce's *Portrait of the Artist as a Young Man* when he was himself a young man, witness his article on Joyce in *DP*, 11 December 1924.
2. For full references for the statements made in this chapter, see *VT, passim*.
3. M. L. Pallares-Burke, 'Gilberto Freyre: a Love Story', in *The European Legacy* 3, no. 4 (1998), 11–31.
4. Pallares-Burke, 'Love story'.
5. C. Hayes, *An Introduction to the Sources relating to the Germanic Invasions* (New York: Columbia UP, 1909), 86.
6. *VT*, 362–4.
7. SL.
8. Pallares-Burke, 'Love Story'.
9. *VT*, 407–12.

10. *VF&C; BI* 47, 49.
11. *VT*, 84–5.
12. *IB*, 34.
13. What follows draws especially on J. Woodall, *The Man in the Mirror of the Book* (London: Sphere, 1996).
14. *VT*, 89–113.
15. P. Levi, *The Search for Roots: a personal anthology* (London: Allen Lane, 2001).
16. *VT*, 102.
17. E. Rugai Bastos, *Freyre e o pensamento hispânico* (Baúru and SP: EDUSC, 2003), 168ff.
18. On Freyre and Germany, V. Chacon, *Freyre: uma biografia intellectual* (Recife: Massangana, 1993); on Sudermann, *VT*, 255–9.
19. R. Bilden, 'Brazil: laboratory of civilization', *The Nation*, no. 3315 (1929).
20. This much quoted passage comes from the first preface to *CGS*, 45.
21. *DP*, 20 March 1921.
22. *DP*, 27 February 1921.
23. O. Montero, *José Martí, An Introduction* (Basingstoke: Palgrave Macmillan, 2004); *Racism in the Republic: Marti and the Legacy of the U.S. Civil War*, Lehman College & The Graduate Center, CUNY, *www.lehman.edu/ciberletras/v07/montero.html*; M. G. Miller, *Rise and Fall of the Cosmic Race* (Austin: University of Texas Press, 2004).
24. E. R. Black, *War against the Weak: Eugenics and America's Campaign to Create a Master Race* (New York: Thunder's Mouth Press, 2003), 19.
25. *VT*, 220–30.
26. J. L. Borges, *The Aleph and Other Stories, 1933–1969: together with commentaries and an autobiographical essay* (London: Cape, 1971), 224.
27. *DP*, 28 October 1923.
28. N. Shakespeare, *Bruce Chatwin* (London: Cape, 1999), 339.
29. L. Hearn, *Kokoro: hints and echoes of Japanese inner life* (Boston: Houghton, Mifflin, 1896).
30. Meneses, a passage probably written by Freyre himself. Cf. M. Hélio, *O Brasil de Freyre: uma introdução à leitura de sua obra* (Recife: Comunigraf, 2000), 61ff.
31. U. Hannerz, *Cultural Complexity: Studies in the Social Organization of Meaning* (New York: Columbia UP, 1992), 260.
32. E. Cabral de Mello, *O norte agrário e o Império, 1871–1889* (RJ: Nova Fronteira, 1984); cf. D. Muniz de Albuquerque, *A invenção do Nordeste* (Recife: Massangana, 1999).
33. The problem of the differences between the lost one-page programme of the Centro Regionalista do Nordeste in 1926 and the version that Freyre published in 1952 remains unsolved. See W. Martins, 'O manifesto regional que não houve' (1965), *http.//www.secrel.com.br/jpoesia/*.
34. *R&T*, 89.
35. C. Lacerda, 'O Menino do Engenho', in J. Lins do Rego, *Ficção Completa* (2 vols, RJ: Editora Nova Aguilar, 1976), vol. II, 1311.

36. C. Braga-Pinto (ed.) *Ligeiros Traços: escritos de juventude, de José Lins do Rego* (RJ: Olympio, 2007); *VT*, 167–78.
37. On the two leaders, A. Dimas, 'Barco de proa dupla: Freyre e Mário de Andrade', in *Imperador*, 849–69.
38. Cf M. Antonio de Moraes (ed.) *Correspondência Mário de Andrade e Manuel Bandeira* (SP: EDUSP, 2000), 221n; cf. Dimas, 'Barco'.
39. A. G. Ramos Nogueira, *Por um inventário dos sentidos: Mário de Andrade e a concepção de patrimônio e inventário* (SP: Hucitec, 2005).
40. G. Freyre, *Manifesto* (7th edn, Recife: Massangana, 1997), 36; cf. *Sociología*, 4th edn (RJ: Olympio, 1967), 77.
41. *DP*, 15 November 1925.
42. J. D. Needell, 'Identity, Race, Gender and Modernity in the Origins of Freyre's Oeuvre', *American Historical Review* 100 (1995), 51–77: *VT*, 267–70.
43. SL also ended with a description of funerals, but the tone was less nostalgic.
44. *VSN*, 148.
45. R. M. Levine, *Father of the Poor? Vargas and his era* (Cambridge: CUP, 1998).
46. On the child project, Peter Burke, 'O pai do homem: Gilberto Freyre e a história da infância', *EC*, 786–96.

Chapter 3: Masters and Slaves
1. D. Ribeiro, 'Gilberto Freyre: uma introdução a *CGS*' (1977; rpr. *EC*, 1026–36).
2. Interview with M. Faerman (1985), BVGF.
3. *VT*, 407–11; W. Pater, 'The Child in the House', in *Miscellaneous Studies* (London: Macmillan, 1910), 178–9; G. Gissing, *The Private Papers of Henry Ryecroft* (1903: rpr. London: Phoenix House, 1953), 79, 84, 90–1, 130–1, 152, 160; cf. J. D. Needell, 'Identity, Race, Gender and Modernity in the Origins of Gilberto Freyre's Oeuvre', *American Historical Review* 100 (1995), 51–77.
4. C. G. Mota, 'Revisitando O Mundo que o Português Criou', in F. Quintas (ed.) *Novo Mundo nos Trópicos* (Recife: Fundação GF, 2000), 248–54, at 249.
5. *CGS*, 48, 55 (from the preface to the first edition, omitted from the English translation); on Zimmern, M. L. Pallares-Burke, 'O Caminho para casa-grande', *EC*, 821–48, at 833–5.
6. Interview (1983).
7. Freyre's preface to S. Buarque, *Raízes do Brasil* (RJ: Olympio, 1936). Cf. A. da Costa e Silva, 'Quem fomos nos no século xx: as grandes interpretações do Brasil', in C. G. Mota (ed.) *Viagem Incompleta: a experiência brasileira 1500–2000* (SP: SENAC, 2000), 19–41.
8. C. da Matta', 'Nota filológica' to EC, xxix–xxxiv.
9. C. Ribeiro Hutzler, 'Antropologia visual em *CGS*', in F. Quintas (ed.) *A Obra em tempos vários: livro comemorativo dos 95 anos de nascimento de Gilberto Freyre* (Recife: Massangana, 1999), 101–12.

10. Note by Freyre to selections from these prefaces, appendix to fortieth edn of *CGS*, 563.
11. *CGS*, 55.
12. On this aspect of the book, G. Gomes, 'A arquitetura em *CGS*', EC 749–70. The sketch was inspired by a book on medieval England.
13. Freyre is more explicit in *S&M*, 16.
14. *CGS*, 49.
15. *O&P*, 448.
16. *CGS*, 475, 52, 51.
17. P. Burke, 'O pai do homem: Gilberto Freyre e a história da infância', EC, 786–96.
18. M. Lopes Gama, quoted in M. L. G. Pallares-Burke, 'A Spectator in the Tropics', *Comparative Studies in Society and History* 36 (1994), 676–701, at 683.
19. *CGS*, 399–401; *M&S*, 360–3.
20. *CGS*, 165–6.
21. A good discussion of this aspect of the book is R. Vainfas, 'Sexualidade e cultura em *CGS*', EC, 771–85.
22. Freyre, letter to Rodrigo de Andrade, 15 November 1932, BVGF.
23. *CGS*, 311; *M&S*, 259.
24. *VT*, 120–39.
25. *CGS*, 83–4. The Putnam translation omits 'gostosamente'.
26. *CGS*, 121–2; *M&S*, 74–5.
27. L. Costa Lima, 'A versão solar do patriarcalismo', *A Aguarrás do Tempo: estudos sobre a narrativa* (RJ: Rocco, 1989); R. Benzaquen de Araújo, *Guerra e Paz: Casa-Grande e Senzala e a obra de Gilberto Freyre nos Anos 30* (RJ: Editora 34, 1994).
28. *CGS*, 495; *M&S*, 446.
29. *CGS*, 372; *M&S*, 323-4.
30. *CGS*, 284; *M&S*, 223.
31. T. E. Skidmore, *Black into White; race and nationality in Brazilian thought* (New York: Oxford University Press, 1974); J. Lesser, *Negotiating National Identity: immigrants, minorities, and the struggle for ethnicity in Brazil* (Durham, NC: Duke UP, 1999).
32. *VT*, 279–82.
33. J. M. Park, *Latin American Underdevelopment: a history of perspectives in the United States, 1870–1965* (Baton Rouge: University of Louisiana Press, 1995), 123.
34. *CGS*, 343; *M&S*, 278 (translation modified).
35. Freyre, *O Camarada Whitman* (RJ: Olympio, 1948), 21–2, 34–7; id., *Dona Sinhá e o Filho Padre* (RJ: Olympio, 1971), 117–18, 134.
36. VSN; *CGS*, 387–91; *M&S*, 343–9.
37. F. Ortiz, *Cuban Counterpoint: tobacco and sugar* (1940: English trans., New York: Knopf, 1947).
38. S. Schwartz, 'Gilberto Freyre e a história colonial: uma visão otimista do Brasil', EC, 909–21.

39. *CGS*, 210; *M&S*, 156–7.
40. *CGS*, 121–2, 393–4, 472–3; *M&S*, 74–7, 330–1, 403.
41. *CGS*, 125; *M&S*, 79–80 (translation modified).
42. H. Spencer, *First Principles* (1867: new edn, London: Routledge, 1996), 486–7, 507ff. and *passim*.
43. *VT*, 359, 374–6.
44. Ribeiro, 'Introdução', 20; *R&T*, 63.
45. M. de Certeau, *The Writing of History* (1975: English trans., New York: Columbia UP, 1988).
46. *CGS*, 203, 327; *M&S*, 146, 224n.
47. *CGS*, 192, 343, 376, 430; *M&S*, 128, 278, 329, 402.
48. *CGS*, 368; *M&S*, 316.
49. *VT*, 370.
50. *CGS*, 155; *M&S*, 66n.
51. *CGS*, 347; *M&S*, 283.
52. *VT*, 332–45.
53. Quoted in L. Stoddard, *The Rising Tide of Colour against White-World Supremacy* (1920: Brighton, Historical Review Press, 1981), 120.
54. *CGS*, 59; *M&S*, xlvi.
55. *CGS*, 382–6; *M&S*, 337–42 (translation modified).
56. *CGS*, 58–9; *M&S*, xlviii. The translator has left out a qualifying 'perhaps'.
57. *CGS*, 182, 189, 391; *M&S*, 113, 125, 350.
58. *CGS*, 61; *M&S*, liii.
59. B. Matamoro, 'Gilberto Freyre: un discurso del método', *Ciência e Trópico* 2 (1974), 249–61; Ribeiro, 'Introdução', 1035–7; M. L. Pallares-Burke, 'Um método anti-metódico', in *Imperador*, 32–45.
60. On pointillism, E. Nery de Fonseca, '*CGS* como obra literária', EC, 870–1. On Conan Doyle, Freyre, *Dona Sinhá e o filho padre* (2nd edn, RJ: Olympio, 1971), 240; cf. C. Ginzburg, 'Clues', *Myths, Emblems, Clues* (London: Hutchinson, 1990), 96–125. On micro-history, R. Vainfas, 'Sexualidade e cultura em *CGS*', EC 771–85, at 785.
61. *CGS*, 50, 202; *M&S*, xxxv, 144.
62. Quoted in T. Glover, *The Jesus of History* (London: SCM, 1917), a passage underlined by Freyre in his copy; K. Burke, *A Grammar of Motives* (New York: Prentice-Hall, 1945), 59.
63. *CGS*, 292; *M&S*, 233.
64. *C&P*, 149.
65. *CGS*, 227; *M&S*, 183.
66. Freyre, letter, 27 November 1921, BVGF.
67. *VT*, 250.
68. Nery de Fonseca, 'Obra literária'.
69. H. White, *Metahistory* (Baltimore: Johns Hopkins UP, 1973).
70. *CGS*, 216; *M&S*, 167.
71. *CGS*, 46; *M&S*, xxx.
72. *CGS*, 216. In the margin of Benson's *Pater* he wrote 'GF' in the margin where Benson noted that Pater was fond of 'beginning a sentence with an em-

phatic phrase and thus inverting the clause'.
73. Y. de Almeida Prado, *Literatura*, 20 January 1934; L. Miguel Pereira, *Gazeta de Notícias*, 7 October 1934. Lins in *O Estado*, 3 February 1934; O. T. de Sousa, *O Jornal* (1934); Arinos in *Estado de Minas*, 11 February 1934.
74. J. Macy, *The Spirit of American Literature* (New York: Modern Library, 1908), 235–6, the pages turned down in Freyre's copy.
75. *CGS*, 404; *M&S*, 366, modifying the unusual sentence structure that we have restored.
76. *CGS*, 506; *M&S*, 461.
77. Nery de Fonseca in 'Obra literária' notes Freyre's 'estilo imagista'.
78. *CGS* 111, 482; *M&S*, 56, 429 (translation modified).
79. *CGS* 265, 482; *M&S* 199, 429 (translation modified).
80. J. C. Reis, *As Identidades do Brasil, de Varnhagen a FHC* (RJ: Fundação Getúlio Vargas, 1999), 51–82.
81. On Romero, A. Candido, *Introdução ao metodo crítico de Silvio Romero* (SP: Rev. dos Tribunais, 1945); Skidmore, *Black*, 32–7.
82. Freyre, *Perfil de Euclides* (RJ: Olympio, 1944).
83. M. A. Rezende de Carvalho, '*CGS* e o pensamento social brasileiro', EC, 877–908.
84. *VT*, 323–4.
85. Meneses, 211.
86. *M&S*, 179.
87. P. Prado, *Retrato do Brasil* (1928: ed. C. A. Calil, SP: Companhia das Letras, 1997), especially 85, 135, 138, 143, 179, 185, 199, 204. He described his book as optimistic in a letter to his son: ibid., 217–18.
88. T. Lima Nicodemo, *Urdidura do Vivido. Visão do Paraíso e a obra de Sérgio Buarque de Holanda na década de 1950* (SP: EDUSP, 2008).
89. *CGS* 52, 55, 94, 135, 163, 202, 231, 370, 406, 406, 449, 451. On Bilden, *VT*, 378–406.
90. *CGS*, 448; *M&S*, 322n,; *VT*, 379–80.
91. *CGS*, 363, 440, 444, 596; *BI*, 65. U. B. Phillips, *American Negro Slavery: a survey of the supply, employment and control of Negro labor as determined by the plantation regime* (New York: Appleton, 1918), viii, 309, 313–14, 321, 327–8. Cf. R. Hofstadter, 'U. B. Phillips and the Plantation Legend', *Journal of Negro History* 29 (1944), 109–24.
92. *VT*, 193–201, 345–52; A. Zimmern, *The Greek Commonwealth: politics and economics in fifth-century Athens* (4th edn, Oxford: Clarendon Press, 1924), 385, 390.
93. M. de Andrade, original preface to *Macunaíma* (not published in the first edn), quoted in A. G. Ramos Nogueira, *Por um Inventário dos Sentidos* (SP: Hucitec, 2005), 119.
94. F. Tannenbaum, preface to *Mansions*, xi.
95. J. Amado, *Estado de SP*, 9 Oct 1971: 'Meu país é uma verdadeira democracia racial'. Id., preface to H. Costa, *Fala Crioulo* (RJ; Record, 1982), 15. Cf. M. G. Miller, *Rise and Fall of the Cosmic Race* (Austin: University of Texas Press, 2004).

96. J. Monteiro Lobato, preface to Meneses (1944); J. Amado, 'CGS e a Revolução Cultural', *CFA*, 30–6; A. Candido, 'Aquele Gilberto' (1987: rpr. in his *Recortes* (SP: Companhia das Letras, 1993), 82–4; E. Nery de Fonseca, *DP*, 3 May 1973.

97. R. M. F. de Andrade, *Diário Carioca*, 20 October 1933.

98. J. Lins do Rego, *O Estado*, 3 February 1934.

99. Letter from Manuel Bandeira, 17 January 1935, BVGF.

100. Skidmore, *Black*, 199.

101. M. Silveira (directed) *CGS*, adapted by José Carlos Cavalcanti Borges.

102. Freyre, interview, *Jornal de Brasil*, 2 September 1973.

103. D. H. P. Maybury-Lewis (1986; rpr. EC, 1111–15); H. Vianna, *The Mystery of Samba: popular music and national identity in Brazil* (Chapel Hill: University of North Carolina Press, 1999).

104. M. Herskovits (1951; rpr. his *New World Negro*, Bloomington: Indiana UP, 1966), 28; P. Martin, *HAHR* 14 (1934), 327.

105. Tannenbaum, *Mansions*, vii, xi.

106. Reported in *DP*, 14 May 1939. Cf. F. Moulin-Civil, 'Les voix croisés de Gilberto Freyre et Fernando Ortiz', EC, 1126–36. M. Moreno Fraginals, *The Sugarmill: the socioeconomic complex of sugar in Cuba, 1760–1860* (1964; English trans., New York: Monthly Review Press, 1976), 9.

107. R. Barthes (1953; rpr. EC, 1100–1).

108. F. Braudel (1943; rpr. EC, 1075–90).

109. *Estado de SP*, interview with Hobsbawm, 12 March 2000.

110. Letter from the translator, E. Tóth, to Freyre, 5 February 1986. Freyre claimed to have been translated into Serbo-Croat and Russian, but these versions may not have been published.

111. Meneses, 255.

112. V. do Rêgo Monteiro wrote in 1933 of 'a mais repugnante pornografia'. Cf. Vainfas, 'Sexualidade'.

113. Needell, 'Identity'; M. Chor Maio, '"Estoque semita": a presença dos judeus em CHS', *Luso-Brazilian Review* 36 (1999), 95–110.

114. On sentimentalism, A. Cândido, 'Prefácio', to 1969 edn of S. Buarque, *Raízes do Brasil*; rpr. his *Teresina e seus amigos* (RJ: Paz e Terra, 1980), 135–52; Ribeiro, 'Introdução', 13.

115. J. Ribeiro, *Jornal do Brasil*, 31 January 1934.

116. C. Rodrigues, *Gazeta de Alagoas*, 4 July 1937.

117. R. Ghioldi, 'Gilberto Freyre, sociólogo reaccionario' (1951; rpr. *Escritos*, 4 vols, Buenos Aires: Anteo, 1975–7), vol. 4, 16–44.

118. Ghioldi, *Gilberto Freyre*, 40.

119. S. B. Schwartz, *Sugar plantations in the formation of Brazilian society: Bahia, 1550–1835* (Cambridge: CUP, 1985); B. J. Barickman, *A Bahian Counterpoint* (Stanford: Stanford University Press, 1998); id., 'Revisiting the *Casa Grande*: Plantation and Cane-Farming Households in Early Nineteenth-Century Bahia', *HAHR* 84 (2004), 619–60.

120. G. Veiga, *Jornal do Comercio*, 7 December 1952.

121. Ghioldi, *Gilberto Freyre*, 20, 24.

122. On settlements of fugitive slaves, *CGS*, 117, 348; *M&S*, 68, 285. On everyday resistance, J. Scott, *Weapons of the Weak: everyday forms of peasant resistance* (New Haven: Yale UP, 1985).

123. Quoted in C. Dunn, *Brutality Garden* (Chapel Hill: University of North Carolina Press, 2001), 129.

124. *CGS*, 392; *M&S*, 351. Freyre's point is that the relation between mistresses and slaves was shaped by the confinement of the mistresses to the view from the veranda. An attempt at the opposite perspective, the view from 'the quarters' may be found in J. W. Blassingame, *The Slave Community: Plantation Life in the Antebellum South* (New York: OUP, 1972).

125. G. Veiga, *Jornal do Comercio*, 10 August 1952; id., *A teoria do poder constituinte en Frei Caneca* (Recife: Universidade Federal de Pernambuco, 1975), 10–11; id., 'Um Pensador dialético', *Ciência e Trópico* 11 (1983), 241–56, at 250.

126. The prefaces to the Brazilian editions, from the second to the twentieth, are conveniently collected in EC, 483–526.

127. *CGS*, 348; *M&S*, 285.

128. *CGS*, 139–40, 331. Milliet's critique is rpr. in EC, 982–4.

129. *CGS*, 137; *S&M*, 164. Cf. Freyre, 'Maternalismo na formação brasileira', *DP*, 24 December 1950, and L. Miguel Pereira, 'A valorização da mulher na sociología histórica de Gilberto Freyre', *CFA*, 350–6.

130. E. Cabral de Mello, 'O "ovo de Colombo" gilbertiano', in *Imperador*, 17–31, at 29.

131. E. and J. de Goncourt, *Les maîtresses de Louis XV* (Paris: Firmin Didot, 1860), preface.

132. D. Boorstin, *The Americans* (3 vols, New York: Random House, 1958–73); R. Hofstadter, 'Conflict and Consensus in American History', in *The Progressive Historians: Turner, Beard, Parrington* (London: Cape, 1969), 437–66.

133. H. Nash Smith, *Virgin Land: the American West as symbol and myth* (Cambridge, Mass.: Harvard UP, 1950); W. Fluck and T. Claviez (eds) *Theories of American Culture, Theories of American Studies* (Tübingen: Gunter Narr, 2003).

134. E. Rugai Bastos, *Gilberto Freyre e o pensamento hispânico* (Baúru and SP: EDUSC, 2003).

135. Freyre's copy of Castro was the 1954 edition, entitled *La realidad histórica de España*. He had published two articles on Castro in *O Cruzeiro* in 1953. Cf. C. Sánchez-Albornoz, *España: un enigma histórico* (Buenos Aires: Sudamericana, 1956), 145.

136. Miller, *Cosmic Race*, 27–44.

137. Vasconcelos is cited in *AAM*, 230.

Chapter 4: A Public Intellectual

1. J. Le Goff, *Intellectuals in the Middle Ages* (1957; English trans., Oxford: Blackwell, 1993); C. Charle, *Naissance des 'intellectuels': 1880–1900* (Paris: Minuit, 1993). The phrase about 'constant movement' comes from the discussion of definitions in S. Collini, *Absent Minds: intellectuals in Britain* (Oxford: OUP, 2006), 45–65.

2. D. Pécaud, *Entre le people et la nation: les intellectuels et la politique au Brésil* (Paris: Maison de Science de l'Homme, 1989), 62; Collini, *Absent Minds*, x; A. Reyes, 'Notas sobre la inteligencia americana', *Sur* (1936). On Brazil, S. Miceli, *Intelectuais à brasileira* (SP: Companhia das Letras, 2001).

3. E. W. Said, *Representations of the Intellectual* (London: Vintage, 1993); id., *Out of Place: a memoir* (London: Granta, 1999).

4. G. A. Moore, *The Coming of Gabrielle: a comedy* (New York: Boni and Liveright, 1921), 219.

5. Freyre, 'A ternura maternal da Bahia'(1943: rpr. in his *Bahia e bahianos*, Salvador: Fundação das Artes, 1990), 43.

6. Miceli, *Intelectuais*, 231.

7. *O&P*, 421–2; *Order*, 148–9.

8. M. L. G. Pallares-Burke, 'A Spectator in the Tropics: a case study in the production and reproduction of Culture', *Comparative Studies in Society and History* 36 (1994), 676–701.

9. On Freyre's activities as a journalist up to 1933, see *VT*, *passim*.

10. *DP*, 10 April 1921.

11. Meneses, 128, 290; F. Morais, *Chatô, o rei do Brasil* (SP: Companhia das Letras, 1994); E. Nery de Fonseca, 'Do Encanamento aos Aflitos', in M. Tavares de Miranda (ed.) *Que somos nos? 60 anos S&M* (Recife: Fundação J. Nabuco, 2000), 25–34, at 28.

12. Freyre, *Modos de homem e modas de mulher* (RJ: Record, 1986), 88; *TM*, 319; cf. A. Vizeu, 'O primeiro manual de redação do Brasil', *Observatório da Imprensa*, 17 July 2007.

13. The BVGF includes a chronological list of articles, but this is nothing like complete, witness the many articles in scrapbooks in the FGF that do not occur in it. We have added what we found in the scrapbooks to the list in the BVGF, but the figures above should only be taken as a minimum.

14. Freyre, 'Modo de ser escritor', *O Cruzeiro*, 30 January 1954; speech at Petrópolis, 24 July 1959; id., letter to José Olympio, 29 June 1964, BUGF. Cf. Miceli, *Intelectuais*, 146–56.

15. Freyre, 'A Inglaterra e os intelectuais modernos', in *Ingleses* (RJ: Olympio, 1942), 148–50.

16. *PBA*, 141–72.

17. Conversation with Freyre's daughter Sonia Maria Freyre Pimentel and his daughter-in-law Maria Cristina Suassuna de Mello Freyre, 2001.

18. *VT*, 224–9 and *passim*.

19. *TA*, I, 19.

20. Bilden, letter to Oliveira Lima, 20 January 1926.

21. Freyre, 'Meredith e os annuncios de jornal', *Correio da Manhã*, 2 November 1939; id., 'A proposito de um romance', *DP*, 30 August 1950.

22. Freyre, 'A propósito de um romance'.

23. Freyre, 'O romantico Mumford', *Correio da Manhã*, 23 July 1938; id., 'Favelas e Mucambos', *O Cruzeiro*, 1 July 1950.

24. Freyre, 'Um livro de Mumford', *Correio de Manhã*, 23 June 1939.

25. Freyre, 'O Velho Boas', *Jornal de Comercio*, 21 January 1943.

26. Freyre, 'Football mulato', *DP*, 17 June 1938. Cf. T. J. F. de Albuquerque Maranhão, 'Apolo versus Dionísio no campo da história: o futebol em Gilberto Freyre', *http://www.efdeportes.com*, Revista Digital – Buenos Aires – vol. 10 (2004).
27. *Order*, xxvi.
28. *DP*, 16 December 1923.
29. Freyre, 'Internationalizing Social Science', in H. Cantril (ed.) *Tensions that Cause Wars* (Urbana: University of Illinois Press, 1950), 139–65.
30. Freyre, 'Internationalizing', 157–8.
31. Lins, letter, 1924.
32. Freyre, 'Dois Livros', *O Jornal*, 27 January 1944.
33. *VF&C*, 156–86.
34. *VT*, 185, 216–17.
35. On the regionalist movement, Meucci, 58–63; R. M. Levine, 'The First Afro-Brazilian Congress', *Race* 15 (1973), 185–93; id., *Pernambuco in the Brazilian Federation 1889–1937* (Stanford: Stanford University Press, 1978), 69–70; A. Romo, 'Rethinking Race and Culture in Brazil's First Afro-Brazilian Congress of 1934', *Journal of Latin American Studies* 39 (2007), 31–54.
36. Freyre, 'O que foi o primeiro congresso', *Estudos Afro-Brasileiros* (2 vols, 1935–7: facsimile rpr., Recife: Fundação Joaquim Nabuco, 1988), vol. 2, 348–52.
37. A. Teixeira, letter, 12 October 1957; cf. letter, 20 April 1959, Biblioteca Virtual Anísio Teixeira.
38. Freyre, letters, BVGF.
39. J. Outtes, *O Recife: Gênese do Urbanismo, 1927–43* (Recife: Editora Massangana, 1997), 49, 54, 67.
40. On Freyre as an employee of SPHAN, Meucci, 109; criticisms of him in *O Jornal*, 14 February 1926, quoted in Levine, *Pernambuco*, 68, 200; Freyre, *Mucambos do Nordeste: algumas notas sobre o typo de casa mais primitivo do Brasil* (RJ: Ministério da Educação e Saúde, 1937).
41. Freyre, 'Favelas e Mocambos'.
42. D. Chaves Panodli, *Pernambuco de Agamenon Magalhães* (Recife: Editora Massangana, 1984); J. A. Ribeiro, *Agamenon Magalhães: uma estrela na testa e um mandacaru no coração* (Recife: Assembléia Legislativa do Estado de Pernambuco, 2001).
43. N. Evenson, *Chandigarh* (Berkeley: University of California Press, 1966).
44. Freyre, *Prefácios* (2 vols, RJ: Cátedra, 1978), vol. 1, 73; *Rurbanização: que é?* (Recife: Massangana, 1982), 121; on Burle Marx, N. Stepan, *Picturing Tropical Nature* (London: Reaktion, 2001), 76–91.
45. Freyre, 'A Brazilian's Critique of Brasília', *The Reporter*, 31 March 1960.
46. Cf. R. Nash, *The Conquest of Brazil* (New York: Harcourt Brace, 1926), a book that Freyre cited and that argued the need for a 'forest policy'.
47. *QP*, 216–38; cf. Freyre, *Rurbanização: que é?*
48. Freyre, 'Roupa de menino', *O Cruzeiro*, 19 May 1951; id., *Modos*, 106.
49. Freyre, interview, 1941; id., *Nos e a Europa germânica* (RJ: Grifo, 1971). Cf. G. Seyferth, 'Nacionalismo e imigração no pensamento de Freyre', in E. V.

Kosminsky, C. Lepine and F. Arêas Peixoto (eds) *Gilberto Freyre em quatro tempos* (Bauru: EDUSC, 2003), 155–80.

50. Freyre, interview 1980; M. Chor Maio, 'O Projeto UNESCO e a Agenda das Ciências Sociais no Brasil dos anos 40 e 50,' *Revista Brasileira de Ciências Sociais* 14 (1999), 141–58, at 150.

51. The manifesto was written at the suggestion of Ulisses Pernambucano. Olívio Montenegro and Sylvio Rabelo supported it: *QP*, 17–18. Cf. Freyre, *Uma cultura ameaçada* (Recife: Officina do Diário da Manhã, 1940).

52. Freyre, 'Exemplo de Lutador', *O Jornal*, 17 June 1944, an obituary of Ulisses; id., 'Atualidade de William Morris', DOPS file, Xerox copy in FGF.

53. Freyre, 'Inimigo da Gente de Cor', *DP*, 5 September 1950.

54. Freyre, *O Jornal*, 25 January 1944.

55. P. Flynn, *Brazil: a Political Analysis* (London: Benn, 1978), 132–49; G. Veiga, 'Na tarde morna de verão, more o herói', *DP*, 3 March 1999.

56. These attacks appeared mainly in the *Folha da Manhã*, a paper owned by Agamenon Magalhães.

57. Freyre, 'Meu rótulo de "comunista"', *DP*, 19 August 1945.

58. Freyre, 'Novas palavras aos baianos', *DP*, 29 August 1945; id., 'Para quem o povo marcha', *DP*, 7 October 1945.

59. Nine speeches are reprinted in *QP*.

60. Freyre, *DP*, 28 July 1945.

61. Freyre, 'A Vitoria do Socialismo na Gra-Bretanha', *Correio de Manhã*, 28 July 1945; id., 'Regresso aos grandes homens', *Correio de Manhã*, 30 July 1940; id., 'Difficil de classificar', *Correio de Manhã*, 1 October 1937.

62. Freyre, interview, 1971; G. Corção, *O Século do Nada* (RJ: Record, 1973).

63. Freyre, 'A Vitória do Socialismo na Grã-Bretanha', *Diários Associados*, 28 July 1945.

64. Freyre, 'Rui Barbosa e a Inglaterra', in *Ingleses*, 165–70; id., 'Rui Barbosa e a Questão social', in *Pessoas, Coisas & Animais* (SP: MPM Propaganda, 1979), 254–91.

65. R. Ghioldi, 'Freyre, sociólogo reaccionario', in *Escritos* (4 vols, Buenos Aires: Anteo, 1975–7), vol. 4, 16–44.

66. G. Veiga, *Jornal do Comercio*, 23 March, 4 May, 8 June, 15 June, 6 July, 10 August, 7 September, 5 October, 12 October, 7 December, 14 December 1952. The quotation from G. Veiga, 'Um pensador dialético', *Ciência e Trópico* (1983), at 253. Interview given by Veiga to the authors in August–September 2001.

67. Quoted in A. Moreira, *Condiciamentos Internacionais da Area Luso-Tropical* (Recife: Massangana, 1984), 4.

68. Cantril, *Tensions*, 7–8.

69. C. Piñeiro Iñiguez, *Sueños paralelos. Freyre y el lusotropicalismo* (Buenos Aires: Grupo Editor Latinoamericano, 1999), 51–7.

70. A. da Costa e Silva, 'Notas de um companheiro de viagem', *A&R*, 14–15.

71. Freyre, 'A propósito de críticas', *O Cruzeiro*, 15 November 1952; *A&R*, 43–5, 156–7.

72. P. Chabal, *Amílcar Cabral: revolutionary leadership and people's war* (Cam-

bridge: CUP, 1983); C. Castelo, 'A Recepção do Luso-Tropicalismo em Portugal', in F. Quintas (ed.) *Novo Mundo nos Trópicos* (Recife: FGF, 2000), 84–95.

73. Castelo, 'Recepção', 93. Cf. A. Enders, 'Le luso-tropicalisme, théorie d'exportation', *Lusotopie* (1997), 201–10; Y. Léonard, 'Salazar et luso-tropicalisme, histoire d'une appropriation', *Lusotopie* (1997), 211–26; id., 'A ideia colonial, olhares cruzados', in F. Bethencourt and K. Chaudhuri (eds) *História da Expansão Portuguesa* (5 vols, Lisbon: Círculo de Leitores, 1998) vol. 4, 521–50; C. Castelo, *"O modo português de estar no mundo"*. *O luso-tropicalismo e a ideologia colonial portuguesa (1933–1961)* (Porto: Edições Afrontamento, 1998); C. Piñeiro Iñiguez, *Sueños paralelos*; A. Moreira and J. C. Venâncio (eds) *Luso-Tropicalismo: Uma Teoria Social em Questão* (Lisbon: Vega, 2000); A. Warley Candeer, *La tropicologie dans l'oeuvre de Gilberto Freyre*, Paris, doctoral thesis, 2002, http://prossiga.bvgf.fgf.org.br/portugues/critica/teses/alessandro_candeas.pdf.

74. A. Cabral, 'Foreword' to B. Davidson, *The Liberation of Guinea* (1969). The critics are in turn criticized by P. Borges Graça, 'A Incompreensão da Crítica ao Luso-Tropicalismo', in Quintas, *Novo Mundo*, 208–12.

75. Rémy Lucas, 'Aventura e Rotina: Gilberto Freyre et l'Afrique', *Lusotopie* (1997) 237–48; Costa e Silva, 'Notas'.

76. Quoted in Piñeiro/Iñiguez, *Sueños paralelos*, 392; Borges Graça, 'A Incompreensão', 209.

77. Flynn, *Brazil*.

78. Freyre, 'Internationalizing Social Science', 148–50

79. Freyre, *Harvard Crimson*, 10 December 1964.

80. F. Morais, *Chatô, o rei do Brasil* (SP: Companhia das Letras, 1994), 653.

81. E. Duarte in WC (a collection of press cuttings kept by Freyre's wife Magdalena; the title probably denotes 'water-closet', the correct place, in her view, for critical reviews of her husband), FGF.

82. Freyre, *Nação e Exército* (RJ: Olympio, 1948); id., *Rio Branco: a Estátua e o Homem* (1946); cf. Meneses, 271–5.

83. DP, 5 February 1922.

84. DP; letter to José Olympio, 27 August 1954.

85. Freyre, 'Um Ano Histórico para o Brasil', *DP*, 26 April 1964; id., *Seis Conferências em busca de um leitor* (RJ: Olympio, 1965); id., preface; *Para um programa da Arena*, 1972.

86. Freyre, interview, 1970.

87. *Sunday Times*, 22 March 1972.

88. Freyre, 'Em louvor de Dom Helder, *O Cruzeiro*, 23 February 1958; id., 27 August 1966; J. de Broucker, *Dom Helder Câmara: la violence d'un pacifique* (Paris: Fayard, 1969), 88; N. Piletti and W. Praxedes, *Dom Helder Câmara entre o poder e a profecia* (SP: Editora Ática, 1997), 339–40.

89. *O Globo*, 8 June 1964.

90. M. C. Carvalho, 'Céu e inferno de Freyre', *Folha de S. Paulo, Mais!*, 12 March 2000, 6–8.

91. Letter to José Olympio, 20 June 1964.

92. A. Candido, 'Aquele Gilberto', *Recortes* (SP:Companhia das Letras 1993), 82–4.
93. Interview with G. Veiga, 2001; E. Veríssimo, letter, 8 January 1972, BVGF.
94. 'O Anarquista construtivo', interview with Freyre, *Veja*, 1981.
95. E. Gaspari, *A ditadura envergonhada* (SP: Companhia das Letras, 2002); id., *A ditadura escancarada* (2004); id., *A ditadura encurralada* (2004).
96. *IB*, xix.
97. Meneses, 254–70; Candido, *Recortes*, 82.
98. Freyre, 'Revolucionário conservador' (1949); *O&P*, 741, 777.
99. Cf. J. G. Merquior, *EC*, 1045.
100. On Vargas, R. M. Levine, *Father of the Poor? Vargas and his Era* (Cambridge: CUP, 1998); B. Fausto, *A Concise History of Brazil* (Cambridge: CUP, 1999), 198–236.
101. Freyre, *Pessoas*, 313.
102. Meucci, 176.
103. Freyre, *O Cruzeiro*, 27 August 1949.
104. Freyre, *DP*, 10 August 1947.
105. Freyre, *New World in the Tropics* (New York: Knopf, 1959).
106. Freyre, *DP*, 28 November 1952.
107. Freyre, 'Difficil de classificar'.
108. Freyre, *DP*, 28 November 1952.
109. P. Geddes, *Cities in Evolution* (London: Williams and Norgate, 1915), 314.
110. Freyre, 'Um livro de Mumford', *Correio de Manhã*, 23 June 1939.
111. L. Mumford, *The Culture of Cities* (London: Secker and Warburg, 1938), 151, 161, 163.
112. R. Wojtowicz, *Lewis Mumford and American Modernism* (Cambridge: CUP, 1996), 39.

Chapter 5: Empire and Republic

1. N. Elias, *Involvement and Detachment* (Oxford: Blackwell, 1987).
2. Freyre, 'Livros Novos', *O Estado de São Paulo*, 10 July 1937.
3. Freyre, *Perfil de Euclides e outros perfis* (1944: 2nd edn, RJ: Record, 1987), 21.
4. *NE*, 26. The book has not been translated into English.
5. Freyre makes reference to Braudel in the 2nd edn of *NE*.
6. Quoted in Meucci, 327; cf the discussion, 215–28.
7. *NE*, 135, 74, 77, 99, 197.
8. *NE*, 64, 176.
9. *NE*, 163.
10. *NE*, 176–7.
11. *NE*, 166.
12. R. Ghioldi, 'Freyre, sociólogo reaccionario', in *Escritos* (4 vols, Buenos Aires: Anteo, 1975–7), vol. 4, 33.
13. *S&M*, 11 (omitted in the English translation).
14. Preface to *Terres du Sucre* (Paris: Gallimard, 1956), the French translation of *NE*.
15. *NE*, 158.

16. *NE*, 89.
17. *NE*, 98. Cf. C. Lévi-Strauss, *The Savage Mind* (1962; English trans., London: Weidenfeld, 1966), 204–7.
18. E Cabral de Mello, 'O "ovo de Colombo" gilbertiano', in *Imperador*, 17–31.
19. *CGS*, 470–4, 489–90.
20. Preface to first edn of *CGS*.
21. *IB*, 134.
22. *Mansions*, xiii.
23. *CGS*, 61.
24. *Diário de Noticias*, 13 April 1939; *Correio da Manhã*, 8 December 1939.
25. Letter to GF, 30 September 1947.
26. E. Cabral de Mello, 'Ovo'. The author gave one of his books to Freyre in 1984 with the inscription, 'Who can, writes *S&M*: who cannot, contents himself with writing works at a second level, like this book.'
27. *O&P* 180, 286; *Order*, 70.
28. *O&P*, 198, 562, 318–39; *Order*, 218, 88–102.
29. *S&M*, 118: *Mansions*, 72.
30. *O&P*, 470, 142, 504, 587–8; *Order*, 247–8, 238.
31. *O&P*, 163, 427, 430; *Order*, 116.
32. *S&M*, 13, 125, 159; *Mansions*, xxv, 73–4, 99; *O&P*, 470; *Order*, 167.
33. *O&P*, 271, 267; *Order*, 54.
34. R. Benzaquen, *Guerra e Paz: CGS e a obra de Freyre nos anos 30* (RJ: Editora 34, 1994), 132.
35. *S&M*, 60; *Mansions*, 26.
36. *S&M*, 65; *Mansions*, xxvii (translation modified).
37. *S&M*, 16; *Mansions*, xxvii; *O&P*, 137, 333–4; *Order*, 99.
38. *S&M*, 600–59; *Mansions*, 354–99; *O&P*, 477; *Order*, 170, 174, 182.
39. *O&P*, 473; *Order*, 170.
40. *S&M*, 615; *Mansions*, 369.
41. *S&M*, 564; *Mansions*, 339; *Order*, 11.
42. *O&P*, 485, 519; *Order*, 174, 188.
43. Freyre, *Artigos de Jornal* (Recife: Mozart, 1935), 69–71.
44. G. Deleuze, *Proust et les signes* (Paris: PUF, 1964).
45. E. P. Thompson, *The Making of the English Working Class* (London: Gollancz, 1963), 12.
46. C. Ginzburg, 'Clues', *Myths, Emblems, Clues* (London: Hutchinson, 1990), 96–125, at 123–4.
47. M. L. G. Pallares-Burke, 'O caminho para a Casa Grande: Freyre e suas leituras inglesas', *EC*, 821–48.
48. *IB*, 39, 44, 295, etc.
49. P. Arbousse-Bastide, preface to Freyre, *Um Engenheiro Francês no Brasil* (1940: 2nd edn RJ: Olympio, 1960), I, 4–6; R. Bastide, quoted ibid., 5–7.
50. L. Venturi, *Painting and Painters – How to look at a Picture from Giotto to Chagall* (New York: Scribners, 1947), 72, 84, 112–15.
51. Cf. H. P. Chapman, *Rembrandt's Self Portraits – a Study in Seventeenth-Century Identity* (Princeton: Princeton UP, 1990), 75.

52. *IB*, 27–9, 37–8.
53. E. Cabral de Mello, introduction to *IB*.
54. L. Costa, 'O Aleijadinho e a arquitectura tradicional' (1929); C. Ribeiro de Lessa, 'Mobiliário Brasileiro dos Tempos Coloniais', *Estudos Brasileiros* 6 (1939).
55. *PBA*, lxx.
56. *TM*, 88.
57. I. Jacknis, 'Franz Boas and Exhibits', in G. W. Stocking (ed.) *Objects and Others* (Madison: University of Wisconsin Press, 1985), 75–111; id., 'The Ethnographic Object and the Object of Ethnology in the Early Career of Franz Boas', in Stocking (ed.) *Volksgeist as Method and Ethic* (Madison: University of Wisconsin Press, 1996), 185–214; E. Kasten, 'Franz Boas: Ethnographie und Museumsmethode', in M. Dürr, E. Kasten and E. Renner (eds) *Franz Boas* (Wiesbaden: Harrassowitz, 1992), 79–102.
58. G. W. Stocking (ed.) *The Shaping of American Anthropology, 1883–1911: a Franz Boas Reader* (New York: Basic Books, 1974), 61–7.
59. Quoted in Jacknis, 'Exhibits', 79, 101; Jacknis, 'Objects', 205. Cf. B. Malinowski, 'Culture', *Encyclopaedia of the Social Sciences* (1930: rpr. New York: Macmillan, 1948), vol. 3, 621–45.
60. F. Boas, *Kwakiutl Ethnography* (Chicago: University of Chicago Press, 1966), 77–104.
61. T. Veblen, *Theory of the Leisure Class* (New York: Huebsch, 1899), 35, 121.
62. Freyre, 'Some Aspects of the Social Development of Portuguese America', in C. C. Griffin (ed.) *Concerning Latin American Culture* (New York: Columbia UP, 1940), 79–103, at 96; id., 'Veblen', *Jornal de Comercio*, 27 April 1943.
63. Freyre, *Seis conferências em busca de um leitor* (RJ: Olympio, 1965), 68.
64. Freyre, 'Sugestões para o estudo histórico social do sobrado no Rio Grande do Sul' (1940: rpr. *PBA*, 84–98; id., 'engenheiro francês'; id., *A Casa Brasileira* (RJ: Grifo, 1971).
65. *IB*, 149–284; *O&P*, 150; *Order*, 138–44.
66. *IB*, 62.
67. *IB*, 56, 73, 174; *O&P*, 590–1, 605.
68. *IB*, 240.
69. On hats, *O&P*, 603; gloves, jackets, coats, *IB*, 57; shoes, *S&M*, 624ff.; underwear, *O&P*, 818; *Order*, 367.
70. *O&P*, 299; *Order*, 79.
71. *O&P*, 845–6; *Order*, 372–3.
72. *S&M*, 12, 132, 760; *Mansions*, a section added in the enlarged edition of 1951.
73. *S&M*, 429–30; *Mansions*, 271 (omitting the anecdote).
74. *S&M*, 16; *Mansions*, xxiv.
75. *S&M*, 215, 222; *Mansions*, 140, 145.
76. *S&M*, 212; *Mansions*, 134–5.
77. On slums, *S&M*, 210f., 666; *Mansions*, 132–4, 406–7; on *favelas*, Freyre, *O Cruzeiro*, 1 July 1950.

78. J. Lins do Rego, *O Moleque Ricardo* (Rio: Olympio, 1935), especially ch. 23.
79. L. Veríssimo, *O Tempo e o Vento* (RJ: Globo, 1949-62).
80. Freyre, 'Sobrado'; id., 'A proposito de um romance', *DP*, 30 August 1950.
81. On the *chácara*, *S&M*, 220, 232; *Mansions*, 107.
82. On the bungalow, *IB*, 57; the chalet, *O&P*, 387; *Order*, 133.
83. *IB*, 19, 86; *O&P*, 627.
84. On the station, *IB*, 128; the hotel, *O&P*, 586-90; *Order*, 238-41.
85. *S&M*, 68, 76, 245-6.
86. *IB*, 79, 173, 195ff.
87. *O&P*, 78, 280f; *Order*, 66.
88. GF, *Dona Sinhá e o Filho Padre* (3rd edn, RJ: Record, 2000), 200.
89. *IB*, 220.
90. *O&P*, 284-5; *Order*, 68-9.
91. Freyre, *O Cruzeiro*, 3 April 1954.
92. *O&P*, 282-3; *Order*, 67.
93. *IB*, 191.
94. Ribeiro de Lessa, 'Mobiliário'.
95. *Order*, xxxiii.
96. *IB*, 187, 200, 221.
97. *S&M*, 455; *Mansions*, 273. Arbousse-Bastide, xiv.
98. The criticism was made by L. Costa Lima, 'A versão solar do patriarcalismo', *A Aguarrás do Tempo*: *estudos sobre a narrative* (RJ: Rocco, 1989), 187-236, at 216. Briggs quoted in M. L. G. Pallares-Burke, *The New History: Confessions and Conversations* (Cambridge: Polity Press, 2001), 41-5.
99. *O&P*, 496-7, 505, 558, 615-6; *Order*, 196-7, 256.
100. VSN, 146-50.
101. *S&M*, 455-6; *Mansions*, 273-4.
102. *IB*, 42, 45, 196-9, 221, 229, etc.
103. *NE*, 166.
104. *IB*, 119-21, *passim*.
105. *IB*, 194-204.
106. *IB*, 134-5.
107. *O&P*, 657, 764-5; *Order*, 330-1.
108. *O&P*, 269-70, 818; *Order*, 55, 367.
109. *O&P*, 272-3; *Order*, 57, 404.
110. F. Ortiz, *Cuban Counterpoint* (1940: English trans., New York: Knopf, 1947). Cf. *S&M*, 508, 784 (sections added for the 1951 edn).
111. *O&P*, 806; *Order*, 356.
112. *IB*, 107, 113, 136, 221.
113. *O&P*, 144, 858-73; *Order*, 376-85.
114. *O&P*, 818, 867; *Order*, 367, 383.
115. Benzaquen, *Guerra*, 139-43; Y. M. Lotman, *Russlands Adel: eine Kulturgeschichte von Peter I. bis Nikolaus I* (1994; German trans., Cologne: Böhlau, 1997).
116. Benzaquen, *Guerra*, 134-5.
117. *IB*, 189. On the 'double life', E. Seidensticker, *Low City, High City: Tokyo from Edo to the Earthquake, 1867-1923* (London: Allen Lane, 1983).

118. *IB*, 221.
119. *O&P*, 287; *Order*, 71.
120. *IB*, 228.
121. E. and J. de Goncourt, *Histoire de la Société Française pendant la Révolution* (Paris: Dentu, 1854), 92–6.
122. Benzaquen, *Guerra*, 137–8.
123. *S&M*, 75.
124. *S&M*, 69, 345, 624; *O&P*, 92, 646–9, 790–2, etc.; *Order*, 267–70, 337–9, 349–51.
125. Freyre, 'Sobrado', 93.
126. First given as a paper in 1934, published in book form as *Escravo*.
127. *Escravo*, 61, 68, 71–2.
128. *Escravo*, 16, 29, 46, 68.
129. J.-P. Aron, P. Dumont, E. Le Roy Ladurie, *Anthropologie du conscrit français d'après les comptes numériques et sommaires du recrutement de l'armée, 1819–1926* (Paris: Mouton, 1972).
130. S. Thyrso, *Cartas de algures* (Lisbon: Portugalia, 1924), 265; Freyre, 'Meredith e os annuncios de jornal', *Correio da Manhã*, 2 November 1939. Freyre himself pays tribute to G. B. Johnson, 'Newspaper Advertisements and Negro Culture', *Journal of Social Forces* (1924–5) and to M. J. Herskovits, *The Anthropometry of the American Negro* (New York: Columbia University Press, 1930). Cf. *Journal of Negro History*, 1 (1916), 163–216.
131. Preface to *S&M*, 19.
132. L. Vauthier, *Diário íntimo*, ed. Freyre (Rio: Olympio, 1940); Freyre, 'Engenheiro francês'; Freyre, *O Velho Felix* (RJ: Olympio, 1959).
133. *O Cruzeiro*, 13 June 1953; *O&P*, 961n., omitted from English translation.
134. *Diário de Noticias*, 13 April 1939; *Correio da Manhã*, 8 December 1939; *O Jornal*, 11 April 1943; *O&P*, 58, 103–31; *Order*, xxxii.
135. F. Znaniecki, *Social Action* (1936; rpr. New York: Russell and Russell, 1967), 638–9; Freyre, *Prefácios desgarrados* (2 vols, RJ: Cátedra, 1978), vol. 2, 958ff.
136. P. Thompson, *The Voice of the Past* (Oxford: OUP, 1978), 78.
137. Freyre, *DP*, 2 July 1942.
138. *O&P*, 149–52; omitted from English translation.
139. *NE*, 90.
140. *S&M*, 15, 68, 76, 624; *Mansions*, xxvi–xxvii, 34.
141. *O&P*, 284–5; *Order*, 69.
142. *S&M*, 230, 235; *Mansions*, 152 – the second passage was omitted from the translation .
143. *O&P*, 764, 282; *Order*, 330.
144. *S&M*, 299; *Mansions*, 181.
145. *S&M*, 125; *Mansions*, 74 (our translation).
146. *O&P*, 810, 948; *Order*, 360.
147. *O&P*, 299, 485; *Order*, 79 (omitting the qualification), 179.
148. F. Braudel, 'A travers un continent d'histoire', rpr. *EC*, 1075–87; E. Cabral de Mello, 'Ovo'; Freyre, interview, 1983.
149. *Order*, xiii.

236   *Notes*

150. S. Buarque de Holanda, 'Sociedade Patriarcal' (1951; rpr. *Tentativas de Mito-logia*, SP: Perspectiva, 1979, 99–105).
151. L.Washington Vita, *Correio Paulistano*, 21 June 1959; Skidmore.
152. D. de Carvalho, *Diário de Notícias*, 28 July 1959; Skidmore, 499.
153. Skidmore, 500; E. Da Costa Viotti, *Brazilian Empire: Myths and Histories* (Chicago: Chicago UP, 1985); F. H. Cardoso, *Capitalismo e escravidão no Brasil Meridional* (SP: Difusão Européia do Livro, 1962); O. Ianni, *As metamorfoses do escravo: apogeu e crise da escravatura no Brasil Meridional* (SP: Difusão Européia do Livro, 1962); F. Fernandes, *A integração no negro na sociedade de classes* (SP: EDUSP, 1965).
154. P. Ariès and G. Duby (eds) *Histoire de la vie privée* (5 vols, Paris: Seuil, 1985–7); F. Novais (ed.) *História de la vida privada no Brasil* (4 vols, São Paulo: Companhia das Letras, 1998–2000). One of the rare references to Freyre comes in the chapter by E. Cabral de Mello.
155. VSN, 101.
156. *CGS*, 51–2.
157. *S&M*, 736–7.
158. *O&P*, 684, 700; *Order*, 286, 300.
159. Freyre, *Em torno de algums túmulos afro-cristãos* (Salvador: Livraria Progresso, n.d. [c.1959]).
160. Noted in the margins of his copy of P. and B. Berger, *Sociology: a biographical approach* (New York: Basic Books, 1972).

Chapter 6: The Social Theorist

1. On Freyre's teaching experience at the Escola Normal and the University of the Federal District, Meucci, 19–180, 326–9.
2. The revisions are discussed in Meucci, 239–43.
3. *C&P*; on anthropology, 23, 83. The title echoes a book by the novelist José de Alencar, *Como e porque sou romancista* (1873).
4. *CGS*, ch. 1, n. 153.
5. On Freyre's attitude to theory, D. Ribeiro, 'Gilberto Freyre: uma introdução a *CGS*' (1977; rpr. EC, 1026–36), at 1032; on method, M. L. G. Pallares-Burke, 'Un método antimetódico: Werner Heisenberg e Gilberto Freyre', in *Imperador*, 32–45.
6. Meucci, 12, and *passim*.
7. E. Hobsbawm, *The Age of Capital 1848–1875* (London: Weidenfeld, 1975), 263; J. W. Burrow, *Evolution and Society* (Cambridge: CUP, 1966), 179–227; G. Hawthorn, *Enlightenment and Despair: a history of sociology* (Cambridge: CUP, 1976), ch. 5.
8. J. A. Hobson, 'Herbert Spencer' (1904; rpr. in M. W. Taylor (ed.) *Herbert Spencer: Contemporary Assessments* (London: Routledge, 1996).
9. VT, 359–70.
10. H. Spencer, *First Principles* (1867: new edn, London: Routledge, 1996), 9–13, 68–97.
11. H. Spencer, 'Replies to Criticism' (1873; rpr. in *Essays: Scientific, Political, and Speculative*, new edn, London: Routledge, 1996), vol. II, 219–43.

12. Freyre, *Novas Conferências em Busca de Leitores* (Recife: Fundação de Cultura da Cidade do Recife, 1995), 37, 96 (articles first published in 1943 and 1969); id., *O Jornal*, 10 November 1942.

13. Freyre, 'Malinowski', *La Nación*, 1 May 1943; id., 'Radcliffe-Brown', *Ingleses* (RJ: Olympio, 1942), 151-5.

14. Freyre, *Jornal de Comercio*, 27 April 1943.

15. On Freyre's relation to Freyer and Simmel, S. Vila Nova, *Sociologías e Possociología em Freyre* (Recife: Massangana, 1995), 69–82; Meucci, 194–5. Cf. D. Frisby, *Sociological Impressionism: a re-assessment of Georg Simmel's social theory* (1981; 2nd edn, London: Routledge, 1992). On Freyre's 'superficial' knowledge of German and his need to read Simmel, Weber et al. in translation, *C&P*, 45. His library included a Spanish translation of Simmel's essays, *Cultura femenina* (1934), including the philosophy of fashion.

16. The passage marked comes from S. Tax (ed.) *Horizons of Anthropology* (London: Allen and Unwin, 1965), 137.

17. V. Chacon, *Gilberto Freyre: uma biografia intelectual* (Recife: Massangana, 1993), 200–01, 261–2; lectures from this period are printed in *PBA*, 3–27 and in Freyre, *Antecipaçoes* (Recife: EDUPE, 2001), 46–55, 71–83.

18. The correspondence between Freyre and Herskovits can be found in the Herskovits papers in the University Archives, Northwestern University. Our thanks to the archivist, Allen Streiker, for supplying copies.

19. S. Miceli (ed.) *História das ciências sociais no Brasil*, vol.1 (SP: Vértice and IDESP, 1989).

20. *Sociología*, vol. 1, 18.

21. *DP*, 3 August 1958.

22. *Sociología*, 16, 281.

23. *Sociología*, 66–7.

24. Letter, 2 February 1946.

25. *Sociología*, 302ff., 337–8, 565ff., 570ff.

26. *Sociología*, 691–7.

27. *S&M*, 740 (from the introduction to the 2nd edn, 1951).

28. Interview with A. Rino Sobrinho, *O Jornal*, 11 April 1943.

29. *Sociología*, 20, 29, 65–6, 99, 587.

30. *Sociología*, 13-16, 30-1, 58, 64-5.

31. J. L. Gillin, 'Franklin Henry Giddings', in H. W. Odum (ed.) *American Masters of Social Science* (New York: Holt, 1927), 191–228; L. Davids, 'Franklin Henry Giddings: overview of a forgotten pioneer', *Journal of the History of the Behavioral Sciences* 4 (1968), 62–73.

32. F. H. Giddings, *Readings in Descriptive and Historical Sociology* (New York: Macmillan, 1906). Cf. *VT*, 362–5, 370–6.

33. *Sociología*, 497-8.

34. *C&P*, 85; E. Roquette-Pinto, *Ensaios de antropologia brasiliana* (SP: Companhia Editora Nacional, 1933).

35. Freyre, *Rurbanização: que é?* (Recife: Massangana, 1982). He was criticized by Wilson Martins (*Jornal do Brasil*, 18 June 1983) for exaggerating his claims

to originality in this domain and for using the term in the opposite way to the Americans who coined it.

36. SL, 599.
37. S&M, 369.
38. IB, 159, 242.
39. G. Gurvitch, *The Spectrum of Social Time* (1958: English trans., Dordrecht: Reidel, 1964). On the more general affinities between Freyre and Gurvitch, Meucci, 266–70.
40. O&P, 83 (omitted from English translation).
41. O&P, 41, 48; *Order*, xxix (second passage omitted).
42. O&P, 235 (omitted from English translation).
43. Freyre, 'On the Iberian Concept of Time', Chapel Hill: United Chapters of the Phi Beta Kappa (1963), 415–30, available in BVGF.
44. AAM, passim.
45. AAM, 67, 86, 155.
46. O&P, 639 (omitted from English translation).
47. PBA, 108.
48. Among many examples, which tended to disappear from the translations, CGS, 110, 303, 393; O&P, 76, 581, 589, 597.
49. D. Arnold, '"Illusory Riches": representations of the tropical world, 1840–1950', in F. Driver and B. Yeoh (eds) *Constructing the Tropics, Singapore Journal of Tropical Geography* 21 (2000).
50. *Escravo*, 41.
51. A&R, 249.
52. O&P, 485–6 (partly lost in translation in *Order*, 180).
53. R. DaMatta, 'For an Anthropology of the Brazilian Tradition', in D. Hess and R. DaMatta (eds) *The Brazilian Puzzle: culture on the borderlands of the Western World* (New York: Columbia UP, 1995), 270–92, at 281; J.-L. Amselle, *Mestizo Logics: anthropology of identity in Africa and elsewhere* (1990; English trans., Stanford: Stanford UP, 1998).
54. CGS,46; O Jornal, 7 May 1943; BI, chapter; 'Has Brazil developed a Racial Democracy?'. Cf. L. Cruz, 'Democracia racial', *http://www.fundaj.gov.br/ tpd/128.html*.
55. M. Chor Maio, 'O Projeto UNESCO e a Agenda das Ciências Sociais no Brasil dos anos 40 e 50,' *Revista Brasileira de Ciências Sociais* 14 (1999), 141–58, at 143–4; R. E. Sheriff, *Dreaming Equality: color, race, and racism in urban Brazil* (New Brunswick: Rutgers UP, 2001); A. S. Guimarães, 'Racial Democracy', in J. Souza and W. Sinder (eds), *Imagining Brazil* (Lanham, MD: Lexington Books, 2005), 119–40, at 119, 125, 127.
56. Guimarães, 'Democracy', 122; Freyre, *Jornal de Comercio*, 25 July 1945.
57. D. Pierson, *Negroes in Brazil: a Study of Race Contact at Bahia* (Chicago: University of Chicago Press, 1942), 331, 345 (with frequent references to Freyre); C. Wagley (ed.) *Race and Class in Rural Brazil* (Paris: UNESCO, 1952), 7 (with a reference to Freyre, 8n.).
58. E. Viotti, 'The Myth of Racial Democracy' (1979; rpr. in her *Brazilian Empire* (Chicago: Chicago UP, 1985), 234–46); M. G. Hanchard , 'Racial

Democracy', in *Orpheus and Power* (Princeton: Princeton UP, 1994) 43–74; H. Vianna, 'A meta mítológica da democracia racial', in *Imperador*, 215–21.

59. R. Ghioldi, 'Freyre, sociólogo reaccionario', in *Escritos* (4 vols, Buenos Aires: Anteo, 1975–7), vol. 4, 16–44, at 40; E. Cabral de Melo in *Imperador*, 24.

60. Cruz, 'Democracia', 2–4.

61. *VT*, 324.

62. R. Bilden, 'Brazil, Laboratory of Civilization', *The Nation*, January 1929.

63. S. Zweig, *Brazil: Land of the Future* (English trans., London: Cassell, 1942), 7–9.

64. Quoted in M. A. do Nascimento Arruda, *Metrópole e Cultura: São Paulo no meio século xx* (Bauru, SP: EDUSC, 2001), 406.

65. C. R. Boxer, *The Portuguese Seaborne Empire* (1969: 2nd edn, Harmondsworth: Penguin, 1973, 283); id., *Race Relations in the Portuguese Colonial Empire*, 1415–1825 (Oxford: Clarendon Press, 1963). Cf. Freyre, 'O Professor Boxer', *O Cruzeiro*, 29 December 1956.

66. M. Chor Maio, 'O Projeto UNESCO'.

67. On Métraux, Bastide and Fernandes, J. B. Borges Pereira, 'Raça e classe social no Brasil', in M. A. d'Incao (ed.) *O Saber Militante: ensaios sobre Florestan Fernandes* (SP: UNESP, 1987), 151–60, at 152.

68. M. Harris, *Town and Country in Brazil* (New York: Columbia UP, 1956).

69. F. H. Cardoso, *Capitalismo e escravidão no Brasil Meridional* (SP: Difusão Européia do Livro, 1962); O. Ianni, *As metamorfoses do escravo: apogeu e crise da escravatura no Brasil Meridional* (SP: Difusão Européia do Livro, 1962); F. Fernandes, *A integração no negro na sociedade de classes* (SP: EDUSP, 1965).

70. Cardoso and Ianni, *Côr*, 277; Ianni, *Raças*, 5, 7, 26, 68.

71. R. Bastide and F. Fernandes, *Relações raciais entre negros e brancos em São Paulo: ensaio sociológico sobre as origens, as manifestações e os efeitos do preconceito de cor no município de São Paulo* (SP: Editora Anhembi, 1955); F. H. Cardoso and O. Ianni, *Cor e mobilidade social em Florianópolis: aspectos das relações entre negros e brancos numa comunidade do Brasil Meridional* (SP: Companhia Editora Nacional, 1960); Florestan Fernandes, *The Negro in Brazilian Society* (1964: English trans., New York: Columbia UP, 1969); O. Ianni, *Raças e classes sociais no Brasil* (RJ: Civilização Brasileira, 1966).

72. Cardoso and Ianni, *Côr*, 247.

73. Bastide and Fernandes, *Relações raciais*, 123–4; Ianni, *Raças*, 61; Fernandes, *Integração*, vol. 2, 161, 199. A copy of this last book remains in the library in Apipucos with an inscription by Florestan referring to his 'profound admiration' for Freyre.

74. F. H. Cardoso, *The Accidental President of Brazil* (New York: Public Affairs, 2006), 48–52.

75. *QP*.

76. Preface to Cardoso and Ianni, *Côr*, xvi.

77. *CGS*, 226, 255; *PT*, 32.

78. A. Zimmern, *The Third British Empire* (London: OUP, 1926).

79. *CGS*, 161–5.

80. A. da Costa e Silva, 'Notas de um Companheiro de Viagem', *A&R*, 13–24, at 18.

81. *A&R*, 25, 293, 295; R. Lucas, 'Aventura e Rotina: Gilberto Freyre et l'Afrique', *Lusotopie* (1997) 237–48; Costa e Silva, 'Notas'.

82. P. Borges Graça, 'A Incompreensão da Crítica ao Luso-Tropicalismo', in F. Quintas (ed.), *Novo Mundo Nos Trópicos* (Recife: FGF, 2000), 208–12, at 211; M. Harris, *Patterns of Race in the Americas* (1964: 2nd edn, New York: Norton, 1974), 67.

83. G. J. Bender, *Angola under the Portuguese: the Myth and the Reality* (Berkeley: University of California Press, 1978), 18; cf. Costa e Silva, 'Notas', 19-21.

84. *BI*, 417–18.

85. *A&R*, *passim*.

86. W. Dalrymple, *White Mughals: love and betrayal in eighteenth-century India* (London: HarperCollins, 2002).

87. He was also aware of K. M. Panikkar, *Asia and Western Dominance: a survey of the Vasco da Gama epoch of Asian history, 1498–1945* (London: Allen and Unwin, 1953) and G. Wint, *The British in Asia* (1947), cited in *TM*, 77, 82.

88. Cf. R. Hyam, *Empire and Sexuality: the British experience* (Manchester: Manchester UP, 1990), 115–33.

89. Freyre, 'Luso-Tropicalism', *Garcia de Orta* 5 (1957), 382–404, at 383.

90. *A&R*, *passim*.

91. *PT*, 33.

92. *R&T*, 51.

93. *AAM*, *passim*.

94. Freyre, 'Iberian Concept'; cf. *AAM*.

95. *AAM*, 103.

96. *I&R*, 62.

97. *I&R*, 100.

98. *Sociología*, 49, 504.

99. Freyre, *Jornal de Comercio*, 1959; id., *Estado SP*, 30 May 1971.

100. D. Chakrabarty, *Provincializing Europe* (Princeton: Princeton UP, 2000).

101. C. Ribeiro Hutzler, 'Antropologia visual em *CGS*', in F. Quintas (ed.) *A Obra em tempos vários: livro comemorativo dos 95 anos de nascimento de Gilberto Freyre* (Recife: Massangana, 1999), 101–12; cf. *C&P*, 78.

102. A. Warley Candeer, 'La tropicologie dans l'œuvre de Freyre', Paris, doctoral thesis, 2002, *http://prossiga.bvgf.fgf.org.br/portugues/critica/teses/alessandro_candeas.pdf*.

103. Freyre, *Um brasileiro em terras portuguesas. Introdução a um possível tropicologia* (RJ: Olympio, 1953).

104. GF, "Internationalizing Social Science", in H. Cantril (ed.) *Tensions that Cause Wars* (Urbana: University of Illinois Press, 1950), 139–65.

105. On the Institute, Meucci, 245–9.

106. These seminars were inspired by Frank Tannenbaum, one of the leading North American specialists on Latin America at that time.

107. *BI*.

108. Freyre, *Arte, Ciência e Trópico* (1962; 2nd edn, Brasília: Instituto Nacional do Livro, 1980), 57.
109. Freyre, *Médicos, Doentes e Contextos Sociais* (RJ: Globo, 1983).
110. L. Costa Lima, 'A versão solar do patriarcalismo', *A Aguarrás do Tempo: estudos sobre a narrative* (RJ: Rocco, 1989), 187–236, at 216.
111. The documents are reproduced in *Imperador*, 227–33.
112. Quoted in *Imperador*, 247.
113. C. G. Mota, *Ideologia da cultura brasileira (1933–1974)* (SP: Ática, 1978), 54.
114. Reported in the *Estado de São Paulo*, 31 March 1979, rpr. *Imperador*, 245–6.
115. Freyre, 'A propósito de sociología' and 'Ainda a propósito de sociología', *DP*, 27 July and 3 August 1958.
116. Joaquim Falcão, 'A luta pelo trono: Gilberto Freyre versus USP', in *Imperador*, 131–67. Cf. Nascimento Arruda, *Metrópole*, esp. 196–8, and Meucci, 239–79.
117. On Duarte, M. Chor Maio, 'Projeto UNESCO', at 127; cf. E. Rugai Bastos, 'A questão racial e a revolução burguesa', in Incao, *Saber*, 140–50.
118. Meucci, 187, 258.
119. J. de Souza Martins, *Florestan: sociología e consciência no Brasil* (SP: USP/ FAPESP, 1998).
120. Meucci, 105–6.
121. F. Fernandes, *A Etnologia e a Sociología no Brasil* (SP: Anhembi, 1958), 202. Cf. O. Ianni, 'Florestan Fernandes e a formação da sociología brasileira' (1986: rpr. in Ianni (ed.) *Florestan Fernandes: sociología crítica e militante*, SP: Expressão Popular, 2004, 15–73, at 26).
122. Freyre, 'Ainda a propósito'.
123. *Sociología*, 77, 66, quoted in Meucci, 189, 250–1.
124. C. Wright Mills, *The Sociological Imagination* (New York: OUP, 1959). Freyre cites Mills in *C&P*, 26.
125. Freyre, 'Microscopic history', *Diogenes* (1957); G. Levi, 'Microhistory', in P. Burke (ed.) *New Perspectives in Historical Writing* (1991; 2nd edn, Cambridge: Polity Press, 2001).
126. Quoted in *Imperador*, 151.
127. F. H. Cardoso, *Mudanças* (1969), 316.
128. G. Veiga, 'A sociología "en negligé"', *Jornal de Comercio*, 26 September 1954. On shirt-sleeves, above, 00. Cf. Veiga, *Jornal de Comercio*, 10 August 1952.
129. L. Rivas, 'A mística do mestre', *DP*, 22 February 1999.
130. On Freyre as an example of conservative thought as described by Mannheim, Meucci, 277–8.
131. *TM*, 225.
132. *R&T*, 211.
133. Cf. L. C. Ribeiro, 'Civilização e Cordialidade. Norbert Elias e Freyre: diálogos sobre um processo', *www.fef.unicamp.br/sipc/anais7/Trabalhos*.
134. C. Geertz, *The Interpretation of Cultures* (New York: Basic Books, 1973). Geertz is cited in Freyre, *Médicos*, 19.
135. L. Gossman, 'Anecdote and History', *History and Theory* 42 (2003), 143–68.
136. A rare exception is R. J. C. Young, 'O Atlântico lusotropical: Freyre e a

transformação do hibridismo', in J. Lund and M. McNee (eds) *Freyre e os estudos latino-americanos* (Pittsburgh: Instituto Internacional de Literatura Iberoamericana, 2006), 99–122.

137. E. Said, *Orientalism* (London: Routledge, 1978); R. Guha, *Elementary Aspects of Peasant Insurgency in Colonial India* (Delhi: OUP, 1983); P. Gilroy, *The Black Atlantic: modernity and double consciousness* (London: Verso, 1993); H. Bhabha, *The Location of Culture* (London: Routledge, 1994); G. Chakravorty Spivak, *A Critique of Postcolonial Reason: toward a history of the vanishing present* (Cambridge, Mass.: Harvard UP, 1999).

138. Of the secondary literature on post-colonial theory, we have found the following most useful: B. Moore-Gilbert, *Postcolonial Theory: contexts, practices, politics* (London: Verso, 1997); R. J. C. Young, *Postcolonialism: an historical introduction* (Oxford: Blackwell, 2001); N. Lazarus (ed.), *Postcolonial Literary Studies* (Cambridge: CUP, 2004).

139. N. Canclini, *Hybrid Cultures: strategies for entering and leaving modernity* (1995; English translation, Minneapolis: University of Minnesota Press, 2005).

140. Chakrabarty, *Provincializing*.

141. E. K. Brathwaite, *The Development of Creole Ssociety in Jamaica, 1770–1820* (Oxford: Clarendon Press, 1971).

142. By 1959 he was referring to M. Cohen, *Pour une sociologie du langage*: 'A lingua portuguesa: aspectos de sua unidade e pluralidade', rpr. *VF&C*. Cf. M. V. Leal, 'Antecipações sócio-lingüísticas em *CGS*', *Congresso Afro-Brasileiro* (Recife: 1985); L. A. Marcuschi, 'Freyre e a sociolingüística', in Quintas, *Obra*, 365–74.

143. *VT*, 106. Cf. *Sociología* (1945), 364.

144. Pallares-Burke, *New History*, 41–5.

Chapter 7: Gilberto Our Contemporary

1. J. Mariás, 'Adios a un brasileño universal', *ABC*, 19 July 1987.

2. Inscription to Freyre of Rosa's *Corpo de Baile* (1956), 'Ao extraordinário ESCRITOR'.

3. Manuel Bandeira and Carlos Drummond, EC, xv, xix.

4. Cf. E. Neff, *The Poetry of History* (New York: Columbia UP, 1947), a book to which Freyre referred in his *Seis conferências em busca de um leitor* (RJ: Olympio, 1965), 143.

5. R. Morse, 'The Multiverse of Latin American Identity, c.1920–c.1970', in L. Bethell (ed.) *Cambridge History of Latin America*, vol. 10 (Cambridge: CUP, 1995), 1–127, at 72; E. Cabral de Melo, 'O "ovo de Colombo" gilbertiano', in *Imperador*, 17–31.

6. W. Otterspeer, *Orde en trouw: Over Johan Huizinga* (Amsterdam: Bezige Bee, 2006), which uses the method of contrasts to study Huizinga himself.

7. J. Huizinga, *Autumn of the Middle Ages* (1919; English trans., Chicago: University of Chicago Press, 1996), 174; S&M, 255; *Mansions*.

8. P. Burke, 'Elective Affinities: Gilberto Freyre and the *nouvelle histoire*', *The European Legacy* 3, no. 4 (1998), 1–10.

9. F. Braudel, 'A travers un continent d'histoire: Le Brésil et l'oeuvre de Gilberto Freyre', rpr. EC, 1075–91.
10. P. Ariès, *Centuries of Childhood* (1960; English trans., New York: Vintage, 1962).
11. P. Ariès, *Un historien de dimanche* (Paris: Seuil, 1980); cf. P. Hutton, *Philippe Ariès and the Politics of French Cultural History* (Amherst and Boston: University of Massachusetts Press, 2004).
12. Ariès, *Dimanche*, 119, 139.
13. On Ariès and *Action française*, Hutton, *Ariès*; on Freyre, V. Chacon, *A Luz do Norte* (Recife: Massangana, 1989), 129.
14. Ariès, *Dimanche*, esp. 14, 18, 58, 84, 171.
15. On comparative political theory, R. L. Euben, *Enemy in the Mirror: Islamic Fundamentalism and the Limits of Modern Rationalism* (Princeton: Princeton UP, 1999).
16. F. Ortiz, *Cuban Counterpoint: tobacco and sugar* (1940; English trans., New York: Knopf, 1947). This section follows P. Burke, 'Don Tabaco e Seu Açúcar', *Folha de S. Paulo: Mais!*, 23 March 1997; cf. F. Moulin-Civil, 'Les voix croisées de Freyre et Fernando Ortiz', EC, 1126–36.
17. NE; cf. K. V. Thomas, *Man and the Natural World* (London: Weidenfeld and Nicolson, 1983).
18. Asa Briggs in M. L. G. Pallares-Burke, *The New History: Confessions and Conversations* (Cambridge: Polity Press, 2001).
19. QP, 179.
20. After coining this phrase we discovered two distinguished predecessors. Braudel hoped that Freyre would write 'Buildings et maisons à bon marché': 'A travers', 1088; F. H. Cardoso, 'À espera de *Grande indústria e favela*', *Senhor/Vogue*, May 1978, 115–21.
21. The title of a song by Jackson do Pandeiro, 1959.
22. Fernanda Abreu, 'Esse o lugar', 1996.
23. M. Harris, *Patterns of Race in the Americas* (1964: 2nd edn, New York: Norton, 1974), 65–78; J. Burdick, *Blessed Anastácia: women, race, and popular Christianity in Brazil* (London: Routledge, 1998), 172.
24. M. G. Miller, *Rise and Fall of the Cosmic Race: the cult of mestizaje in Latin America* (Austin: University of Texas Press, 2004); M. Hanchard (1994) *Orpheus and Power: the Movimento Negro of RJ and SP, 1945–88* (Princeton: Princeton UP, 1994).
25. Quoted in VT, 325.
26. VT, 340.
27. S. Péna, 'Retrato molecular do Brasil', in *Imperador*, 283–300; R. Ventura Santos and M. Chor Maio, 'Race, Genomics, Identities and Politics in Contemporary Brazil', *Critique of Anthropology* 24 (2004), 347–78.
28. J. M. Spencer, *The New Coloured People: the mixed-race movement in America* (New York: New York UP, 1997).
29. T. Garton Ash, 'In Brazil I glimpsed a possible future in which there is only one race', *Guardian*, 12 July 2007. Text and blogs accessible at *http://www. guardian.co.uk/Columnists/Column/0,,2124284,00.html*.

30. *O Globo*, 26 July 87, quoted in V. Chacon, *Freyre: uma biografia intelectual* (Recife: Massangana, 1993), 45; F. H. Cardoso, 'Livros que inventaram o Brasil', *Novos Estudos* 37 (1993), 21–36. Cf. his interview by R. Pompeu de Toledo, 'Construindo a Democracia Racial', *http://www.planalto.gov.br/publi_04/colecao/racial1e.htm*, and M. C. Carvalho, 'FHC fala sobre Freyre', *Folha de S. Paulo: Mais!*, 12 March 2000, accessible in BVGF.

31. P. Fry, *Para Inglês ver: identidade e política na cultura brasileira* (Rio: Zahar, 1982); id., *The Persistence of Race* (Rio: Civilização Brasileira, 2005); id., 'Sobre a pertinência de S&M para a compreensão da dinâmica racial no Brasil contemporâneo: ou o sorriso do mulato', in F. Quintas (ed.) *Novo Mundo Nos Trópicos* (Recife: FGF, 2000), 255–9; id., 'A democracia racial infelizmente virou vilã', *O Globo*, 18 June 2005.

32. 'Vida, paixão e banana do tropicalismo', discussed in C. Dunn, *Brutality Garden: Tropicália and the Emergence of a Brazilian Counter-Culture* (Chapel Hill: University of North Carolina Press, 2001), 128-9. Cf. C. Piñeiro Iñiguez, *Sueños paralelos. Freyre y el lusotropicalismo* (Buenos Aires: Grupo Editor Latinoamericano, 1999), 405ff.

33. *http://www.samba-choro.com.br/s-c/tribuna/samba-choro.0301/0016.html*; Veloso quoted in Dunn, *Garden*, 214.

34. H. Vianna, *The Mystery of Samba* (1995; English trans. Chapel Hill: University of North Carolina Press, 1999), 105.

35. R. E. Sheriff, *Dreaming Equality: color, race, and racism in urban Brazil* (New Brunswick: Rutgers UP, 2001), 200–6, 218, based on fieldwork in a *favela* in Rio de Janeiro.

36. Sheriff, *Dreaming*, 190, 201–2, 218; L. Sansone, 'The New Politics of Black Culture in Bahia, Brazil', in C. Govers and H. Vermeulen (eds) *The Politics of Ethnic Consciousness* (Basingstoke: Macmillan, 1997), 277–309. A rather different view is expressed by A. S. Guimarães, 'Racial Democracy', in J. Souza and W. Sinder (eds), *Imagining Brazil* (Lanham, MD: Lexington Books, 2005), 119–40.

37. J. Amado, preface to H. Costa, *Fala, Crioulo* (RJ: Record, 1982).

38. P. A. Taguieff, *The Force of Prejudice* (1987; English trans., Minneapolis: University of Minnesota Press, 2001), esp. 213–29.

39. Freyre, 'Internationalizing Social Science', in H. Cantril (ed.) *Tensions that Cause Wars* (Urbana: University of Illinois Press, 1950), 139–65, at 142–3.

Further Reading

Most of the voluminous secondary literature on Freyre is in Portuguese, and a good deal of it is cited in the notes. The following list, on the other hand, is confined to works in English (and occasionally in French), not only on Freyre himself but on the Brazil of his time.

J. A. de Almeida, *Trash* (1936), trans. R. L. Scott-Buccleuch (London: P. Owen, 1978).

J. Amado, *Tent of Miracles* (1969), trans. B. S. Merello (New York: Knopf, 1971).

P. Ariès, *Centuries of Childhood* (1960), trans. R. Baldick (New York: Vintage, 1962).

K. M. Balutansky and M.-A. Sourieau (eds) *Caribbean Creolization* (Gainesville: University of Florida Press, 1998).

B. J. Barickman, *A Bahian Counterpoint* (Stanford: Stanford UP, 1998).

——, 'Revisiting the *Casa Grande*: Plantation and Cane-Farming Households in Early Nineteenth-Century Bahia', *HAHR* 84 (2004), 619–60.

R. Bastide, 'Lusotropicology, Race and Nationalism', in R. H. Chilcote (ed.) *Protest and Resistance in Angola and Brazil* (Berkeley: University of California Press, 1972), 225–42.

——, 'The Present Status of Afro-American Research in Latin America', *Daedalus* 103 (spring 1974), 111–23.

G. J. Bender, *Angola under the Portuguese: the Myth and the Reality* (Berkeley: University of California Press, 1974).

R. Benzaquen, 'The Praise of Folly: ambiguity and excess in Freyre's *The Masters and the Slaves*', in Luiz E. Soares (ed.) *Cultural Pluralism, Identity and Globalization* (RJ: IPC, 1996), 156–73.

J. Bernabém, P. Chamoiseau and R. Confiant, *Eloge de la créolité* (Paris: Gallimard, 1971)

E. R. Black, *War Against the Weak: Eugenics and America's Campaign to Create a Master Race* (New York: Four Walls Eight Windows, 2003).

D. Borges, 'The Recognition of Afro-Brazilian Symbols and Ideas, 1890–1940', *Luso-Brazilian Review* 32 (1995), 59–78.

C. R. Boxer, *Race Relations in the Portuguese Empire, 1415–1825* (Oxford: Clarendon Press, 1963).

E. K. Brathwaite, *The Development of Creole Society in Jamaica, 1770–1820* (Oxford: Clarendon Press, 1971).

F. Braudel, 'A travers un continent d'histoire: Le Brésil et l'oeuvre de Gilberto Freyre' (1943; rpr. EC, 1075–90).

A. Briggs, 'Gilberto Freyre and the Study of Social History' (1981); rpr. *Collected Essays* (2 vols, Brighton: Harvester, 1985), vol. 2, 272–87.

I. N. Bulhof, 'Johan Huizinga, Ethnographer of the Past', *Clio* 4 (1974–5), 201–24.

P. Burke, 'Elective Affinities: Gilberto Freyre and the *nouvelle histoire*', *The European Legacy* 3 (1998), no. 4, 1–10.

——, 'The Place of Material Culture in *Ingleses no Brasil*', in F. Quintas (ed.) *Novo Mundo nos Trópicos* (Recife: FGF, 2000), 140–5.

N. Canclini, *Hybrid Cultures* (1990: English trans., C. L. Chiappas and S. L. López, Minneapolis: University of Minnesota Press, 1995).

A. Warley Candeer, 'La tropicologie dans l'oeuvre de Gilberto Freyre', Paris, 2002, doctoral thesis, online, http://prossiga.bvgf.fgf.org.br/portugues/critica/teses/alessandro_candeas.pdf.

D. Cannadine, *G. M. Trevelyan* (London: Fontana, 1993).

D. Chakrabarty, *Provincializing Europe* (Princeton: Princeton UP, 2000).

D. Cleary 'Race, nationalism and social theory in Brazil: rethinking Gilberto Freyre', *www.transcomm.ox.ac.uk/working%20papers/cleary.pdf*.

E. da Cunha, *Revolt in the Backlands* (1902); trans. S. Putnam (Chicago: University of Chicago Press, 1944).

R. DaMatta (1979) *Carnival, Rogues and Heroes: an Interpretation of the Brazilian Dilemma* (1979); trans. J. Drury (Notre Dame, Ind.: University of Notre Dame Press, 1991).

J. Dávila, *Diploma of Whiteness. Race and Social Policy in Brazil, 1917–1945* (Durham, NC: Duke UP, 2003).

C. Degler, *Neither Black Nor White: Slavery and Race Relations in Brazil and the US* (1971); 2nd edn, Madison, Wis.: University of Wisconsin Press, 1986.

C. Dunn, *Brutality Garden: Tropicália and the Emergence of a Brazilian Counter-Culture* (Chapel Hill: University of North Carolina Press, 2001).

P. L. Eisenberg, *The Sugar Industry in Pernambuco. Modernization without Change, 1840–1910* (Berkeley: University of California Press, 1974).

B. Fausto, *Concise History of Brazil* (Cambridge: CUP, 1999).

L. Febvre, 'Brésil, terre d'histoire' (1952); rpr. EC, 1091–1100.

P. Flynn, *Brazil: a political analysis* (London: Benn, 1978).

M. Moreno Fraginals, *The Sugarmill: the socioeconomic complex of sugar in Cuba, 1760–1860* (1964); trans. C. Belfrage (New York: Monthly Review Press, 1976).

G. Freyre, *The Masters and the Slaves* (1933); trans. S. Putnam (New York: Knopf, 1946).

——, *The Mansions and the Shanties* (1936); trans. H. de Onís (New York: Knopf, 1963).

——, 'The Negro in Brazilian Culture', *Quarterly Journal of Inter-American Relations* 1 (1938), 69–75.

——, 'Social and Political Democracy in America', *American Scholar* 19 (1940), 228–36.

——, 'Aspects of Social Development in Portuguese America', in C. Griffin (ed.) *Concerning Latin American Culture* (New York: Columbia UP, 1940), 79–103.

——, *Brazil: an Interpretation* (original English text, New York: Knopf, 1945).

——, 'Brazil, racial amalgamation and problems', *Yearbook of Education* (1949), 267–85.

——, 'Internationalizing Social Science', in H. Cantril (ed.) *Tensions that Cause Wars* (Urbana: University of Illinois Press, 1950), 139–65.

——, *Order and Progress* (1959); trans. R. W. Horton (New York: Knopf, 1970).

——, *New World in the Tropics* (original English text, New York: Knopf, 1959).

——, *The Portuguese in the Tropics* (Lisbon: Commission to Commemorate Prince Henry, 1961).

——, *Americanism and Latinity in Latin America*, trans. S. Alexandre (Montreal: Diogenes, 1963); Portuguese edn, 1966.

——, 'Ethnic Democracy: the Brazilian Example', *Américas* 15 (December 1963), 1–6.

——, 'On the Iberian Concept of Time', *American Scholar* 42 (1963), 415–30.

——, *Mother and Son* (1964: trans. S. Putnam, New York: Knopf, 1967)

——, *The Racial Factor in Contemporary Politics* (original English text, Brighton: University of Sussex, 1966).

The Freyre Reader (1971); trans. B. Shelby (New York: Knopf, 1974).

P. Fry, 'Politics, Nationality and the Meanings of Race in Brazil', *Daedalus* 129, no. 2 (2000), 83–118.

R. Graham, *Britain and the Onset of Modernization in Brazil 1850–1914*, Cambridge: CUP, 1968.

A. S. Guimarães, 'Racism and Anti-Racism in Brazil: a Post-modern Perspective', in B. P. Bowser (ed.) *Anti-Racism in World Perspective* (Thousand Oaks, CA: Sage, 1995), 208–27.

A. S. Guimarães, 'Racial Democracy', in J. Souza and W. Sinder (eds), *Imagining Brazil* (Lanham, MD: Lexington Books, 2005), 119–40.

D. T. Haberly, *Three Sad Races* (Cambridge: CUP, 1983).

M. Hanchard, *Orpheus and Power: the Movimento Negro of Rio de Janeiro and São Paulo 1945–88* (Princeton: Princeton UP, 1994).

L. Hanke, 'Gilberto Freyre: Brazilian Social Historian', *Quarterly Journal of Inter-American Relations* 1 (1939), 24–44.

D. J. Hellwig (ed.) *African-American Reflections on Brazil's Racial Paradise* (Philadelphia: Temple UP, 1992).

A. Hennessy, 'Gilberto Freyre and the Reshaping of the Latin American Past', *Times Literary Supplement*, 14 July 1989.

R. Hofstadter, *The Progressive Historians: Turner, Beard, Parrington* (New York: Knopf, 1969).

J. Huizinga, *The Autumn of the Middle Ages* (1919); trans. R. J. Payton and U. Mammitzsch (Chicago: University of Chicago Press, 1996).

P. H. Hutton, *Philippe Ariès and the Politics of French Cultural History* (Amherst: University of Massachusetts Press, 2004).

R. Janine Ribeiro, 'The Paradoxical Asset of a Weak National Identity' *http://www.renatojanine.pro.br/LEstrangeira/identity.html*.

P. C. Johnson, *Secrets, Gossip and Gods: the transformation of Brazilian Candomblé* (Oxford: OUP, 2002).

L. Lauerhass Jr (1986) 'You must go home again: Gilberto Freyre and the Brazilian Past', introduction to 1986 edn of *Order*.

R. Lemaire, 'Rereading Gilberto Freyre', in *Alterity, Identity, Image*, ed. R. Corbey and J. Leerssen (Amsterdam-Atlanta: Rodopi, 1991), 139–50.

J. Lesser, *Negotiating National Identity: Immigrants, Minorities and the Struggle for Ethnicity in Brazil* (Durham, NC: Duke UP, 1999).

R. M. Levine, 'The First Afro-Brazilian Congress', *Race* 15 (1973), 185–93.

——, *Father of the Poor? Vargas and his Era* (Cambridge: CUP, 1998).

J. Lins do Rego, *Plantation Boy* (1932: trans. E. Baum (New York: Knopf, 1966).

M. Chor Maio, 'UNESCO and the Study of Race Relations in Brazil', *Latin American Research Review* 36 (2001), 118–36

A. K. Manchester, *British Preeminence in Brazil* (Chapel Hill: University of North Carolina Press, 1933).

D. H. P. Maybury-Lewis (1986) 'The Masters and the Slaves', rpr. EC, 1111–15.

M. G. Miller, *Rise and Fall of the Cosmic Race: the cult of mestizaje in Latin America* (Austin: University of Texas Press, 2004).

R. M. Morse, 'Balancing Myth and Evidence: Freyre and Sérgio Buarque', *Luso-Brazilian Review* 32 (1995), 47–57.

——, 'The multiverse of Latin American Identity, c.1920–c.1970', in L. Bethell (ed.) *Cambridge History of Latin America* 10 (Cambridge: CUP, 1995), 1–127.

R. Motta, 'Paradigms in the Study of Race Relations in Brazil', *International Sociology* 15 (2000), 665–82.

F. Moulin-Civil, 'Les voix croisées de Gilberto Freyre et Fernando Ortiz', EC, 1126–35.

J. D. Needell, 'Identity, Race, Gender and Modernity in the Origins of Gilberto Freyre's Oeuvre', *American Historical Review* 100 (1995), 51–77.

——, 'History, Race and State in the Thought of Oliveira Viana', *HAHR* 75 (1995), 1–30.

F. Ortiz, *Cuban Counterpoint: tobacco and sugar* (1940); trans. H. de Onís (New York: Knopf, 1947).

M. L. G. Pallares-Burke, 'Gilberto Freyre: a Love Story', *The European Legacy* 3, no. 4 (1998), 11–31.

M. R. Querino, *The African Contribution to Brazilian Civilization* (1918); English trans. Center of Latin American Studies, University of Arizona, Special Studies no. 8 (1978).

J. H. Rodrigues, 'Capistrano de Abreu and Brazilian History', in E. Bradford Burns (ed.) *Perspectives on Brazilian History* (New York: Columbia UP, 1967), 156–80.

A. Romo, 'Rethinking Race and Culture in Brazil's First Afro-Brazilian Congress of 1934', *Journal of Latin American Studies* 39 (2007), 31–54.

L. Sansone, 'The New Politics of Black Culture in Bahia, Brazil', in C. Govers and H. Vermeulen (eds) *The Politics of Ethnic Consciousness* (Basingstoke: Macmillan, 1997), 277-309.

S. B. Schwartz, *Sugar Plantations in the Formation of Brazilian Society: Bahia 1550–1835* (Cambridge: CUP, 1985).

R. Schwarz, *Misplaced Ideas*, trans J. Gledson (London: Verso, 1993).

R. E. Sheriff, *Dreaming Equality: color, race, and racism in urban Brazil* (New Brunswick: Rutgers UP, 2001).

T. E. Skidmore, 'Gilberto Freyre and the Early Brazilian Republic: Some Notes on Methodology', *Comparative Studies in Society and History* 6 (1963–4), 490–505.

——, *Black into White: Race and Nationality in Brazilian Thought* (1974); revised edn (Durham, NC: Duke UP, 1993).

—— (1996) 'The Essay: architects of Brazilian national identity', in *Cambridge History of Latin American Literature*, vol. 3, Cambridge: CUP, 19xx), 345–62.

F. Tannenbaum, 'Introduction' to Gilberto Freyre, *Mansions and Shanties* (New York: Knopf, 1963), vii–xii.

R. Ventura Santos and M. Chor Maio, 'Race, Genomics, Identities and Politics in Contemporary Brazil', *Critique of Anthropology* 24 (2004), 347–78.

E. Veríssimo, *O Tempo e o Vento* ('Time and the Wind, 1949–62): vol. 1 trans. L. L. Barrett (London: Arco, 1951).

H. Vianna, *The Mystery of Samba* (1995: English trans., Chapel Hill: University of North Carolina Press, 1999).

N. H. Vieira, 'Hybridity vs Pluralism: Culture, Race and Aesthetics in Jorge Amado', in K. Brower et al. (eds.) *Jorge Amado* (London: Routledge, 2001), 231–51.

E. Viotti, 'The Myth of Racial Democracy'(1979); rpr. in *Brazilian Empire: Myths and Histories* (Chicago: University of Chicago Press, 1985), 234–46.

H. Wesseling, 'From Cultural Historian to Cultural Critic: Johan Huizinga and the Spirit of the 1930s', *European Review* 10 (2002), 485–500.

D. Williams, *Culture Wars in Brazil: The First Vargas Regime, 1920-45* (Durham, NC: Duke UP, 2001).

R. J. C. Young, *Postcolonialism: an historical introduction* (Oxford: Blackwell, 2001).

Index